India–Myanmar Relations

This book provides a comprehensive evaluation of India's multi-faceted relations with Myanmar. It unravels the mysteries of the complex polity of Myanmar as it undergoes transition through democracy after a long military rule. Based on meticulous research and understanding, the volume traces the trajectory of India–Myanmar associations from ancient times to the present day, and offers a fascinating story in the backdrop of the region's geopolitics. An in-depth analysis of the India–Myanmar–China triangle brings out the strategic stakes involved.

It will be of great interest to researchers and scholars of international relations, peace and conflict studies, defence and strategic studies, politics, South and Southeast Asian studies, as well as policy-makers and political think tanks.

Rajiv Bhatia served as Director General of the Indian Council of World Affairs (ICWA), New Delhi, India, and is former Ambassador to Myanmar. He is a distinguished former diplomat, an active figure in India's strategic community and a prolific commentator on foreign policy. As Director General, he imparted considerable dynamism to the ICWA, a premier think tank on international affairs. He was Senior Visiting Fellow at the Institute of Southeast Asian Studies (ISEAS), Singapore, during 2011–13. As India's ambassador to Myanmar from 2002–05, he had a ringside view of developments in the region. He has published over 125 articles in newspapers and journals and has a rich experience of Track-II dialogue and diplomacy.

India–Myanmar Relations

Changing contours

Rajiv Bhatia

NEW DELHI LONDON NEW YORK

First published 2016
by Routledge
1 Jai Singh Road, New Delhi 110001, India

by Routledge
2 Park Square, Milton Park, Abingdon, Oxon OX14 4RN

and by Routledge
711 Third Avenue, New York, NY 10017

Routledge is an imprint of the Taylor & Francis Group, an informa business

© 2016 Institute of Southeast Asian Studies

The right of Rajiv Bhatia to be identified as author of this work has been asserted in accordance with sections 77 and 78 of the Copyright, Designs and Patents Act 1988.

All rights reserved. No part of this book may be reprinted or reproduced or utilised in any form or by any electronic, mechanical, or other means, now known or hereafter invented, including photocopying and recording, or in any information storage or retrieval system, without permission in writing from the publishers.

Trademark notice: Product or corporate names may be trademarks or registered trademarks, and are used only for identification and explanation without intent to infringe.

British Library Cataloguing-in-Publication Data
A catalogue record for this book is available from the British Library

Library of Congress Cataloging-in-Publication Data
A catalog record has been requested for this book

ISBN: 978-1-138-92959-3 (hbk)
ISBN: 978-1-315-68110-8 (ebk)

Typeset in Sabon
by Apex CoVantage, LLC

 Printed and bound by CPI Group (UK) Ltd, Croydon, CR0 4YY

Dedicated to Kumkum's parents and my parents,
one of whom – my Mother – shared our three
extraordinary years at 'India House', Yangon

Contents

List of tables	viii
List of maps	ix
Foreword by Shyam Saran	xi
Preface	xiv
Acknowledgements	xvii
List of abbreviations	xix

1	Changing Myanmar	1
2	Deciphering Myanmar: an Indian perspective	15
3	India–Myanmar relations: from antiquity to Raj	63
4	India–Myanmar relations: from independence to military rule	89
5	India–Myanmar relations: during reform period	121
6	Bilateral relationship: present state-of-play	161
7	India–Myanmar–China triangle	191
8	Bilateral relations: future directions	215

Epilogue	229
Appendices	231
Bibliography	239
Index	251

Tables

6.1	Recent high-level visits	169
6.2	Myanmar's trade with ASEAN and neighbouring countries	174
6.3	India–Myanmar trade	175
6.4	India's major imports from Myanmar	175
6.5	India's major exports to Myanmar	176
6.6	India–Myanmar border trade	177
6.7	Recent government of India-assisted developmental projects in Myanmar	185

Maps

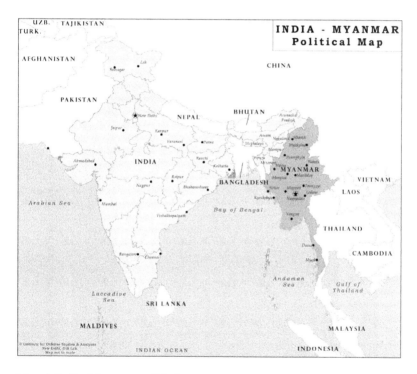

Map 1 India–Myanmar political map.

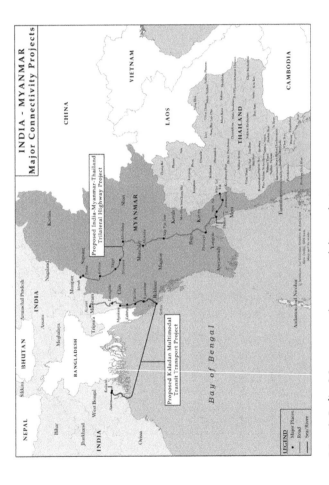

Map 2 India–Myanmar major connectivity projects.

Foreword

Ambassador Rajiv Bhatia is one of those rare individuals who has been able to straddle the disparate worlds of diplomacy and scholarship with comfortable ease and consummate skill. This quality is important since much of the craft of diplomacy lacks the benefit of academic research and historical analysis. Conversely, academic work often suffers from being bereft of the sense of realism and practical statecraft, which a diplomatic practitioner possesses. The value of Ambassador Bhatia's well-researched and comprehensive book on India–Myanmar relations, titled *India–Myanmar Relations: Changing Contours*, lies precisely in his bringing together the perspectives of a diplomat and a scholar to a subject of considerable contemporary importance. The Institute of Southeast Asian Studies (ISEAS), Singapore, should be complimented for commissioning this volume.

Having served in Myanmar as India's Ambassador just before Ambassador Bhatia's own very successful assignment, I am more than conscious of the complexity that characterises India's relations with Myanmar. The book has done well to present, in some detail, the historical background of these relations, which stretch back to dawn of history. There are the close affinities born out of the shared religious and cultural legacy of Buddhism. For the people of Myanmar, majority of whom are devout devotees of Sakyamuni, India is the revered and hallowed land of pilgrimage. The Ramayana too, is popular among its people, though it is embellished with local colours and flavour. Then there is the more recent history when both our countries fell under colonial rule. The last Emperor of India, Bahadur Shah Zafar, spent his final years in exile in Yangon. The last King of Burma, Thibaw, was similarly exiled to Ratnagiri in India, where he lived and died a penurious and embittered man. Colonial rule also brought a large number of Indians to Myanmar as peasants, labourers and traders. Colonial Rangoon, now Yangon, was almost an Indian city with 60 per cent of its population at one time being of Indian origin. Ambassador Bhatia delves into this rich and varied history and shows how the past has coloured our present perceptions of each other; there are strong affinities but one must not neglect some lingering antipathies as well.

During his tenure as India's Ambassador from 2002 to 2005, Rajiv Bhatia had a ringside view of some of the most significant political developments taking place within Myanmar as well as in India–Myanmar relations. His interaction with Myanmar's military leaders, his extensive travels within the country and his background as a former Joint Secretary in the Ministry of External Affairs, in charge of Myanmar, provide raw material for some of the more fascinating insights and hitherto unknown facts about the country and its relations with India. There are sections of the book that would be invaluable to scholars and researches looking for the backdrop to the more momentous political changes that we have witnessed in the recent period of 2011–14.

There is no doubt that for much of Asia, but particularly South-East Asia, the dynamics of the India–China relationship is a constant and running theme. While China may see itself as regaining what it believes is its historical primacy in the region, India views the future of Asia somewhat differently – a more multipolar Asia if you will, in line with its innate preference for a multipolar world order. Nowhere do we see a jostling for these two different approaches to the region than in Myanmar. It is apparent as Ambassador Bhatia points out, why Myanmar is important to India. We share a 1,600-km long boundary, which on the Indian side abuts four of our sensitive North Eastern states of Arunachal Pradesh, Nagaland, Manipur and Mizoram. There exist strong ethnic, kinship and cultural links between tribes that lie astride the border. India and Myanmar share the strategic ocean space of the Bay of Bengal and with the launch of India's Look East Policy in 1992, Myanmar also became India's gateway to ASEAN. It is these geopolitical realities that led India to review and adjust its earlier policy of unstinted support to the democracy movement led by Aung San Suu Kyi and to shun any engagement with the country's military leaders. India realised that the non-engagement policy had only created congenial space for China to quickly establish a predominant position in a sensitive neighbouring country with serious implications for India's own security. Since then, India has been involved in not only engaging the military leadership in Myanmar but in building strong political, economic, cultural and military links with the country, providing a countervailing presence to China. Ambassador Bhatia played a key role in piloting this important transition in India's relations with Myanmar.

The book spells out the implications of the recent reform and opening up of Myanmar. This has created opportunities but perhaps there is a much more complex and competitive environment in which we need to pursue our interests. The insights which Rajiv Bhatia provides, based not only on his earlier experience but also recent interactions in Myanmar as Director General, Indian Council for World Affairs (ICWA), are a very valuable guide to policymakers, scholars and also those seeking business opportunities. He has made some substantive recommendations for our Myanmar policy covering government-to-government, business-to-business and people-to-people engagement. These merit close attention.

India–Myanmar Relations: Changing Contours is a very timely and valuable addition to the emerging corpus of literature on Myanmar. It is unique in providing an Indian perspective on the country and that too, a perspective which brings the rigour of scholarship together with the hard-nosed realism of a practicing diplomat in a most productive manner. I have no doubt that this book will remain a source of reference and a guide to policy for many years to come.

Shyam Saran
Chairman, RIS
Former Foreign Secretary
November 2014

Preface

It was the last week of June 2011. I undertook a long and exhausting journey that began in Seattle, and it took me through Toronto, Paris, Delhi and Bangkok, and finally ended in Yangon. If even one of the four flight connections had been missed, my participation in the international seminar would have been impossible. On the following morning, during a brisk walk in the verdant garden of Inya Lake Hotel, I took in the beautiful view of the lake. I had visited this place for the first time two decades earlier. On that maiden visit to Myanmar, I was struck by the country's magic and mystique. Later, while living in Yangon, I came to this picturesque spot on many occasions.

On that humid June morning, a few guests were busy taking their morning walk, while enjoying the invigorating effect of the green foliage and crystal-blue lake, kissed by the rising sun. I spotted the familiar face of a person whom I had seen, though not met, at a conference in New Delhi three months earlier. As our paths crossed, we introduced ourselves. I was pleased to meet Ambassador K. Kesavapany, director of the Institute of Southeast Asian Studies (ISEAS), Singapore. A short while later, we both made our presentations at the seminar. At breakfast the following day, he strongly suggested my writing a book on India–Myanmar relations.

I was tempted. It was an irresistible proposition due to two reasons. Myanmar was the country that fascinated me the most, of all the nine countries where I had served as a diplomat during a 37-year long career. It was now in the process of undergoing a major transformation. General elections were held in November 2010, followed by the release of democracy icon Aung San Suu Kyi from house arrest, formation of a new 'civilian' government under President Thein Sein, his announcing an ambitious reform agenda and a widening perception that the country faced a historic transition combined to make the task of studying and writing about the country, both fascinating and timely. The second reason was a strong, ingrained desire to address a personal challenge head on – that of turning a diplomat into a scholar again, thus completing the cycle which, in my case, had begun over 45 years back when I was a university student and then a college lecturer.

Candidly speaking, there were two concerns though. Soon after my retirement from the Indian Foreign Service, I had begun publishing articles on foreign policy issues in some of the most prestigious national dailies of India. But I knew that writing articles was easier than accepting the commitment of researching and authoring a full-length book. An affable and persuasive diplomat-scholar, Kesavapany assured me that the entire exercise was wholly doable and it would be intensely enjoyable too.

The other concern was whether there would be an audience, a readership interested in a book on Myanmar, written from the Indian perspective. Students and academics interested in international relations, officials, diplomats and media people, both in India and abroad, take interest in India's foreign policy, especially as it pertains to her neighbours. Yet, among them, Myanmar seemed to be receiving much less attention than it deserved. Somehow the country had fallen off the radar of an average educated Indian or South Asian.

I remembered an unforgettable experience which a Mexican ambassador had at Delhi airport as he prepared to board his flight, on his way to Yangon for a short holiday. Trying to obtain a SIM card for his mobile phone, he asked the young Indian salesgirl for one which would be usable in 'Myanmar'. 'Where, sir?' she enquired politely. He patiently repeated the country's name a couple of times, then went on to explain that 'Burma' was its previous name. Neither 'Myanmar' nor 'Burma' rang any bells to the salesgirl. The hassled ambassador left without getting the SIM card, dismayed by the salesgirl's ignorance about India's immediate neighbours.

I am glad I accepted the challenge, drawing inspiration from Nelson Mandela's immortal words: 'It always seems impossible until it's done.'

This book attempts to analyse the essential features of Myanmar as a nation and a society and the transformation it has been going through in recent years. In this backdrop, it presents a comprehensive story of the development of India–Myanmar relations from ancient times to early 2015. After an introductory chapter, the next chapter examines the essence of social, cultural, economic and political facets and foreign policy profile of Myanmar. The three chapters that follow trace the evolution of India–Myanmar relations from precolonial times to the present, with Chapter 6 analysing the current state-of-play. The next chapter deals with the India–Myanmar–China triangle. The last chapter looks at future contours and directions of the bilateral relationship and presents a set of policy recommendations.

This work is meant not only for academics but also for policymakers, diplomats, business leaders and all young scholars interested in India's relations with one of its most important neighbours. I hope that this book interests everyone who is curious about and cares for Myanmar. It is especially meant for those who will have a role to play in managing, monitoring or just savouring India's emergence as a great power. To do this, they will certainly need to appreciate what drives our vital, though neglected, neighbour in the east and its complex relationship with India and the world.

The book draws from my years of study and research but also from my rich experience of living, working and travelling in Myanmar as India's ambassador from June 2002 to August 2005. Prior to those years, I handled India's relations with Myanmar as the head of the concerned division in the Ministry of External Affairs in the early 1990s. Following my retirement from the Indian Foreign Service in 2009, I observed and wrote about Myanmar as a member of the strategic community. In this venture, I have greatly benefitted from my countless discussions with Myanmar watchers in India and abroad. Above all, my personal interactions with the people of Myanmar ranging from the man on the street to the high and mighty of the land, including Senior General Than Shwe, chairman of SPDC and Nobel laureate Aung San Suu Kyi, have moulded the assessment offered in this work.

My fundamental purpose is to analyse and present objectively the complexities and dynamics of India–Myanmar relations in a rapidly changing environment, and to help create a firm basis for better and stronger relations between the two governments and peoples. India and Myanmar have always been neighbours, occasionally strangers and, for a while during 1988–91, their governments behaved as though they were adversaries. There is, however, little doubt that the two nations have always desired to be dependable friends and close partners. Their shared destiny is one of constructive dialogue, mutual understanding, cooperation and partnership.

Acknowledgements

Writing op-ed articles, making PowerPoint presentations and delivering public lectures is an easy task for many. Authoring a book, however, is a far bigger challenge. It requires deep curiosity and interest, stamina for research and commitment. Many persons helped me in this demanding venture.

I express my deep appreciation to the Institute of Southeast Asian Studies (ISEAS), Singapore, for giving me assistance to write this book and for the access to its amazing library. I am indebted to Ambassador K. Kesavapany, the then director of ISEAS, who inspired me to undertake this challenging task. Other colleagues at ISEAS, particularly Ng Kok Kiong and Y. L. Lee, were very helpful. Three anonymous reviewers who went through the manuscript helped me to enhance its value through their constructive suggestions. I benefitted greatly from my interaction with a vast number of experts on Myanmar in India and abroad.

Without perhaps knowing it, numerous editors encouraged me by publishing my articles on Myanmar and other foreign policy issues. Debates and deliberations at India's leading think tanks gave me new insights.

The three years spent in Myanmar, working and travelling in the country and interacting with ordinary Burmese, members of the elite and top leaders, deepened my understanding and affection for their nation. Without knowing them, this book would not have been possible. I am thankful to all of them.

I gratefully acknowledge the constant encouragement given by Honourable Mohammad Hamid Ansari, Vice President of the Republic of India and President of the Indian Council of World Affairs (ICWA). He made it possible that my acceptance of the position as director general of ICWA in June 2012 did not entail the abandonment of this book project.

I am profoundly thankful to Ambassador Shyam Saran, former foreign secretary, for contributing the foreword.

My sincere gratitude is expressed to all colleagues at Routledge, Taylor & Francis Group for their unflinching support.

My good friend, late Ambassador Jagdish Chandra Sharma, instilled in me a special fascination for Southeast Asia. My brother, Vineet, had predicted that a book would flow from my pen a decade before it actually did! Our children, Siddharth and Kanishk, and their wives, Mridula and Vijiti, helped me immensely through their sustained interest and moral support.

Above all, I express the deepest gratitude to my wife, Kumkum, who helped me in multiple ways to produce this work. It is as much hers as mine.

Abbreviations

ABLC	Army Border Liaison Committee
ACARE	Advanced Centre for Agricultural Research and Education
ADB	Asian Development Bank
AEP	Act East Policy
AFPFL	Anti-Fascist People's Freedom League
ARF	ASEAN Regional Forum
ASEAN	Association of Southeast Asian Nations
ASEM	Asia-Europe Meeting
AYUSH	(Department of) Ayurveda, Yoga and Naturopathy, Unani, Siddha and Homoeopathy
BCIM	Bangladesh–China–India–Myanmar
BIMSTEC	Bay of Bengal Initiative for Multi-Sectoral Technical and Economic Cooperation
BIPA	Bilateral Investment Promotion Agreement
BJP	Bharatiya Janata Party
BNA	Burma National Army
BP	Boundary Pillars
BSM	Bangladesh, Sri Lanka, Maldives and Myanmar
BSPP	Burma Socialist Programme Party
CII	Confederation of Indian Industry
CLMV	Cambodia, Laos, Myanmar and Vietnam
COSC	Chairman Chiefs of Staff Committee
CPB	Communist Party of Burma
DFI	Direct Foreign Investment
DTAA	Double Taxation Avoidance Agreement
EAS	East Asia Summit
EOV	Explanation of Vote
EU	European Union
FESR	Framework for Economic and Social Reforms

GAIL	Gas Authority of India Limited
GCSS	General Cultural Scholarship Scheme
GDP	Gross Domestic Product
GSP	Generalised Scheme of Preferences
HRD	Human Resource Development
IAI	Initiative for ASEAN Integration
ICCR	Indian Council of Cultural Relations
ICWA	Indian Council of World Affairs
IDSA	Institute for Defence Studies and Analyses
IIGs	Indian Insurgent Groups
IIT	Indian Institute of Technology
INA	Indian National Army
INC	Indian National Congress
IPCS	Institute of Peace and Conflict Studies
IPR	Indo-Pacific Region
ISEAS	Institute of Southeast Asian Studies
ISRO	Indian Space Research Organisation
IT	Information Technology
ITC	Industrial Training Centre
ITEC	Indian Technical and Economic Cooperation
ITLOS	International Tribunal for the Law of the Sea
KIA	Kachin Independence Army
KIO	Kachin Independence Organisation
KNU	Karen National Union
LDC	Least Developed Country
LEP	Look East Policy
LSR	Lady Sri Ram College for Women
LTTE	Liberation Tigers of Tamil Eelam
MEA	Ministry of External Affairs
MEB	Myanmar Economic Bank
MFTB	Myanmar Foreign Trade Bank
MGC	Mekong–Ganga Cooperation
MGCSS	Mekong Ganga Co-operation Scholarship Scheme
MICB	Myanmar Investment Commercial Bank
MIEDC	Myanmar–India Entrepreneurship Development Centre
MISIS	Myanmar Institute of Strategic and International Studies
MOFA	Ministry of Foreign Affairs
MOGE	Myanmar Oil and Gas Enterprise
MSR	Maritime Silk Route
NDA	National Democratic Alliance
NDTV	New Delhi Television Limited
NEC	North Eastern Council

NER	North East Region
NLD	National League for Democracy
NLM	National Level Meeting
NSA	National Security Advisor
NUP	National Unity Party
ODA	Official Development Aid
OVL	ONGC Videsh Limited
PIOs	Persons of Indian Origin
PMO	Prime Minister's Office
PUCL	People's Union for Civil Liberties
RBC	Regional Border Committee
RIL	Reliance Industries Ltd.
RIS	Research and Information System for Developing Countries
RITES	Rail India Technical and Economic Service
SAARC	South Asian Association for Regional Cooperation
SEZ	Special Economic Zone
SLM	Sectoral Level Meetings
SLORC	State Law and Order Restoration Council
SPDC	State Peace and Development Council
TCIL	Telecommunications Consultants India Ltd.
TCS	Tata Consultancy Services
TERI	The Energy and Resources Institute
UNDP	United Nations
UNHCR	United Nations High Commissioner for Refugees
UNHRC	United Nations Human Rights Council
UNSC	UN Security Council
UPA	United Progressive Alliance
USDA	Union Solidarity and Development Association
USDP	Union Solidarity and Development Party
YMBA	Young Men's Buddhist Association

Chapter 1

Changing Myanmar

> Our heritage is proud and strong, but our true history lies ahead.
> – U Nu[1]

International relations is a vast and ever-evolving subject that covers global, regional and subregional issues. But one of its most basic segments is the study and analysis of relations between two or more states. Understanding and interpreting relations between two neighbouring countries in the light of regional and international developments; social, cultural, economic, political and strategic factors; and the history of evolution of those relations constitutes its essential part.

Relations among neighbouring nations are much at stake, including security, peace, development and well-being of the peoples concerned. In the case of individuals, neighbours, like relatives, are a given; unlike friends, they cannot be chosen. This applies to nations too. Hence investing in strengthening the relations with neighbours is wise. Such endeavours are moulded not only by the two neighbours in question, but also by other nations in the region and outsiders. What is noteworthy is that often management of ties between them transcends the domain of foreign policy, thus taking us into a deeper realm of national psyche, belief, identity, perception and mutuality of interests that bind the two societies and the two peoples. Bilateral relations thus are not merely a foreign policy matter; they touch upon a more fundamental layer of bonds.

India's relationship with Burma/Myanmar is a case in point. At its root lies an enduring affinity created by geographical contiguity, civilisational linkages, cultural interaction and shared political experiences. A commonality of strategic, political and development perspectives impacts as well as sustains their relations or what may be called their linked destiny.

2 Changing Myanmar

Defining South Asia

In South Asia, there exists, buried under a thick blanket of diversities, differences, disputes and dogmas, an innate sense of unity, created by the region's clearly defined geographical features, shared spiritual and cultural heritage and common historical experience. A continuing jostling between the two elements – unity and diversity – and the failure of the region's leaders and elites to achieve an adequate harmonisation between the two elements as a basis of common action might explain why the region is yet to begin playing the role that it should, on the world stage.[2] From this perspective, a study of India's relations with its neighbours enjoys an extraordinary importance that goes well beyond the region.

The significance of India's neighbours in its foreign policy cannot be overemphasised. As Muchkund Dubey, former foreign secretary, aptly put it: '. . . a country is judged by the world through the prism of its neighbours' perception. And India is no exception to this.'[3]

Even a fleeting look at South Asia's map is enough to convince one that the region is bigger than the geographical spread of the South Asian Association for Regional Cooperation (SAARC), and that the country with two names – Burma and Myanmar – forms as much a part of South Asia as of Southeast Asia. Hence it has rightly been depicted as 'the gateway', 'the bridge' between the two regions or 'the crossroads' where India, China and Southeast Asia 'meet', creating an array of linkages as well as risks and opportunities for various stakeholders.

Among India's seven 'immediate' or 'next door' neighbours in SAARC and Myanmar (which has the status of 'Observer' in the regional grouping), it is possible to point to a special subcategory of four nation-states that were linked uniquely in the past. They are India, Pakistan, Bangladesh and Myanmar. The first three were one country – 'India' – until the partition in 1947 when Pakistan emerged as a new state. In 1971, East Pakistan broke away from Pakistan to emerge as Bangladesh. What is often forgotten is that pre-partition India had Burma as its component for 52 years from 1885 when the Raj annexed it to British India, governing it first from Calcutta and then from Delhi. This ended in 1937 when Burma became a self-standing British colony, having been separated from India after considerable debate and agitation.[4]

In recognition perhaps of this historical legacy and of Myanmar's status as an immediate neighbour with which India shares both land and maritime borders, India's Ministry of External Affairs (MEA) gives to its eastern neighbour a special position. The ministry's Bangladesh,

Sri Lanka, Maldives and Myanmar (BSM) division, unlike those divisions that handle bilateral and regional issues relating to other member-states of the Association of South East Asian Nations (ASEAN), was supervised directly by the foreign secretary. As the highest ranking civil servant in the ministry and its chief coordinator, he or she reports to the political leadership in discharging his or her responsibility to manage relations with all the states in South Asia, as defined by the ministry.[5]

Mutual importance

Although often in discussions on India–Myanmar relations, more attention is paid as to why Myanmar is important to India, one may begin by examining first the nature and magnitude of India's importance to Myanmar.

Religion and ethnicity may be considered as the most powerful factors in this context. To those living in Yangon and thus exposed to the heartland of Bamar or Burman (i.e. the majority ethnic group) culture, it is evident that the Buddhist connection has been the most compelling and lasting bond between the two societies. The legend of the Shwedagon Pagoda – that in its womb are buried strands of Lord Buddha's hair, gifted by him to two Burmese merchants – lives on.[6] The belief that Buddha visited the land, that India's King Ashoka built pagodas in the country and the knowledge that Buddhism originated in India are widely shared. The dream of an average Buddhist in Myanmar is to visit, pray and pay obeisance, at least once in a lifetime, at Bodh Gaya in Bihar, the site where Siddhartha achieved enlightenment, thus becoming the Buddha over 2,500 years ago. History tells us that Buddha relics, Buddhist texts and monks, brought later from Sri Lanka in the eleventh century, contributed to the revival and spread of Buddhism. Theravada Buddhism became the dominant faith. This makes Sri Lanka, too, a special partner and friend for the Burmese, but India undoubtedly enjoys the pre-eminent position as a truly sacred land, the fountain of the path to spiritual salvation – nirvana.

A collective memory of interaction and exchanges – philosophical, spiritual, cultural and commercial – between the two lands persists. The connections established during the Raj and freedom struggle as well as after the attainment of independence are remembered. The presence of a large Indian origin population in Yangon and other urban centres and villages is a reality that cannot be ignored. Respect for India as a rising power and a fast-growing economy is acknowledged widely.[7] From a geopolitical viewpoint, Myanmar has always been aware of the risks of proximity to its giant neighbour in the north – China. Relations with India, on the one hand, and with ASEAN, on the other, represent critical elements in the country's endeavour to maintain its independence. A combination of multiple factors thus motivates Myanmar's policymakers as well as the Burmese people to recognise that India is highly relevant to the country's national interests.

Seen from India, Myanmar's importance may be somewhat unclear, but it has been explained very well by experts. Dr Rupakjyoti Borah, an academic, listed five specific reasons in this context.[8] J. N. Dixit, former foreign secretary, identified five different factors, calling them the 'truisms of Indo-Myanmar relations of contemporaneous history'.[9] Myanmar's relevance to India is best appreciated by measuring the weight of geographical contiguity and ethnic affinity. Long before the two countries became independent nation-states, diverse tribes such as Mizos, Nagas, Kukis, Tangkhul and Paites living in the border regions enjoyed – as they do even now – close familial, community-related, linguistic, religious and cultural ties. They visited and traded with each other freely, shifted residence, shared farming and grazing fields and generally helped each other in times of need or adversity. Only when the British arrived to govern the region, the modern concept of national borders was introduced.

Myanmar's military and strategic significance for India can hardly be overemphasised. If this country were to be under the control of another power, it could pose a serious threat to India's security. Writing in 1943, at the time of Japanese occupation of Burma, K. M. Panikkar, the renowned scholar-diplomat, observed:

> the defence of Burma is in fact the defence of India and it is India's primary concern no less than Burma's to see that its frontiers remain inviolate. In fact no responsibility can be considered too heavy for India when it comes to the question of defending Burma.[10]

Many years after India and Burma had attained independence, international boundaries were finalised and demarcated. But the inexorable logic of geography and ethnicity and their strong combined impact on history continues to be felt today, leading to a widely held view that the security, stability and socio-economic development of India's North East Region (NER) are inextricably linked to those of western Myanmar, especially parts of the Sagaing division, Kachin, Chin and Rakhine states that are situated along the four Indian states – Arunachal Pradesh, Nagaland, Manipur and Mizoram.

Myanmar's attractiveness in India's eyes has gone up considerably in the past two decades, particularly after the South Block turned its gaze eastwards, launching India's Look East Policy (LEP).[11] It is neither an accident nor a coincidence that both the LEP and the strategic shift from India's exclusive engagement with the pro-democracy movement to stepping up the level and range of relationship with the military government in Myanmar came around the same time, that is in the early 1990s. All these developments are attributed aptly to the then prime minister P. V. Narasimha Rao. Myanmar's position within ASEAN has strengthened progressively. With the ASEAN chair for 2014 held by Myanmar, the country's appeal for India increased further. Moreover, while looking at the larger region, India and Myanmar have continued to strive for stronger connectivity and cooperation within various subregional frameworks.

'The China factor' operates from both sides of the India–Myanmar border. Given an essentially adversarial relationship between India and China, which is also marked by substantial elements of cooperation and competition, it is quite natural for India – as indeed for China – to be engaged in a continuing process to seek Myanmar's friendship. For India, it is not merely a question of winning political or economic advantage; it impacts directly on India's national security. Myanmar is perceived as 'a buffer state', one that should not be used as a base for activities injurious to internal security or to India's defence against external threats. Of late, the traditional concepts of security and defence appear to be evolving in the direction where they are seen as linked to, and dependent on, economic development of the region concerned. The argument of this school of thinking is that instead of raising walls, it would be desirable to bring them down and ensure integrated development of the border areas, involving all relevant neighbours – Bangladesh, China, India, Myanmar and others. The case for broader, transborder connectivity and joint development projects is a compelling one, but it is not backed by consensus yet, least of all in India. Nevertheless its time may be approaching, particularly with China and India having reached a broad agreement on the BCIM Economic Corridor.[12]

Another factor explaining Myanmar's significance for India has been the former's size and economic attractiveness. It is not a small neighbour (Map 1). Myanmar's land area is about 20 per cent of India's, and its population is less than 5 per cent of India's 1.2 billion people. Traditionally Indians, especially those living in Myanmar, refer to Burma as 'the land of Lord Brahma',[13] endowed with richness and creativity, and also as a part of 'the *Suvarnabhumi*' or 'the

6 Changing Myanmar

Golden Land'.[14] For centuries, Indians travelled to this fabulous land. In British times, hundreds of thousands of Indians were taken there, to be employed as labourers and farmers. Others went there on their own volition, attracted by the economic opportunity it offered, to work as government officials, professionals and private entrepreneurs. The lure of the market beckons Indian entrepreneurs even now, perhaps more than in the past. Besides, being vulnerable on the energy security front and with rising appetite for oil and natural gas, India has a special interest in resource-rich Myanmar.

The new era

Mutual attractiveness and importance rose sharply as Myanmar entered a new era of transition to democracy in November 2010. This phenomenon brought Myanmar back on India's radar. Media paid more attention to the emerging change. Strategic and academic community made special efforts to monitor the new phase in the country's political development.[15]

Elections for the national parliament and state assemblies took place peacefully on 7 November 2010. Even though the elections were marked by notable irregularities and condemned by many as 'neither free nor fair', they turned out to be the first stage of an exciting, new journey that the country had embarked upon. A week later, on 13 November, Daw Aung San Suu Kyi, secretary general of the National League for Democracy (NLD) as well as a national and international icon, was released after being kept under house arrest for years. The world greeted the news enthusiastically. US President Barack Obama hailed her as 'a hero of mine and a source of inspiration'.[16] Nearly four months after the elections, Thein Sein, a retired general and former prime minister, was elected on 4 February as the new president. He took over the highest office on 30 March 2011, as the previous ruling military junta named the State Peace and Development Council (SPDC) was dissolved. Thein Sein delivered a historic speech on the same day before Pyidaungsu Hluttaw, the national parliament, spelling out his bold and wide-ranging agenda of reform. He identified securing national reconciliation and inclusive governance, accelerating economic progress and conducting foreign policy on the basis of the Five Principles of Peaceful Co-existence as his government's priority goals.

In June 2011, an international seminar on 'Myanmar and the International Community – the Way Forward' was hosted by the Myanmar

Institute of Strategic and International Studies (MISIS), a part of the Ministry of Foreign Affairs, and Friedrich-Ebert-Stiftung, an independent German foundation. Participants (including this author) proceeded from the unspoken assumption that Myanmar was on the cusp of a major change. They appeared to agree with Foreign Minister U Wunna Maung Lwin who asserted that Myanmar had turned 'a new chapter in its history'.[17] Following detailed deliberations on the polity's internal and external dimensions, a broad consensus emerged on what might follow regarding a new equation between Myanmar and the world. Veteran expert Robert H. Taylor called on the international community to recognise that change was on its way in Myanmar, which needed a suitable response.[18] Echoing this, Thant Myint-U emphasised that Myanmar faced 'multiple watersheds' and expressed the hope that a pragmatic and flexible approach would be adopted by all concerned.[19] The country was clearly in the midst of a complex transition.[20]

Subsequent weeks witnessed very little change, fuelling the view of pessimists that nothing of substance had changed. Suu Kyi, through her two 2011 Reith lectures, seemed to confirm this perception. There were 'no real changes', she said, only 'lots of very beautiful words, but these are not enough'.[21] Just when optimists began losing hope, a transformational event took place. As a sequel to preliminary discussions between Suu Kyi and Minister of Labour Aung Kyi, President Thein Sein held a historic meeting with her at the presidential palace in the new capital – Naypyitaw – on 19 August 2011. Both sides sent out the signal that a basic understanding had been reached. It would allow the main opposition party, NLD, and its supreme leader to play a role in political affairs. Earlier, the party had decided not to participate in the 2010 elections, which resulted in the military-backed Union Solidarity and Development Party (USDP) winning a vast majority of seats in the parliament. Even more important than the meeting's outcome was the powerful symbolism of Thein Sein and Suu Kyi standing in front of a portrait of Aung San, her father, the revered war hero and architect of Burma's independence.[22] It conveyed a message of reconciliation that the whole nation understood.

The following months saw the reform process gaining traction. Political and other prisoners were released in phases. Restrictions on media were eased gradually. An agreement was reached with the NLD. This enabled it to re-register itself as a political party after the electoral law was amended, which had disbanded it earlier. The way was thus paved for its participation in the by-elections. Dialogue was started

8 Changing Myanmar

with ethnic minority armed groups, resulting in the signing of ceasefire or peace agreements with most of them, including the Karen National Union (KNU). Economic liberalisation unfolded as labour and financial sector reforms as well as measures for easing of trade, investment and foreign exchange regulations were announced.

Claiming to bow to the people's wishes, President Thein Sein 'suspended' the construction of Myitsone hydroelectric dam project, thereby causing a major surprise and serious setback to China.[23] Besides, an exceptionally dynamic phase began in the management of foreign affairs and the conduct of diplomacy, with Myanmar leaders visiting a large number of countries and receiving a seemingly endless series of VIP visitors. An early gain was the announcement by ASEAN of its decision to award its 2014 chair to Myanmar. Among the visits by foreign dignitaries to the country, the one that stood out was that of Hillary Clinton, the US secretary of state. This was the first visit at this level from the US since 1955. President Thein Sein called it a historic milestone. Clinton held discussions first with the president in Naypyitaw and then with Suu Kyi in Yangon. The two women embracing each other warmly was a gripping visual that demonstrated the depth of change Myanmar was going through.

The first quarter of 2012 was dominated by the high-profile campaign for by-elections, launched by NLD under the charismatic leadership of Suu Kyi. Despite many difficulties encountered by the opposition party, the campaign was run in an atmosphere of considerable freedom. Even as the world watched with fascination the intimate and intense manner in which Suu Kyi connected with the people, travelling through the length and breadth of the land, political uncertainty loomed, forcing most observers to avoid predicting the electoral outcome. A respectable organisation nevertheless felt bold enough to observe that NLD would win 'maybe 60%' of available seats.[24]

When results of 1 April 2012 elections came out, they showed a landslide victory for NLD, which was, in relative terms, even of a bigger magnitude than in the 1990 elections. This time NLD had won 96 per cent of the vacancies, even though it gave the party barely 6 per cent of total seats in the parliament. Despite relating to a rather small number of seats in the overall context, the electoral verdict confirmed that Suu Kyi's bond with people was intact. She called the by-election outcome 'the triumph of the people' and expressed the hope that it would mark 'the beginning of a new era'.[25] As significance of this development was debated in and outside Myanmar, a prestigious national daily in India termed it as 'the watershed moment in

Myanmar's history'.[26] Most observers in India greeted the change with realistic optimism. K. Yhome, a promising young scholar, wrote aptly:

> While one cannot say for sure whether the changes will lead to a democratic Myanmar, one can be sure that the changes taking place in the country are real and the country is evolving a new future for itself which will hopefully be better than the past.[27]

Meaning for India

As a few journalists from India had gone to Myanmar to cover the elections, news about Suu Kyi's victory as well as her messages and those from the government camp reached audiences in India directly. Responding to a question from NDTV's Sreenivasan Jain about her expectations from India, Suu Kyi observed: 'I always expect more, more and more from India. India is the largest democracy in the world . . . India can never do enough for democracy in Myanmar.'[28] The Myanmar government's view was presented by Prashant Jha of *The Hindu* through his interview with Ko Ko Hlaing, President Thein Sein's chief political advisor who, while urging Indian investors to explore business opportunities in Myanmar, observed: 'If you hesitate now, it may be too late.'[29] Assessing what she saw and heard during a week-long stay in the country, Suhasini Haidar, senior editor of CNN-IBN, argued that India's 'middle-path policy was outdated now', adding that engaging modern Myanmar would 'mean writing a whole new script'.[30]

Well before the by-elections, India's official reaction to the transition to democracy had come under sharp scrutiny. The South Block refrained from expressing any view on 7 November 2010 elections until the release of Suu Kyi a week later. External Affairs Minister S. M. Krishna welcomed Suu Kyi's release, stating:

> We hope that this will be the beginning of the process of reconciliation in Myanmar. The recent elections in Myanmar are an important step in the direction of the national reconciliation process being undertaken by the Government of Myanmar. We have always encouraged them to take this process forward in a broad-based and inclusive manner.[31]

In June 2011, Krishna travelled to Myanmar to hold discussions with the government of Myanmar on a wide-ranging agenda of bilateral, regional and international issues. This visit opened an era of vastly stepped-up interaction between the two countries in the subsequent years.

NLD's entry into the political mainstream, Suu Kyi's emergence as the key leader of opposition in the parliament, her willingness to cooperate with the government up to a degree, her emerging collaboration with Speaker Thura Shwe Mann, her determination to amend the 2008 Constitution in order to reduce the military's dominance of political life and pave the way for her own candidature for the presidency as well as the rise of the parliament's assertiveness vis-à-vis the executive branch of the government combined to represent a seminal stage in Myanmar's political development. The reform process, which began in 2011, showed not only its potential but also its risks and limitations, especially as religious strife and ethnic dissentions came to the fore, drawing not only national but also international attention. Since about mid-2013, angst jostled with hope as the nation experienced serious competition (and some conflict) between those who favoured more reform and the advocates of the status quo on a wide range of issues.

The changing situation created at least three powerful reasons for India to re-appraise its Myanmar policy.

First, it meant that, as the world's largest democracy next door, India was expected to contribute actively to the consolidation of democracy and democratic forces in Myanmar. As part of this larger process, a fresh dialogue and renewed cooperation with NLD appeared essential. 'India, which has sidelined Ms. Suu Kyi and the NLD in its eagerness to engage with the junta', asserted *The Hindu* editorial, 'now has the task of re-building relations with Myanmar's democratic forces'.[32]

Second, economic reform measures and progressive lifting of sanctions created new space. Policymakers in New Delhi needed to factor this in, with a view to motivating India Inc. to abandon its caution and reticence when it came to penetrating the Myanmar market.

Third, the transition to democracy heralded marked shifts in Myanmar's external relations. These included a rapprochement with the US and EU, a new-found respect in ASEAN, evidence of new stress in China–Myanmar relations, and brightening prospects of fresh aid and investment flows from partners, new and old, such as Japan, Australia, Canada, as well as the World Bank and the International Monetary Fund (IMF). This implied that 'business as usual' might no longer be an adequate policy response by the South Block to the changing political and diplomatic landscape. It underlined the need for modifications in India's policy approach. Prominent experts such as Shyam Saran[33] and Harsh V. Pant made useful suggestions in this context.[34] Another view was that India should pursue a middle path that falls somewhere between China and the West.[35]

In sum, it seemed that the period 2011–14 was an ideal moment to monitor closely the changing dynamics in and relating to Myanmar as well as to attempt a comprehensive assessment of the state of India's relations with Myanmar – their past, present and future – in a wider context.

Notes

1 Addressing Rangoon University, 22 December 1951, as cited by Hugh Tinker, *The Union of Burma*, London: Oxford University Press, 1959, p. 379.

2 Deb Mukharji, 'Transitions in Southern Asia: Implications for India', *Indian Foreign Affairs Journal*, Vol. 8, No. 2 (April–June 2013), p. 186. 'South Asia offers an extremely complex web of relationships. It cannot be equated with Europe where each nation had a distinct historical identity and experience. Some South Asian nations do, but not all.'

3 Muchkund Dubey, *India's Foreign Policy: Coping with the Changing World*, Delhi: Pearson, 2013, p. 50.

4 Even before 1885, parts of Burma were administered by the British following their victories in the First Anglo-Burmese War (1824–26) and the Second Anglo-Burmese War (1852).

5 In January 2014, BSM division was broken into two divisions – BM (Bangladesh and Myanmar) and SM (Sri Lanka, Maldives and the Indian Ocean). Both are supervised by the foreign secretary. Another point is noteworthy here. For decades, the joint secretary (South) dealt with the region stretching from Thailand to Australia, whereas the joint secretary (East Asia) dealt with China, Japan, Republic of Korea and Democratic People's Republic of Korea. In view of the increasing salience of ASEAN in India's foreign policy, a new division – ASEAN-Multilateral – was created a few years back, with a separate joint secretary heading it who reports to secretary (East). This division has played a significant role in addressing multilateral issues, within the ASEAN context, pertaining to Myanmar, even as the BM division continues to deal with all bilateral matters relating to the eastern neighbour.

6 Myint-U Thant, *Where China Meets India*, London: Faber & Faber Ltd., 2011, p. 9. In a concise statement of this legend, Thant Myint-U wrote: 'Twenty-five centuries ago, two merchant brothers named Tapussa and Bhallika met the Buddha, by chance, just days after his Enlightenment at Bodh Gaya, in northern India . . . The Buddha gave them eight strands of hair from his head. The Burmese believe that Tapussa and Bhallika were from lower Burma and that on their return home they placed the hairs in a jewelled casket and enshrined the casket deep within what would become the Shwedagon pagoda.'

7 'Perspectives', *The New Light of Myanmar*, 30 May 2012. Given as Appendix II.

8 Rupakjyoti Borah, 'India's Huge Stakes in Myanmar', *Russia & India Report*, 23 April 2012. The author highlighted the following: (i) For

12 Changing Myanmar

India, Myanmar is a land bridge to ASEAN, (ii) Myanmar can help curb insurgency on India–Myanmar border, (iii) India needs Myanmar's rich oil and natural gas resources, (iv) India needs to curb China's influence in the region, and (v) 'Myanmar is crucial for India's land connectivity with the rest of the Southeast Asian region'. http://indrus.in/articles/2012/04/23/indias_huge_stakes_in_myanmar_15552.html (accessed on 25 April 2012).

9 J.N. Dixit, *My South Block Years*, New Delhi: Pauls Press, 1996, p. 165. These truisms are: (i) cultural interaction between India's Northeast and Myanmar, (ii) Buddhist period was one of 'deep cultural and intellection interaction', (iii) Burma formed part of British India, (iv) large Indian community of traders and professionals, and (v) leaders of the freedom struggle – Nehru, Aung San and U Nu – formed close, personal relationships.

10 K.M. Panikkar, *The Future of South-East Asia: An Indian View*, New York: The Macmillan Company, 1946, pp. 40–1.

11 In November 2014, Prime Minister Narendra Modi began giving a new orientation to the policy and called it 'Act East Policy'.

12 Joint Statement – A vision for future development of India–China strategic and cooperative partnership, 23 October 2013, para 4: 'Pursuant to the understanding reached between the two leaders in May 2013, India and China have each established a Study Group on the BCIM [Bangladesh, China, India and Myanmar] Economic Corridor. The visit of the Chinese delegation to India in this regard was noted as a positive step. Further discussions on concepts and alignment of the economic corridor are envisaged. Both India and China would continue to discuss with the other parties to this initiative, and hold the first BCIM Joint Study Group meeting in coming December to study the specific programs on building the BCIM Economic Corridor.' http://www.mea.gov.in/bilateral-documents.htm?dtl/22379/Joint+Statement (accessed on 16 November 2013). Between the end of 2013 and the end of 2014, two meetings of the BCIM Joint Study Group consisting of representatives of the four governments strove to take the project forward.

13 Brahma, the creator, is part of the Hindu Trinity, with Vishnu and Shiva being its other deities. The phrase refers to the natural beauty and richness of resources of the country; it was often used by Burmese of Indian origin in conversations with the author.

14 R.K. Dube, 'Suvarnabhumi and Suvarnadvipa: Origin, Identity and its Richness in Gold in Ancient and Mediaeval Times', *Bulletin of Metals Museum*, Vol. 36 (2003), pp. 3–22. 'Suvarnabhumi and Suvarnadvipa are conjugate Sanskrit terms, having literal translation as "The land of Gold" and "The Island of Gold" respectively. It has been shown through definite evidences that greater part of Myanmar, Malay Peninsula and Sumatra were designated by a common name of Suvarnabhumi.'

15 Between mid-2010 and end-2012, this author participated, in New Delhi alone, in 20 seminars, conferences and lectures on the developments in Myanmar and its relations with India. Among them, the more important events were hosted by the Commonwealth Journalists' Association (13 December 2010), National Maritime Foundation (10 August 2011), Vivekananda International Foundation (19 September 2011), joint event by Jamia Millia Islamia and Tampadipa Institute (30–31 January 2012), Global India Foundation (15 February 2012), Society for Indian Ocean

Studies (14 April 2012), Foreign Policy Forum co-managed by Ministry of External Affairs and Federation of Indian Chamber of Commerce and Industry (17 April 2012), Institute of Peace and Conflict Studies (19 April 2012), Aspen Institute India (4 May 2012), Indian Council of World Affairs (10 May 2012), Association of Indian Diplomats (22 August 2012) and Jamia Millia Islamia (5 December 2012).

16 'Statement by the President on the Release of Aung San Suu Kyi', The White House, 13 November 2010, 'While the Burmese regime has gone to extraordinary lengths to isolate and silence Aung San Suu Kyi, she has continued her brave fight for democracy, peace, and change in Burma. She is a hero of mine and a source of inspiration for all who work to advance basic human rights in Burma and around the world. The United States welcomes her long overdue release.' http://www.whitehouse.gov/the-press-office/2010/11/13/statement-president-release-aung-san-suu-ky (accessed on 16 November 2013).

17 From my notes of discussions at the international seminar, held in Yangon, 24–25 June 2011.

18 Ibid.

19 Ibid. Than Myint-U's latest book, *Where China Meets India: Burma and the New Crossroads of Asia*, was released a short while after the seminar, drawing international attention to Myanmar's strategic importance and the complexities of its political and economic situation in a difficult neighbourhood.

20 My op-ed article in *The Hindu* (5 July 2011) ended with the following conclusion: 'I returned with a clear impression that Myanmar is passing through a complex transition: the old era of the State Peace and Development Council rule has ended and the new era of "civilian" rule, with all its imperfections, has begun.'

21 Reith Lectures 2011: Securing Freedom. Aung San Suu Kyi. Lecture one: Liberty, first broadcast on BBC radio 4 at 0900 hrs, 28 June 2011. Lecture two: Dissent, first broadcast on BBC radio 4 at 0900 hrs, 5 July 2011, http://www.bbc.co.uk/reithlectures (accessed on 30 July 2011).

22 'Suu Kyi "Satisfied" with Thein Sein Talks', *The Irrawaddy*, 20 August 2011.

23 The Republic of the Union of Myanmar, President's Office, 30 September 2011. The president stated: 'As our government is elected by the people, it is to respect the people's will. We have the responsibility to address public concerns in all seriousness. So construction of Myitsone Dam will be suspended in the time of our government.' http://www.president-office.gov.mm/en/?q=briefing-room/statements-and-releases/2011/09/30/id-230 (accessed on 30 July 2011).

24 Euro-Burma Office, Analysis Paper No. 1/2012, https://euroburmaoffice.s3.amazonaws.com/filer_public/45/34/4534ba66-b414-42b0-9edc-64078c1e6076/ebo_analysis_paper_no_1_2012.pdf (accessed on 25 April 2015).

25 *Indian Express*, 3 April 2012. 'It is not so much our triumph as a triumph of the people who have decided that they have to be involved in the political process in this country', Suu Kyi said. 'We hope this will be the beginning of a new era.'

26 *The Times of India*, 3 April 2012.

14 Changing Myanmar

27 K. Yhome, 'Myanmar's Transition: A Comment' *Strategic Analysis*, Vol. 37, No. 1 (January–February 2013), p. 114.

28 Sreenivasan Jain, 'Power of One: We Expect More from India, Says Aung San Suu Kyi', NDTV Profit, 7 April 2012, http://www.ndtv.com/video/player/power-of-one/power-of-one-we-expect-more-from-india-says-aung-san-suu-kyi/228660 (accessed on 25 April 2015).

29 *The Hindu*, 4 April 2012.

30 Suhasini Haidar, 'Why India Needs a New Script for Modern Myanmar', *The Hindustan Times*, 5 April 2012. She argued that as Myanmar people celebrated 'the change', for India 'to be a part of this change will need more than a subtle shift in posture. So far its middle-path policy of engaging the military while urging for more reforms has only ended up with it ceding space to China and the ASEAN on investment and trade, and giving up the moral high ground on freedom and human rights to the U.S. and the European Union'.

31 Statement by the External Affairs Minister on the release of Daw Aung San Suu Kyi, 13 November 2010, http://www.mea.gov.in/press-releases.htm?dtl/1634/Statement_by_EAM_on_release_of_Daw_Aung_San_Suu_Kyi (accessed on 19 October 2013).

32 *The Hindu*, 7 April 2012.

33 Shyam Saran, 'Through the Valley of Shadows', *Business Standard*, 18 April 2012. The author opined: 'India has much to contribute to Myanmar's exciting but as yet fragile march towards democracy and economic recovery.'

34 Harsh V. Pant, 'Reading Myanmar Reforms', *Indian Express*, 7 February 2012. He argued that India's Myanmar policy had travelled a long way in 'just the past two years', but he added: 'It is for India to take cognisance of the rapid changes taking place in the periphery and find its own unique role and voice.'

35 Chietigj Bajpaee, 'India Likes What It Sees in Myanmar', *Asia Times*, 1 May 2012. 'India still has the potential to adopt a middle-path toward Myanmar between the irrational exuberance now plaguing the West and recent frictions in Myanmar's relations with China.' http://www.atimes.com/atimes/South_Asia/NE01Df04.html (accessed on 30 June 2012).

Chapter 2

Deciphering Myanmar
An Indian perspective

When the great Prayer for the Three Refuges
rang from sky to sky across deserts and hills and distant shores,
the awakened countries poured their rejoicings
in great deeds, and noble temples,
in the rapture of self-dedication,
in mighty words,
in the breaking of the bond of self.

– Rabindranath Tagore[1]

In order to obtain an accurate understanding of India's complex relationship with Myanmar, it is essential first to appreciate an Indian perspective on Myanmar society, nation and state. Just as British, Chinese and scholars of other countries view Myanmar from their angles and experiences, it may be maintained that Indian experts do likewise. They too are influenced by the manner in which Burma/Myanmar has been perceived and presented in their own country for generations. The portrayal of the country has been attempted by those Indians who studied it, lived and worked in it, or had an opportunity to interact with its people. This author was privileged to have been engaged in all these activities over a fairly long period.

Contemporary India's Burma/Myanmar experts owe a debt of deep gratitude to the rich tradition of Southeast Asian studies in the country and abroad. From ancient times, scholars, pilgrims and monks wrote about their travels and experiences. This material forms a valuable source of knowledge. In the modern period, Indology, nurtured in German, British, Indian and other universities, contributed to the study of Southeast Asia. Writers paid attention to the fascinating linkage that developed between Bengal and the adjacent regions of Burma. Based on her painstaking research, Swapna Bhattacharya

(Chakraborti) traced, in her seminal work *India–Myanmar Relations 1886–1948*, the development of this tradition through the works of numerous scholars, both foreign and Indian. This rich list includes E.H. Johnston, G. Luce, C. Duroisell, Pamela Gutman, N.R. Ray, D.C. Bhattacharya, W.S. Desai, R.C. Majumdar, Kalidas Nag, K.M. Panikkar, D.C. Sarkar, Jayanta Kumar Ray and many others.

What follows is a detailed examination of Myanmar's socio-cultural, political, economic and foreign policy profile as a prelude to the book's comprehensive analysis of the development of India's multifaceted relations with Myanmar.

Myanmar has five neighbours and its shores are washed by the waters of the Bay of Bengal and the Andaman Sea. Its location helps in identifying its socio-cultural character as a nation. On the west, moving from south to north, it is surrounded by Bangladesh, India and China, which borders both on its north and east. Laos and Thailand are its other eastern neighbours, with the latter's boundary touching Myanmar's narrow land strip as it juts into the Andaman Sea. From Bangladesh in the west to Thailand in the east, there is a long coast line. It makes Myanmar's maritime dimension far more important than it is usually appreciated.[2] As to land boundaries, Thailand, China, India, Bangladesh and Laos are the immediate neighbours.[3]

Socio-cultural portrait

History indicates an unbroken inflow of socio-cultural influences that moulded Myanmar as a society. Its impact has been prominently noticeable in border regions – for example, among Chins bordering with Mizos of India, Kachins bordering with the Chinese in Yunan and Shans bordering with communities living in Thailand. But the influence of neighbours extended through the centuries to the heartland as well. The bulk of human migration occurred from the north as people from Tibet and the southern regions of China travelled southwards in phases to settle, attracted by empty but fertile plains washed by the mighty Irrawaddy and the richness of land. Links with and inflows from the east and west too mattered. As a result, Myanmar society reflects these ancient influences and connections in beliefs, culture, arts, costumes, cuisine and way of life.

Nevertheless, it would be erroneous to suggest that this nation is merely a mirror of Chinese, Indian and Thai cultures. Down the ages, Myanmar has shown a remarkable genius for absorbing and synthesising external influences and developing an independent, unique style of its own. Probably from this innate feature of the national psyche emanates the dual inclination to be friendly to neighbours and to assert independence. This impulse, however, is not always translated into practice due to tensions and complexities of its neighbourhood.

Without presenting a survey of Myanmar's history here, reference may be made to the division of 'the first millennium between the founding of the kingdom of Bagan around AD 849 and the last Konbaung in 1885' into four subperiods.[4] This sets the backdrop to the colonial period. Both precolonial history and the British Raj combined to mould what we see as contemporary Burma or Myanmar.

Myanmar is a cultured, conspicuously diverse and complex society. Its culture has been deeply influenced by religion and history. Apart from the well-known Shwedagon Pagoda and temples of Bagan, it has other symbols of past glory that came to light through the archaeological finds in Tagoung, Srikhestra, Visanno, Halin, Mrauk Oo, among other sites. This explains the richness and diversity of its culture that permeates the day-to-day life of its people.

With nearly 89 per cent of the population being adherents of Buddhism – mostly of the Theravada school – Buddhist philosophy, institutions and practices shape the thinking and behaviour of people in a far more visible manner than seen elsewhere. Other religions have been of importance too – Christianity, Islam and Hinduism. Their followers are substantial in overall numbers – 11 per cent of the total population.[5] Of them, Christians, largely present in border regions such as Chin, Kachin, Shan and Karen states, have fared better than Hindus and Muslims in preserving their position and heritage. Hindus, among the minority religions, found it easy to coexist with Buddhism, with Lord Buddha's image displayed in almost every Hindu temple.[6] Followers of Islam did poorly due to historical and political reasons.

Like much of Southeast Asia, Myanmar received and absorbed gifts of Hinduism from a very early period. The story of Ramayana forms an integral part of the country's cultural landscape. The Ramayana's influences came not only from India but also from the eastern neighbours, Thailand and Laos. Rama's story never fails to enthral audiences in Myanmar. They are particularly attracted to it 'because of the gorgeous, colourful costumes and the striking masks and too [*sic*] differentiating the two groups of good and bad characters'.[7]

Role of religion

In the popular mind, Myanmar is perceived as a Buddhist country.[8] This is both a correct and flawed perception. An overwhelming majority of the population is Buddhist, but a strong minority exists that owes

18 Deciphering Myanmar: an Indian perspective

allegiance to other religions. Besides, pre-Buddhist faith in Animism and *nat* worship has a continuing hold on most people. Hence a holistic way is to look at the full, complex picture that the society presents, especially in the manifestation of its ethnic dimensions, which are deeply connected to its religious identity. Put simply, Buddhism explains much about Burma – but not everything.

In Southeast Asia, Burma has been a unique example where Theravada Buddhism flourished well during the monarchical period for many centuries and where the factor of religion played a major part during colonial and post-colonial times as well. Its relevance to contemporary endeavours towards reform of the polity too cannot be minimised.[9]

As independence approached, the country was faced with the choice between modern and traditional conceptions of the role of religion in political affairs. It was a clash of visions between Aung San and the traditionalists. The latter wanted Buddhism to be recognised as the state religion, a demand that Aung San firmly rejected because such a step would jeopardise national unity in a pluralistic society. His view prevailed, with the initial draft constitution stipulating that the state would observe neutrality in religious matters and extend assistance to all religious institutions. Following his assassination, the traditionalists gained by getting their view accepted, though not fully.

This delicate balance, however, came under severe stress throughout the 1950s, partly due to the pressures built by the Buddhist Council meetings, but mainly because the country's top political leader and the successor to Aung San, Prime Minister U Nu, convinced himself that Buddhism must be accepted as the state religion. At the height of his endeavours in this direction, the minorities did what they could to oppose them, but failed. U Nu's flawed approach caused considerable damage to nation-building efforts in the crucial first decade. Later, in running his military rule, Ne Win, as Donald Eugene Smith argues, faced the need to reconcile 'the conviction that religion and politics ought to be kept separate' and 'the belief that governmental intervention was required to eliminate religious attitudes and practices which were clearly detrimental to the building of a modern . . . socialist society'.[10] The regime sought to introduce 'the Burmese Way to Socialism', which both opposed and compromised with the expression of Buddhist faith in public life. An uneasy arrangement prevailed.

The next strong man, Than Shwe, put a stamp of his own on this delicate but vital question. His fellow generals and he had little time for socialist ideas; they were in the business of survival and self-aggrandisement. But he was a devout Buddhist who, as a political leader, understood the appeal of religion to the people. He showed extraordinary acumen in keeping the Buddhist clergy happy and subdued, except in 2007 when 'the Saffron Uprising' broke out.

The 2008 Constitution recognises 'the special position of Buddhism as the faith professed by the great majority of the citizens of the Union'. But it also recognises Islam, Christianity, Hinduism and Animism as 'some of the religions existing in the Union . . .'[11] In the country not seeking retribution against the excesses of Than Shwe regime after its demise, the generals' astute handling of Buddhism in public life might have played a crucial role. The present president, Thein Sein, is well known for his Buddhist piety. So is opposition leader Aung San Suu Kyi, hailed by a few even as the 'female Bodhisattva'.[12]

Buddhism alone does not explain the entire universe of Burmese beliefs. The influence of Hinduism remains visible, not only in the temples of Bagan and elsewhere but in many Buddhist rituals as well as in the people's faith in astrology and the power of gems to ward off calamity and bring good fortune. Impact of Tantric and Mahayana rituals is also evident in some practices. But, perhaps none of these influences is as powerful as the worship of *nats* (i.e. spirits). The Burmese love the Buddha, but they fear the *nats* who need to be propitiated all the time.

Nat worship existed well before Buddhism became widely prevalent. The two learnt to coexist since then, even though staunch Buddhists preferred to disassociate themselves from rituals of *nat* worship. *Nat* possibly derives from the Sanskrit word *natha* (i.e. lord or guardian). Spirits are believed to be of various kinds, but the common feature for all of them is that they need to be kept happy by offerings of food, flowers, incense and money lest they got upset and harmed those who ignored them. Of various categories, *nats* are guardians of nature, considered to be enjoying hegemony on specific rivers, lakes, forests and mountains. Other *nats* are a few Hindu gods, such as *Ganesha* and *Saraswati*, establishing the Indian connection. Yet others are those ancestors who had met violent deaths and whose spirits hover around specific regions.

As the *Glass Palace Chronicles* puts it: '. . . looking to the future, the Buddha is worshipped', while 'looking to the present, one worshippeth . . . spirit(s).'[13]

Unity in diversity

Diversity has been a defining feature of Myanmar society, with its footprint visible in the realm of geography, religion, culture, arts,

20 Deciphering Myanmar: an Indian perspective

food, music and social behaviour. It is known as a country with 135 'national races'. It is composed of eight main ethnic groups, namely Bamar, Shan, Kachin, Chin, Karen, Kayah, Mon and Rakhine.[14] Of them, the Bamar are 68 per cent of the total population.[15] It follows that other ethnic groups, seen individually, are quite small in comparison to the majority group, but collectively they account for nearly 32 per cent of the Burmese people. Hence they represent a power to reckon with, if viewed from the prism of accepted democratic norms. The importance of the divide between the Bamars and other ethnic groups needs to be appreciated from the viewpoint of their habitation pattern. The bulk of Bamars live in Lower and Upper Burma, a region that was known as 'Ministerial Burma' during the British times. On the other hand, most minority ethnic people live in the horseshoe region of hills and border regions, which were called 'Frontier Areas' by the British. The fact of mixing of Bamars and other communities in some areas should be taken note of, but segregation forms a general pattern. Nevertheless, as Shelby Tucker, points out: 'Burma's demography has been further complicated by cultural assimilation and cross-breeding.'[16]

Colonial rulers governed 'Ministerial Burma' directly from Rangoon, the new colonial capital established in 1886, which functioned first under the control of Calcutta and New Delhi (until Burma's separation from British India in 1937) and then directly from London. The hill regions, however, enjoyed ample local autonomy, with freedom granted to local rulers as the British provided only limited supervision. This allowed ethnic groups the opportunity to retain their past patterns of living and governance. It also prevented the development of a shared sense of cultural identity and national unity.

Thus before independence in 1948, there were fears that only a truncated Burma might emerge as an independent country, while the British rule might continue in the border regions. It goes to the credit of Bogyoke Aung San, who combining in his personality, at age 32, several elements of Nehru, Patel and Bose – the famous trio of leaders of India's freedom struggle – managed successfully to win the trust of key ethnic groups at the time.[17] Thanks to the success of the second Panglong Conference, which resulted in the historic agreement on 12 February 1947, a single nation was created as representatives of the Shan, Kachin and Chin communities agreed with the Burman leaders to establish the Union of Burma.[18] The 1947 Constitution formalised arrangements of power-sharing between the majority and minority groups, albeit unsatisfactorily. It granted to the Shan and Kayah states the right to secession from the Union after ten years of staying together, if they chose to separate. But other important ethnic groups such as the Karens were not present in Panglong as full participants. The first Constitution, therefore, had little to offer them and other groups.

Thus when a most serious challenge stared at the Burmese leaders in 1947, they addressed it boldly, if unsatisfactorily, and managed to weld together a single nation. However, as the subsequent history was to show, diversity remained an overarching trait of the Myanmar society. The element of unity in 'unity in diversity' has not been adequately strong. Nation-building began, not ended, as the British departed, and Burma embarked on its journey as an independent nation.

Complex people

By labelling Myanmar as a complex society, the intention is to highlight certain special characteristics of the people, shaped by the circumstances in which they have lived. Generally speaking, Myanmar people carry their age well. Even as they advance in years, their faces do not reveal their true age, enabling them to retain their youthfulness. This provides them with an air of agelessness. This characteristic may be due to their physiognomy, bone structure, food intake or geographical and climatic conditions, or a combination of these factors, but it does make them a case apart.

Another special feature is the Burmese ability to conceal his feelings and views, expressing them as little as possible, especially to foreigners, until they begin to trust the latter. Perhaps this is the trait the Burmese share with the people of Indo-China – the Vietnamese, Cambodians and Laotians who speak and reveal less so that fewer complications arise and self-preservation is ensured. Besides, it is considered a sign of culture to first think and then speak, or probably think more and speak less.

An important factor behind the people's inclination to be less communicative was the long military rule, which was accompanied by monitoring, surveillance and repression perpetuated by the army, especially the Military Intelligence. For 50 years, the common man has had to live with the fear that his or her remarks may be reported to the authorities, which may put him or her in harm's way. From this arose the tendency of speaking less and showing preference for coded words. It was risky to use the name 'Aung San Suu Kyi'. Thus developed the peculiar practice of calling her 'The Lady'. It was simply safer. Not just ordinary folks, but even those in power were very careful in what

22 Deciphering Myanmar: an Indian perspective

they said, rarely going beyond the known positions. But, in informal surroundings such as on a golf course, they were more frank and less guarded. In the reform era that brought a civilian government and freedoms, the situation improved, but old habits die hard.

Finally, since independence, Myanmar society has undoubtedly experienced much suffering, denial, deprivation and fear. Ill effects of Ne Win's brutal rule have been well documented, although public memory of that time may be fading now. The period from 1988 to 1990 was the painful transition when the biggest popular uprising in the country's history was put down mercilessly. Extensive fear was created as a result, enabling the military to rule the country without openly using much force against the civilian population. Its favourite weapons were interrogation and imprisonment of people who opposed it. Insein Jail symbolised repression by the junta. The most well-known dissident of them all, Suu Kyi, had to spend 15 of 21 years from 1989 to 2010 under house arrest in extremely trying circumstances.

The military's terrible actions against the Burmans as well as non-Burman ethnic groups have been analysed extensively. What is also noteworthy is that ethnic rebels and their armed groups too have been found guilty of oppression that they fought against. As a result, forced labour, indiscriminate use of torture and violence, crimes against women, illicit production and smuggling of drugs, illegal transborder trade and irresponsible practices that triggered spread of HIV/AIDS have all combined to cause massive misery and hardship to people. When this is measured against the backdrop of loss of basic freedoms and violation of human rights as well as poverty, misuse of national resources, corruption and inadequate facilities for health, education and social welfare, one begins to get some idea of the long, dark night the people of Myanmar lived through.

Position of women

In an attempt to understand Myanmar society, the role of women cannot be ignored. Despite Buddhism's stress on equality, not everyone is equal in places of worship. For example, at the famed Ananda Temple in Bagan, only monks could use the inner corridor, closest to the Buddha images; only royalty used the middle corridor; and others had to be content with praying from the farthest corridor. Even in modern times, women were generally not allowed to enter the inner space of a pagoda where Buddha images were placed. The ultimate wish of women devotees, it seemed, was to pray for rebirth in the next life as men, for women were considered to have a lower status.[19]

Nevertheless, it may be noted that Burmese women are not exactly an exploited lot. Literature is full of the conventional picture of Burmese men as timid, lazy and inclined less to do hard work than to enjoy a nice meal followed by a long *cheroot*, sipping tea and exchanging gossip. In contrast, women handle shops, work in offices and rule at homes. In short, they are considered smarter than men. To quote F. Tennyson Jesse:

> Completely free from purdah or caste, free to marry whom she likes, and to divorce when she pleases, still keeping her own property and her children, the Burmese woman is a privileged being who rarely abuses her privileges. She often controls the family business and has a say in all matters domestic, and it is the final say.[20]

In a well-argued paper, Daw Thein Thein Nyunt expressed the view that women enjoyed social status equal to men.[21] Although active and successful in many fields, women were not much visible in the government. During the author's tenure, there was no woman in the cabinet; none was a deputy minister; the highest women managed to reach was the director general level. And, of course, no woman was present in the country's highest and most powerful institution, State Peace and Development Council (SPDC). As if to soften this all-male dominance of the government, much media attention was paid to public role of the wives of the three most important generals: Than Shwe, Maung Aye and Khin Nyunt.

In course of Women's Day celebrations, protocol was in evidence when it came to the distribution of awards. What was also revealing in the awards ceremony was the diversity of talents that were recognised and appreciated at the national level. Those watching the award ceremony and listening to the speeches extolling the contribution of women leaders in history were driven to reflect on the tragic irony that the best-known woman of contemporary Myanmar, Suu Kyi, and the military unfortunately remained caught, for too long, in a hopeless political confrontation, thereby sapping the nation's ability to move forward.[22]

Internal politics

Nation-building

In June 2012 Suu Kyi spoke of her country before an international gathering: 'Some of us call it Burma, some of us call it Myanmar.'[23]

24 Deciphering Myanmar: an Indian perspective

This country with two names has struggled with the fundamental issues of national identity, nation-building and legitimacy (or its lack) in the governance structure.[24] This struggle continues at the end of 2014, impacting the country's internal politics, economy and foreign policy. Issues facing Myanmar have been rooted 'in the country's complex and often contested institutions and history'.[25] A critical analysis of this theme is instructive in deepening our understanding of what has been termed as 'a divided society'.[26]

Before the phased takeover by Great Britain in the nineteenth century, Burma emerged gradually as a country, welding a string of city-states into powerful kingdoms. The last to rule Burma was the Konbaung dynasty (1752–1885). King Thibaw of this dynasty was overthrown by the British. The colonial rule introduced modern tools of administration. It also modernised agriculture and commerce. Despite its bane, the Raj pulled the country into the twentieth century, bringing in its wake education and economic progress, and turning Rangoon, the capital, into a regional hub for sea and air travel between London and Southeast Asia. Nation-building, however, was a task that was left unfinished.[27]

Independence could have brought national unity, but it did not. It became a wasted opportunity, although it did not seem so in the beginning.[28] In India's case, many assets were available such as cultural, spiritual and philosophical unity, cemented by a collective memory of a few all-India empires – Ashoka, the Guptas and the Mughals – as well as of the freedom movement that increasingly became mass-based under the leadership of Mahatma Gandhi. Besides, India's exposure to British administration lasted for nearly 200 years. In contrast, in Burma's case, these assets were not available to the same optimal degree. The divide between the majority community and minorities remained deep. The Raj, in fact, deepened it further. The polity had a relatively short-lived experience of self-government under the British. The freedom movement was anchored in a comparatively narrow geographical base. Besides, it 'showed definitely religious traits with all the strength but all the weaknesses that that implies'.[29] In this backdrop came the efforts of '30 Comrades' led by Aung San, who were trained and supported by a foreign power, Japan. They returned to engineer the overthrow of the colonial rule. They created an army that has been playing a dominating role ever since. True nation-building thus happened neither at the arrival of independence nor in the subsequent decades.

The story of recent decades is a work in progress. Fissiparous tendencies, sustained by the society's innate diversity, and its unique political experience marked by authoritarian rule during 1962–2010, unrest and disturbances, ethnic rebellions and civil wars, have made the nation's inner fibre rather brittle. A land of many ethnic nationalities has evolved as a weak nation-state. Without resolving the key challenge of defining nationhood and ensuring that the minorities feel a sense of belonging as much as the majority community, Myanmar may still remain a troubled nation. Ethnic and national reconciliation, equitable power-sharing and inclusiveness are the prerequisites for its well-being.

Legitimacy

Underneath the incomplete process of nation-building lies the issue of legitimacy.[30] The very first government led by Prime Minister U Nu faced this as the communists, Karens and a section of the army raised the flag of rebellion. But it was a democratic government whose legitimacy would be confirmed by the elections of 1951–52.[31] Later as the government faced serious disaffection again in 1958, it invited the army to take over the administration temporarily. By making Ne Win as a caretaker prime minister under the 1947 Constitution, legitimacy was conferred on this transitional arrangement. The army respected the people's authority by returning to the barracks voluntarily in 1960, after holding elections and transferring power to the elected leaders. The subsequent period of 1960–62 witnessed tensions and rifts within the political class on the degree of autonomy that should be given to ethnic minorities. Whether this factor or the army's power lust, or a combination of the two, led to the coup by Ne Win in 1962 remains a subject of debate. The army action was illegitimate, an unjustifiable act, regardless of attempts by the apologists to justify it.

Whatever limited legitimacy the Ne Win regime had earned through governing the country for 26 years was lost completely in mid-1988 when the people's discontent spilled over into demonstrations and protests on the streets, marked by large-scale violence. The crackdown was accompanied by another army coup. An illegitimate coup against those who were in power illegitimately was regarded as completely lacking in legality, but Mao's dictum stipulates: 'Power flows from the barrel of a gun.' So it did in Burma during 1988–90. Following the elections held in 1990 and the army's failure to transfer power and respect the people's wishes, debate on legitimacy became even sharper. This debate lasted for long due to sustained opposition of the army rule by a combination of political parties, ethnic groups, civil society and the exiles' movement as well as international actors.

26 Deciphering Myanmar: an Indian perspective

However hard the army tried, it could not secure legitimacy through the National Convention process. From it emerged the draft constitution of 2008.[32] The referendum in May 2008, even as Cyclone Nargis had devastated the country, was held under peculiar conditions. The new draft constitution was on offer to the people on a 'take-it-or-leave-it' basis. As expected, the draft constitution won popular approval. Although the constitution was the army's gift and not a product of the labours of the people's elected representatives, the government formed under it could claim some legitimacy due to the referendum, and the elections of November 2010, however flawed they were.

The claim by Thein Sein government that 'a new era' had begun might not have convinced many, but for the fact that his reform agenda began to make a dent in a country stilled by oppression and cynicism. His notable act of forging accommodation with Suu Kyi and NLD and their agreement to cooperate with him as reflected in the party's participation in the by-elections combined to increase the quotient of legitimacy. The Western governments' decision to lift sanctions reflected acceptance of the new political reality.

The debate about the country's name – Burma or Myanmar – relates more to the realm of political legitimacy rather than etymology or linguistics. It has been 'highly divisive'.[33] Advocates of 'Myanmar' argue that it is inclusive of all ethnic groups and is indigenous, whereas 'Burma' is narrow and colonial, a view contested by the 'Burma' camp. But the latter's principal objection has been that an illegitimate military regime had no right to change the country's name, an act that needs popular approval.

Political triangle

Myanmar's post-independence politics, especially during the State Law and Order Restoration Council (SLORC) and SPDC era and later, can be best appreciated with reference to a triangle in which three arms are the army, the political parties and the minority ethnic groups. Each arm of the triangle has maintained a complex and changing relationship with the other two arms; each arm has within itself a bundle of differences and tensions; and the three arms are *not* equal in terms of political weight and power. A critical examination of the interrelationship of the three actors is the best way to appraise the country's political development.

Some may argue that there is the fourth arm represented by Myanmar organisations and citizens, exiles, refugees and activists based outside its national borders. Their presence in neighbouring countries, such as Thailand and India, and their activities in the West, particularly in countries such as Norway, UK and US, have had an impact on the political scene.[34] But it is difficult to accept that they stand as an independent pole of power. Their close links with the two poles, political parties and ethnic groups, and their hostility towards the third pole, the army, should, however, be factored in.

Tatmadaw

In Myanmar's political triangle, the *Tatmadaw* has been the most important component, the very base of the power pyramid. The army rightly claims credit for having made a significant contribution for the attainment of independence. The supreme leader of the era, General Aung San, is remembered by people very fondly. There is little doubt that his aura and glory have, in due course, been inherited by his daughter, Suu Kyi. She often invokes his name, recalling his leadership during the war and post-war years to assert that he was the architect of independence as well as of the modern army. She does this with another purpose in mind: to project the view that she loves the military as an institution and would like to work with it, preferring it to play a conventional, apolitical role, and hoping that it would someday vacate space to the political class and return to the barracks. On the other hand, the *Tatmadaw*'s top leaders ranging from Ne Win through Saw Maung to Than Shwe have nurtured an altogether different conception of the army's role in the country's affairs.

While policy differences among the generals and other senior figures of both the Ne Win era and post–Ne Win era cannot be ignored, those leaders broadly agreed on the need and desirability of a dominant and overarching role for the military in political, social and economic fields. Their basic belief seems to be that since the *Tatmadaw* brought independence, set up the Union of Myanmar, saved it from disintegration on many occasions, strove ceaselessly to safeguard the country's unity and territorial integrity and introduced economic development, it has both the duty and the right to play a guiding role in public affairs.[35] In effect, their argument, although never stated explicitly, has been that power stems from the military, not the people.[36] To those who might argue that even if this philosophy had existed in the past, it is passé now, that is, in the reform period, it may be stressed that this thinking is reflected in several provisions of the present Constitution, safeguarding the military's dominant position in the political system.[37]

28 Deciphering Myanmar: an Indian perspective

Thus, Aung San's successors turned his view of the army on its head, for he had stated unambiguously:

> The armed forces have not been created for the purpose of persecuting the people, nor for the purpose of exercising power with weapons. The army is the servant of the country. The country is never the servant of the army.[38]

Within the military, internal tensions and rifts have been a fact of life, although the tradition of a strong military culture with its stress on obedience and discipline has generally allowed the army to project a picture of unity and strength. Its ability to spend an enormous portion of the government budget on itself, in addition to financial resources generated through business and corruption, helped it to keep its officers and men happy. Consequently, they showed a high degree of morale and readiness to battle against ethnic groups and in putting down popular protests.

The military consistently tried a carrot-and-stick policy in order to deal with political parties and ethnic groups. This strategy showed poor results, considering that during the Than Shwe era neither the vexed relations between military and political parties nor the complicated majority–minority community question led to any lasting solution. Only when Thein Sein took up the reins and laid greater stress on dialogue, reconciliation and cooperation that the rays of hope appeared.

Parties

Political parties, the second arm, have had a chequered history. Parties are the life blood of a democracy, but in Myanmar's case, many of them let down the cause of democracy.

During the final phase of the independence struggle, the Anti-Fascist People's Freedom League (AFPFL) was the dominant player. Established in 1944 as a broad front against the Japanese who had reneged on giving freedom to Burma, it was home to nationalists, liberals, socialists and communists who were all welded together to achieve the common purpose – the end of foreign rule. After Japan's defeat, it served as the principal opposition to the return of British rule, eventually becoming the first ruling group after independence. AFPFL went through several splits and disintegrated later. 'The democracy era' (1948–62) was marked by deep and persistent factionalism within the ruling combine and strong opposition to it by the Communist Party, which had earlier been a component of AFPFL. Broad consensus on national issues eluded the parties, thus making the democracy vulnerable.

Ne Win established the Burma Socialist Programme Party (BSPP) in July 1962. Burma remained under one-party rule until the end of Ne Win era. It was 'the king's party' but the people wanted choice. Pro-democracy movement in the late 1980s called for a multiparty system, arguing that, without options, democracy could not function properly. The military granted this demand without realising what it was getting into. It set up a new party of its own, the National Unity Party (NUP). When results of the 1990 multiparty elections came out, NUP was trounced and the National League for Democracy (NLD), the party that had emerged from the cobbling together of divergent groups – students, monks, discontented generals and other dissidents – was a clear winner. It never attained power, much like a client who visited the bank with a fat cheque but was not permitted to encash it.

During the SLORC/SPDC period, the government ruled without the help of any political party. But towards its end, the army, knowing the future in which it planned to lead the country, began to prepare itself well. It set up the Union Solidarity and Development Association (USDA) in 1993, which became the Union Solidarity and Development Party (USDP) on 2 June 2010. 'The king's party' was back without the ideological rhetoric associated with BSPP, but essentially its role was the same – to provide a political garb to the army rule. Besides, the army had not forgotten the lessons of 1990. Consequently, when it permitted multiparty elections in November 2010, it simply managed to ensure that NLD stayed away from the elections. The NLD had put forward a few conditions for its participation, which the military regime rejected. Electoral results demonstrated that the army had succeeded in getting what it wanted: a decisive victory for USDP. A notable feature was the appearance of a few smaller parties. The more important among them secured seats in the national parliament and state assemblies. They did not have much political weight, but at least the country showed semblance of a political alternative.

By-elections followed in April 2012 after the Thein Sein government found a way to allow NLD's participation in the polls. Despite years of suppression of NLD and determined attempts to isolate its top leader Suu Kyi from her party and people, the regime failed to make a dent into the icon's hold on the masses. The NLD victory showed that the people wanted a real option. In contrast, USDP came out as a

30 Deciphering Myanmar: an Indian perspective

complete failure, not winning any seat. Although NLD demonstrated its popular appeal once again, it was not free from vulnerabilities. At its party congress in March 2013, it sought to address them, but its success was partial. The party has been dominated by its chairperson Suu Kyi; its executive committee still has too many 'uncles'; and it lacks a second line of leadership. It needs to revitalise itself for a bigger fight – the elections in 2015. On the other hand, the serious jolt USDP received meant that its patron, the army, would need to go back to the drawing board in order to craft a new strategy for its future.

Ethnic groups

As a multiethnic society, Myanmar's diversity is reflected in the multiplicity of its ethnic groups. In the political triangle, ethnics are represented by their political parties, armed groups and civil society organisations that combine to create an important pillar of the polity. Ethnic groups have had a long history of strife with each other and also of tensions and conflicts within several of them. Nevertheless, they have managed to exist within the overall umbrella of a nation-state, the Union of Myanmar. Aung San deftly employed the tools of dialogue and reconciliation for this purpose and was able to create the Panglong arrangements. After encountering great perils to national unity, U Nu's Burma showed some progress towards decentralisation and federalism.

But the thinking of elected leaders clashed with the philosophy of Ne Win and the succeeding generals. The latter's preferred option was to maintain a strong centre and hold the Union together with the force of arms. As a result, Myanmar became the battlefield for several civil wars, punctuated by periods of cessation of hostilities. First, under SLORC in the early 1990s, Khin Nyunt negotiated ceasefire agreements, which brought armed battles between the *Tatmadaw* and most ethnic armed groups to an end. The basic idea was to create a modus vivendi, which stipulated that ethnic groups would recognise the central government's authority in return for ample operational autonomy within their own regions. Subsequently a major innovation was attempted by SLORC/SPDC through the National Convention. The Constitution of 2008, stemming from this process, provided for regional legislatures for states. But the fighting never fully stopped. Hostilities continued. Serious impasse developed on the key issue of merger of ethnic armies into the national armed forces on which the Than Shwe regime insisted, a demand that was rejected by several armed groups.

Since March 2011, the approach anchored on concluding ceasefire agreements was attempted again. Media announced, week after week, the successive signing of ceasefire agreements with the ethnic groups. The agreement with the Karen National Union (KNU) was rightly hailed as a historic landmark because until it was signed in April 2012, this ethnic group had remained engaged in hostilities against the government since independence. The Thein Sein government succeeded in concluding ceasefire agreements with all groups. However, as the country traversed through 2012–14 period, clashes between Muslim and Buddhist communities in the Rakhine state, outbreak of hostilities between the army and Shan groups and the Kachin Independence Army (KIA), and spread of tensions and disturbances between Muslims and Buddhists in central and northern parts of Myanmar cast dark shadows on the government's plan to secure ethnic reconciliation.

History shows that ceasefire agreements by themselves are not adequate to establish and preserve peace. For sustaining it, a lasting political settlement is essential. From the viewpoint of the army and indeed the majority Burman community, the bottom line is national unity. The idea of secession, which was favoured by the Karens, Kachins and others in the past, enjoys little support today. But, what ethnic groups want is genuine autonomy and power-sharing. Many of them would prefer a federal model, whereas federalism is an anathema to the army's strategists.

Therefore, logic and common sense suggest that all stakeholders need to work towards defining, through dialogue, the contours of autonomy in such a manner that national unity is preserved and promoted and, at the same time, regional diversity and the minorities' ability to develop themselves through self-government are accommodated. For achieving this goal, dialogue involving the government, political parties and ethnic organisations is a must, after the conclusion of the armed conflict. The government has been engaged in conducting this dialogue. Some progress was reported. A draft national ceasefire agreement was negotiated, which awaited approval by the ethnic groups' coalition and the central government by the end of 2014.

Economy in transition

Myanmar has widely been known as a country of rich natural resources and poor people. It was a land of plenty and yet in precolonial times, it had essentially been a subsistence economy, largely dependent on agriculture. The British Raj modernised the economy, with profit for the colonial power as the driving motivation, and in this process the country got incredibly entwined with its neighbour, India. World War II devastated the country's economy.

After independence, the new rulers grappled with economic challenges of the 1950s. 'The country began life in economic and political crisis from which it has never really recovered.'[39] This assessment was made on the basis that the subsequent regime of Ne Win brought untold setbacks to economic development through its policy of the Burmese Way to Socialism. In 1987, Burma was recognised by the United Nations (UN) as a Least Developed Country (LDC). Economic failings provided the trigger for political change. The new military rule since 1989 pursued policies that attracted some foreign investment, but the regime failed to make any significant impact.

This was the background in which the reform era since 2011 placed a special focus on economic reform. In his inaugural speech, President Thein Sein emphasised the need for making changes to 'financial and tax policies for the evolution of market economy and improvement of the socio-economic status of the people'.[40] The market economy of his conception was one where all economic forces including the state, regional organisations, cooperatives and private companies could 'work in harmony'.[41] He pledged to give strong encouragement to small and medium enterprises, to open doors, make reforms and invite investments. While recognising Myanmar as an agro-based country and the critical importance of agriculture in its economy, he made it clear that 'agricultural development alone is not enough'.[42] Therefore, the country had to move fast on the path of industrialisation that created new employment opportunities and high per-capita income.

As experts have pointed out, in effecting economic reforms the new government had to address two fundamental challenges: first, how to shift to a system that is more inclusive without attracting hard resistance by the previous beneficiaries such as individuals and companies close to the military, the military itself, and the ruling party USDP; and second, how to introduce sufficient political liberalisation so that Western economic sanctions could be removed, thus paving the way for foreign investments and international assistance.[43] The reform era represents the story of the government's success and its limitations.

Soon after its formation, the government launched the Framework for Economic and Social Reforms (FESR) covering legal reforms, land reform, budgetary, taxation, monetary and exchange rate reforms and reforms to create jobs and attract foreign investments. This strategy also highlighted development priorities including agricultural production, livestock and fishery, rural productivity and cottage industries, microsavings and credit, rural cooperative, rural socio-economy, rural energy and environmental conservation. The chief feature of the reform strategy, according to the government, was its people-centred approach with the aim of poverty reduction. The objective was to reduce poverty levels in Myanmar from 26 per cent in 2013 to 16 per cent in 2015.

Economic growth accelerated at an estimated 7.5 per cent in financial year (FY) 2013–14 from the revised figure of 7.3 per cent in FY 2012–13. Projections indicated GDP growth to be 7.8 per cent in FY 2014–15 and in FY 2015–16.[44] Investment climate improved through government measures, resulting in a higher flow of foreign direct investment (FDI). In September 2014, the government revised its estimate for FDI flow in FY 2014–15 from $4 billion to $5 billion.[45]

The World Bank nevertheless placed Myanmar at the 182nd position among 189 countries in its report on *Doing Business 2014* in terms of 'ease of doing business'.[46] Business leaders expressed concern that Myanmar was failing to ensure rapid job creation that was essential for bringing sustainable economic growth. This indicated the long road ahead for economic reform.

Changing external relations

We may now explore Myanmar's endeavour to connect with the world, a task that takes us to a general appraisal of the country's foreign policy. It may be useful to examine first the perception issue, then the basic principles of foreign policy and finally the development of a few key external relationships in recent years.

Like the rest of the government, Ministry of Foreign Affairs (MOFA) too was shifted to Naypyitaw, the new capital. While this change occurred in 2006, new trends in the nation's foreign policy became visible since 2011.

Perceptions: external and internal

The general view of those studying Myanmar from the outside suggests that the country has not shown much interest in the world at large. Prime Minister U Nu was an exception as he strove to play a role on the international stage and was active in projecting Burma's soft power, leveraging its moral and political influence and preserving its national interests. His successor Ne Win was widely seen as the leader who turned Burma into a hermit state, cutting off its links with

34 Deciphering Myanmar: an Indian perspective

much of the world. It 'became the dark house of the neighbourhood, huddled behind an impenetrable, overgrown fence', wrote Amitav Ghosh.[47] The military junta that replaced Ne Win was subjected to isolation by Western nations through the imposition of sanctions. During its rule Myanmar became deeply dependent on China. Later, it created some room for manoeuvre by building relations with its other neighbours – India and ASEAN – as they adopted the policy of constructive engagement. The reform period, however, witnessed new trends. The government gently applied brakes on its burgeoning relationship with China; took pains to build cooperative ties with the US, EU and Japan responding to their major policy initiatives; and also strove to expand relations with ASEAN, India and many other countries.

As opposed to this external discourse is the self-perception, the view presented by the Myanmar government of its foreign policy, especially its raison d'être and its evolution over the years. The external policy has been changing while retaining its core character, according to two centres of authority, namely MOFA and the current president.

MOFA's official website, in its article on 'Emergence of Foreign Policy', projected that a state's domestic and foreign policies 'intended to attain objectives of national interest'. Besides, they were 'interrelated and mutually reinforcing'. It went on to classify foreign policies of states under three categories, namely isolationism, nonalignment and polarisation. After achieving independence and 'for quite some time thereafter', Myanmar adopted and practiced 'independent' and 'nonaligned' foreign policy. The development of the objectives of this policy was depicted in a systematic manner.[48]

Main principles

Tracing the policy's subsequent evolution, it was asserted that 'beginning in 1971 Myanmar transformed its independent and non-aligned Foreign Policy into an independent and active Foreign Policy'. Later, SLORC, through its Declaration 3/88 of 18 September 1988, announced its adherence to 'the independent and active foreign policy'. Referring to the policy followed since then and particularly during the reform period, MOFA listed the following principles:

- Respect of and adherence to the principle of equality amongst peoples and among nations and the Five Principles of Peaceful Co-existence
- Taking a nonaligned, independent and just stand in international issues

- Maintaining friendly relations with all nations, and good neighbourly relations with neighbouring countries
- Continued support of, and active participation in, the United Nations and its affiliated organisations
- Pursuance of mutually beneficial bilateral and multilateral cooperation programmes
- Regional consultation and beneficial cooperation in regional economic and social affairs
- Active participation in the maintenance of international peace and security and the creation of an equitable economic order and opposition to imperialism, colonialism, intervention, aggression and hegemonism
- Acceptance of foreign assistance that is beneficial to national development provided there are no strings attached.[49]

Another authoritative view of the country's foreign policy was presented in President Thein Sein's inaugural address, delivered before the newly elected parliament. Two specific paragraphs were devoted to this subject. He began, in the first paragraph, by pointing out that since independence successive governments practiced 'different political and economic policies and concepts', but on foreign affairs they all followed the nonaligned, independent and active foreign policy and dealt with other countries in line with the Five Principles of Peaceful Co-existence. He emphasised that the previous governments did not come under the influence of any foreign powers, remained neutral in international relations, at no time did they either permit deployment of foreign troops on Myanmar soil or launch aggression against or interfere in internal affairs of any other country, and they posed no threats to international and regional peace and security. 'These points', the president stressed, 'are the pride of Myanmar's foreign affairs policy'.[50]

Then, shifting his attention on the policy line that his government would follow in future, he observed:

> Our government will also adhere to this honourable foreign policy and continue the relations with all the countries. Moreover, our country will stand firm as a respected member of the global community while actively participating in the international organizations, including the UN, ASEAN, BIMSTEC and other regional organizations. This is why I invite and urge some nations wishing to see democracy flourish and the people's socio-economy grow in Myanmar to cooperate with our new government that emerged in line with the constitution by accepting and recognizing

36 Deciphering Myanmar: an Indian perspective

Myanmar's objective conditions and ending their various forms of pressure, assistance and encouragement to the anti-government groups and economic manipulations.[51]

Thus, Thein Sein spoke both about the past and the future.

Key relationships

India–Myanmar relations need to be studied within the larger framework of Myanmar's external relations. Its most important external relationship (i.e. with China) will be evaluated in a subsequent chapter. Here it may be useful to analyse some of the other important partnerships Myanmar has been able to develop, especially before and during the reform period. In this context, the focus is on Myanmar's changing ties with ASEAN, US, EU, Japan and Australia on the one hand, and its immediate South Asian neighbours (excepting India) on the other. This is relevant to the evaluation of India's place in Myanmar's foreign policy.

ASEAN

Laos and Myanmar joined ASEAN as members on the 30th anniversary of ASEAN in 1997. Vietnam had come in earlier, and Cambodia followed later, thus completing the formation of the special subgroup known as CLMV (Cambodia, Laos, Myanmar, Vietnam). In granting entry to Myanmar, to what extent was ASEAN driven by the motive to help the pro-democracy movement and protect human rights? Many in ASEAN argued that a policy of engagement would help because the generals, through exposure to democratic rule in their neighbouring countries, would be encouraged to compromise with the opposition forces. But, this did not happen. Myanmar took protection under ASEAN's standard policy of noninterference in internal affairs of member states, maintaining that the ASEAN membership could not be used to force it to open its political system. Besides, Yangon knew that its economic liberalisation, executed in the early 1990s, would attract the ASEAN countries, particularly Singapore, Thailand and Malaysia.

Two other points are relevant here. First, most ASEAN democracies, marked at the time by a varying degree of authoritarianism, were hardly in a position to put pressure on Myanmar to liberalise politically. Second, ASEAN's relations with the pro-democracy movement were not particularly close, except in the case of Thailand, which gave shelter to many dissidents and ethnic groups fighting against the military. Suu Kyi in particular was critical of ASEAN's policy of constructive engagement.

In the first decade of Myanmar's membership of ASEAN, much bonhomie marked relations between Myanmar ministers and officials, on the one hand, and ASEAN diplomats and visiting delegations on the other. They projected themselves as part of a large common family. ASEAN diplomats were careful to respect the military's sensitivities and avoided criticising it. Malaysia was active in promoting mediation by special UN envoy for Myanmar, Rezali Ismail, but his mission eventually failed to bridge the huge gap between the minimum demands of the SPDC government and the NLD. Singapore played a leading role in fostering economic ties. It was also a favourite destination for Myanmar generals for their health care needs and personal financial dealings. Indonesia seemed passive, whereas Philippines barely concealed its disappointment with the frozen political situation.

During the period 2006–10, the ASEAN–Myanmar relationship faced several challenges. At the time of the 'Saffron Revolution' in 2007, the SPDC regime came under tremendous international pressure. Western governments, in particular, voiced strong criticism of the ASEAN approach, urging Myanmar's neighbours to recognise the ugly realities and gather courage to censure the generals. The US Senate, for example, adopted a resolution that called for the suspension of Burma from ASEAN. A number of ASEAN leaders found their voices and criticised Myanmar's crackdown of Buddhist monks and the people at large.[52] Individual ASEAN leaders expressed 'horror' and 'anger' over actions by the Myanmar government; some depicted them as indefensible and others pointed out that the unrest was due to a 'flawed democratization process'.[53] But the organisation found a way to remain civil and consistent, content with only a mild criticism of Myanmar.[54]

In May 2008, when Cyclone Nargis struck Myanmar, its government was found to be completely unprepared to deal with the effects of the massive natural disaster and utterly insensitive to the people's misery. Its negative mindset came into sharp focus through its refusal to accept international humanitarian assistance, except from a few countries such as India. This strange impasse provided a rare opportunity for ASEAN. Driven by creative dynamism, it succeeded in persuading Myanmar to join a trilateral task force, comprising representatives of ASEAN, Myanmar and the international community. This task force handled the responsibility of coordinating and supervising the entry and distribution of relief supplies.

38 Deciphering Myanmar: an Indian perspective

By 2009, indications were available regarding Nyapyitaw's plans to hold elections as part of its roadmap to democracy. The ASEAN impressed on the Myanmar government of the need to make elections free, fair and inclusive, but it was hardly in a position to do more. When eventually elections took place on 7 November 2010, albeit without the participation of NLD and with Suu Kyi still under house arrest, ASEAN had missed a great opportunity, according to its critics. As the results came in, confirming the landslide win for the military-supported USDP and as Western governments condemned the elections as 'neither free nor fair', ASEAN found a way to welcome them. It expressed the hope that they would lead to political change and national reconciliation. The outcome, of course, caused disappointment, not surprise, in ASEAN circles.

In evaluating ASEAN's Myanmar 'problem', the basic question to be addressed is: did the policy of constructive engagement or its later version promoted by Thailand, namely 'flexible engagement', achieve its objectives? Evidently, if preventing close relations between Myanmar and China was a key objective, the policy did not succeed much because during the 1989–2010 period, China–Myanmar cooperation developed extremely well. Defenders of ASEAN might argue that without ASEAN's engagement policy Myanmar by now would have become 'China's satellite'. If securing economic benefits was a driver, ASEAN no doubt gained, with Thailand and Singapore emerging as the top investment and trading partners of Myanmar. The host country too benefitted, as it kept its economy going with the triangular assistance of China, India and ASEAN. But, politically the policy achieved little, according to its critics, who claimed that positive political change finally happened only due to the pressure of Western sanctions and censure. Expectedly, advocates of the policy disagreed. Najib Razak, prime minister of Malaysia, recalled that ASEAN was 'on the receiving end of very public diplomatic scoldings' for long, adding:

> But Asean members took a more nuanced view believing that constructive engagement and encouragement were just as effective, if not more, than sanctions and isolation in creating change . . . sure enough, after quarter of a century of isolation, Myanmar is starting to head back into the democratic fold.[55]

Kilian Spandler argued that ASEAN deserves 'credit for substantially contributing to a political climate that is favourable of Burmese democratisation', and in this context he highlighted three elements of ASEAN's Burma policy: 'the concept of constructive engagement, moderate diplomatic pressure and criticism, and the creation of institutional incentives to policy change'. His conclusion was that as 'the West provided the stick, ASEAN fed the carrot – an unintended division of labor, but one that worked.'[56]

Examining arguments of both the camps, one may conclude objectively that neither sanctions nor engagement per se convinced the Myanmar military leadership to shift gears and opt for a new strategy. The change arose from within, from the political elite's careful assessment that the SPDC approach had run the ship of economy aground; that the country's economic revival demanded Western aid, capital and technology; and that these essentials would never be made available to Myanmar without the military reaching a functional compromise with Suu Kyi. As Marie Lall noted, 'This was a local process, devised and controlled by the military.'[57]

Under Thein Sein's presidency, the government embraced reform, and ASEAN acted swiftly to accept the new Myanmar as its future leader and chair for 2014. The decision to do so was taken at its 19th Summit in Bali, Indonesia on 17 November 2011. President Thein Sein received the chairman's gavel at the Summit in Brunei on 10 October 2013. For ASEAN, engagement was the natural and sensible policy to follow from the beginning. With Myanmar largely on the same political and economic wavelength now, ASEAN stood more empowered and Myanmar was set to shine on the regional platform.

The US

America did not have an ambassador in Burma/Myanmar for 22 years until Derek J. Mitchell presented his credentials to President Thein Sein on 11 July 2012. Other facts are equally revealing. The last visit by a US secretary of state to Burma was by John Foster Dulles in February 1955, before Hillary Clinton arrived in the country on 30 November 2011 for a three-day visit. Between the visits of Ne Win in September 1966 and Thein Sein in May 2013 to the US, nearly 47 years had elapsed. When Barack Obama arrived in 'the Golden Land' on 19 November 2012, he became the first American president in history to visit the country. He visited it again to participate in the East Asia Summit in November 2014.

While delivering a historic speech before the joint session of the Indian parliament in November 2010, Obama observed:

> But when peaceful democratic movements are suppressed – as they have been in Burma, for example – then the democracies of the

world cannot remain silent. . . . Faced with such gross violations of human rights, it is the responsibility of the international community – especially leaders like the United States and India – to condemn it. And if I can be frank, in international fora, India has often shied away from some of these issues.[58]

A casual observer might wonder if Obama or his advisers imagined that the US policy was on the verge of a dramatic change within the next few months. A year after Obama's speech, Secretary of State Hillary Clinton shook hands with the president of Myanmar. Having completed a review of its Myanmar policy, Washington, while continuing sanctions, was in the process of engaging with the leaders of Myanmar. The Obama Administration's message was simple: 'If you change, we too shall change.' The story of how the US policy changed, step by step, is fascinating. It shows that the executive decided to lead, winning the support and approval of the Congress. The US government took control of the policy, which had been 'outsourced' earlier to Aung San Suu Kyi and the human rights constituency.

As a backdrop, it may be recalled that the US maintained appropriate and cordial relations with the Burma of U Nu and Ne Win. However, post-1988 and especially since 1990 when SLORC refused to transfer power to NLD, the winner of elections, a new age in world politics had begun. The Cold War was over. The US was now the world's only superpower. Between 1990 and 2008, for a period of 18 years that saw three presidents in office – George H. W. Bush, Bill Clinton and George W. Bush – US–Burma relations came under severe stress. In 1990, Washington downgraded diplomatic relations from the level of ambassador to chargé d'affaires. It progressively adopted a punitive policy of comprehensive economic, financial and travel sanctions against Burma. As Nehginpao Kipgen pointed out, 'Sanctions on Burma were specified under five federal laws, a series of Presidential Executive Orders and determinations.'[59] The US extended support for adoption of resolutions at the UN and other multilateral fora 'to mobilise international attention on the deplorable human rights situation'.[60] Besides calling for the restoration of democracy, release of all political prisoners including Suu Kyi, and stoppage of violation of human rights, the US had other grievances against the Burmese regime. These included its involvement in international drug trafficking, illegal money laundering, oppression of its ethnic minorities, perceived links with or encouragement of international terrorism and suspected ties of cooperation with North Korea to produce nuclear weapons.

Denying legitimacy to the regime, the US government refused to use 'Myanmar', the name given to the country by the military government, and insisted on calling it by its earlier name 'Burma', the one preferred by Suu Kyi and supporters of the democracy movement.

Essentially the regime was viewed as a public enemy. A US secretary of state (Condoleezza Rice) called it 'the outpost of tyranny'.[61] Another (Madeleine Albright) personally championed the cause of making sanctions effective. This policy received strong support from the Congress. Nevertheless, those opposed to sanctions continued to argue that it was a flawed policy that had failed to achieve the results expected of it.[62]

A pertinent question that presents itself here is whether the US denied, or deliberately chose to ignore, the strategic importance of Myanmar in Southeast Asia and, more specifically, whether it cared at all that its policy would drive Burma closer into China's arms. This argument was used again and again, by Myanmar's neighbours, particularly ASEAN and India, in their diplomatic conversations, but apparently it had little effect in Washington until the last phase of the Bush presidency. Only the Obama White House, faced with the challenge to deal with an assertive, rising China in 2009, seemed willing to listen and factor in this strategic dimension.

Obama took office, hoping to make changes in the US foreign policy and looking for new successes in the field of external relations. He sent a direct signal to authoritarian governments that his administration wanted to 'extend a hand if you are willing to unclench your fist'.[63] The generals in Burma could not have missed it. Soon a review of the Burma policy was ordered, an exercise in which a large number of stakeholders in the US, Burma and elsewhere were consulted.[64] The review took months to complete. Finally, in September 2009 Secretary of State Clinton announced the new policy. She frankly acknowledged that neither the policy of sanctions nor that of engagement had achieved the goal of democratic change in Burma.[65] Hence the new 'dual-track' policy would be governed by a combination of two elements: sanctions would continue, but the US would step up dialogue and engagement in order to press for change. Americans seemed to have concluded that they could do business with Thein Sein who was the prime minister at the time; they might have even sensed that forthcoming elections could provide a rare window for at least some change.

Two important occasions were created for dialogue in September and November 2009. First, a meeting between Kurt M. Campbell, assistant secretary for East Asian and Pacific Affairs, and U Thaung, minister for science and technology and a former ambassador to the US, was held in New York (on 29 September). This was the first political level contact between the Obama Administration and the government in Naypyitaw. Second, extensive discussions were held during Kurt Campbell's visit to Myanmar (3–4 November).[66] These two rounds of dialogue must have helped both sides to conclude that a modus vivendi could be crafted.[67]

When elections took place in 2010, the world took notice of Obama's criticism of them being 'neither free nor fair', but many missed the importance of a significant sentence in this statement: 'The United States will continue to implement a strategy of pressure and engagement in accordance with conditions on the ground in Burma and the actions of the Burmese authorities.' He ended the statement with the familiar reiteration of the fundamental US demands.[68] What followed between this statement and President Obama's visit to Burma two years later was Naypyitaw's sustained endeavour to come up to the standards set by Washington. As the attempt succeeded, the US took reciprocal action to ease sanctions and start building up ties.[69]

In this behind-the-scene dialogue between the two governments, there was a third party – Suu Kyi. Her agreement to play by the rules set for the new game was critical. Following her release on 13 November 2010, she gave indications that she would study and reflect on the new situation and consult around before addressing the changed environment. During the period between her release and her meeting with President Thein Sein on 19 August 2011, American interlocutors may have played an active role in bringing the trilateral dialogue to a positive conclusion. Probably this role contributed towards the success of Suu Kyi–Thein Sein meeting, which culminated in a mutual assurance of cooperation. Later in the year as US–Myanmar relations improved, Obama saw the 'flickers of progress'.[70] He publicly exhibited his recognition and respect for Suu Kyi's contribution by telephoning her from Air Force One, while flying from Australia to Bali, to ascertain her concurrence for Hillary Clinton's visit to Burma in November 2011.[71] Surely Derek Mitchell and the State Department would have completed the groundwork in advance of that much publicised telephone call. Expectedly enough, the president received a positive response. The visit by Clinton followed and left an imprint.

In November 2012, Obama's historic visit carried its own powerful symbolism. Besides representing an important landmark in the history of US–Burma relations, the president's visit would be remembered for three of its important features: the superbly crafted speech he delivered at the University of Yangon[72]; the photograph, which showed 'the most powerful man' walking barefoot on the marble floor of Shwedagon Pagoda[73]; and his brave, successful attempt to kiss Aung San Suu Kyi on her cheeks.[74] Even if everything is scripted for presidential visits down to the last detail, the presidential kiss was surely in defiance of the State Department's advice regarding Asian protocol and values.

US–Myanmar relations should also be assessed in light of the visits of President Thein Sein and Suu Kyi to the US. Thein Sein visited the US twice in September 2012 and May 2013, whereas Suu Kyi undertook a 17-day, coast-to-coast tour in September–October 2012. The president, on his first visit, essentially focussed on his participation in UN-related work. He, however, had a meeting with Hillary Clinton, the US secretary of state, though not with the US president who found time to receive Suu Kyi at the White House. Thein Sein and Suu Kyi had a meeting of their own in New York, possibly to convey that they enjoyed a cordial relationship and strove to work together. Their visits unfolded in the backdrop of considerable international criticism of Myanmar and also Suu Kyi concerning their positions on the Buddhist–Muslim communal strife in the Rakhine state. Speaking from the podium of the General Assembly, Thein Sein observed that within 'a short time' the Myanmar people were able 'to bring about amazing changes', but he stressed that the democratic transformation process would be 'a complex and delicate one that requires patience'.[75] On the second visit, Thein Sein was received by President Obama at the White House, who expressed appreciation and support for Myanmar's reform programme.

Suu Kyi's visit was in the nature of an international celebrity travelling to be feted by admirers and supporters. She collected the Congressional Gold Medal that was awarded to her four years earlier. At an event in New York, Henry Kissinger, former US secretary of state, welcomed her as the embodiment of how 'societies became great when they turn confrontation into reconciliation'.[76] She gave a calibrated evaluation of the state of change in her country: 'We are not yet at the end of our struggle, but we are getting there.'[77]

During his visit to Myanmar in August 2014, US Secretary of State John Kerry acknowledged that the country had made 'a significant amount of progress' in recent years, but emphasised that there was 'still obviously a lot of work to be done' to end the civil wars, expand space for civil society and protect the media, and prevent intercommunal violence. He highlighted the importance of 2015 elections as

44 Deciphering Myanmar: an Indian perspective

'a benchmark moment for the whole world to be able to assess the direction that Burma is moving in'.[78] Interestingly, according to an expert, the US dignitary made seven references to 'Burma' and nineteen references to 'Myanmar' in his statement to the press and answers to questions.[79] It was a balancing act of its own.

EU

A macro view of the EU policy indicates that European countries juggled through the years, balancing their values and interests while dealing with the military regime. The overall outcome favoured an edge for interests over values in most cases. Key EU states maintained diplomatic relations at the ambassadorial level and allowed their companies to trade with and invest in Myanmar, but at the same time they participated in the sanctions regime managed by the EU. For long, the Myanmar question cast its shadows on EU–ASEAN relations.

Since 1996, the EU policy was governed by the 'Common Position on Burma', which revolved around the notion that in order to support NLD in its battle against the generals and help the country move towards democratic change, the EU must impose and administer a variety of sanctions.[80] Further, Generalised Scheme of Preferences (GSP) benefits for industrial and agricultural products from Burma were withdrawn in April 1997. The EU also supported NLD's position opposing tourism to Burma.

Against this backdrop, the manner in which the EU policy began to undergo a shift since 2010, culminating in a noticeable transformation by 2013, needs to be analysed here. Given its inner differences, pulls and pressures, the EU had a hard time crafting its reaction to 2010 elections. This was reflected in the declaration issued on 7 November 2010 by Catherine Ashton, the high representative for foreign affairs and security policy. The EU, on the one hand, expressed regret that the authorities failed 'to ensure a free, fair and inclusive electoral process' but, on the other hand, it noted that 'civil society could partially organize itself politically, notwithstanding many difficulties'. From this nuanced perspective, the EU called for the unconditional release of all those detained for 'their political convictions' and for 'a more inclusive phase' in governance.[81]

After Thein Sein became the president, the Council of European Union called on the new government to assume responsibility for 'a peaceful transition to democracy and respect for human rights and fundamental freedoms'. It favoured the launching of 'an inclusive dialogue' with the political opposition within the parliament and stakeholders outside such as NLD. The EU also decided to extend the sanctions or 'restrictive measures' as they were called euphemistically, for another year, but it added that it could respond to 'improvements in governance and progress . . .' Significantly visa ban on a few officials, including the Myanmar foreign minister, was lifted as also the ban on high-level visits to the country. Finally, the Council reiterated its readiness 'to develop a high-level dialogue with the new institutions and with opposition figures across the spectrum'.[82] A year later, the Council's conclusions, issued on 23 April 2012, duly reflected the country's political progress as by-elections had just taken place, resulting in NLD's impressive victory and Suu Kyi's entry into the parliament, which were preceded by a year of political and economic reforms.[83] Catherine Ashton visited the country and inaugurated an EU Office in Yangon in April 2012.

Suu Kyi's first visit to Europe in June 2012 had a huge impact. Covering Switzerland, Norway, Ireland, the UK and France, she connected extremely well with her diverse audiences and received a red carpet welcome wherever she went. In her public pronouncements, she recognised the recent positive changes in her country, while emphasising that it was the beginning of a long and difficult road. Whether she would succeed in leading her people towards real democracy was the question uppermost in everyone's mind. Immediately after the visit, this author had the opportunity to pose the question to Madeleine Albright, former US secretary of state, at her lecture in New Delhi, who replied: 'The story is not over yet.'[84]

By the time the next Council conclusions were finalised and issued on 22 April 2013, the EU had moved forward further. It took the plunge in deciding 'to lift all sanctions with the exception of the embargo on arms which will remain in place'. It congratulated the government of Myanmar/Burma on its achievements, while noting that there were 'still significant challenges to be addressed'. Looking to the future, it stressed that the period before general elections in 2015 was 'critical for the country's overall transition'.[85]

President Thein Sein undertook his first official visit to Europe covering Norway, Finland, Austria, Belgium and Italy in February–March 2013. He visited Brussels and held discussions with the EU leaders. A joint statement was issued on 5 March, reflecting the views of Herman Van Rompuy, president of European Council; Manuel Barroso, president of the European Commission; and President Thein Sein on the broad theme of 'Building a Lasting EU–Myanmar Partnership'. The bottom line was they all agreed to work in partnership to 'make Myanmar into a modern democracy'.[86] In July 2013, Thein Sein visited Europe

46 Deciphering Myanmar: an Indian perspective

the second time, a voyage that took him to the UK and France. These two countries had paid special attention as changes began. Both the UK and France stepped up their political and economic cooperation as reforms gathered momentum in Myanmar.

British Prime Minister David Cameron became the first major Western leader to visit the country in April 2012. During subsequent British–Myanmar talks in London, Cameron expressed support for the reform process, adding that Britain was ready to assist in the economic and political transition. Referring to the changes, Thein Sein observed: 'Over the last two and half years, we have embarked upon a transformation which I believe is unprecedented.'[87]

Earlier Alain Juppé, the French foreign minister, visited Myanmar in January 2012. Thein Sein, while visiting France, discussed matters of mutual interest with President François Hollande and Prime Minister Jean-Marc Ayrault. The French side emphasised the need to release all the political prisoners. On this issue, the visiting president assured the French, as he had done the British earlier, of his 'guarantee' that all the political prisoners would be released by the end of 2013. Myanmar continued to be criticised in Europe on account of the strife in the Kachin and Rakhine states.[88]

Suu Kyi undertook the second trip to Europe in October 2013. She collected from the European Parliament in Strasbourg the Sakharov Prize for Freedom of Thought, nearly a quarter century after it was awarded to her in 1990. 'We have made progress since 1990, but we have not made sufficient progress,' she said. The NLD leader called for changes to the Myanmar Constitution in order to make it 'a truly democratic one'.[89] She also visited Brussels and London to meet EU leaders whom she urged to persuade Myanmar's government to amend the Constitution.[90] While in the UK, Suu Kyi visited the Royal Military Academy at Sandhurst, triggering some criticism by human rights groups. Others, however, saw in the visit, an attempt to woo the leadership of Myanmar defence forces.[91]

Japan

History, Buddhism and common bonds as Asian nations combine to create the perception of 'a special relationship' between Japan and Burma in the post-independence period. For the Burmese side, Japan's wealth and generosity and for the Japanese side, Burma's geostrategic location and shared history were the key determinants. Aid flowed, which increased steadily through the 1960s and 1970s.[92]

Serious strains, however, appeared in the relationship, following convulsions in Burma during 1988–90. Reacting to the military coup, Japan decided to suspend its Official Development Aid (ODA) 'in principle' and to restrict new aid to projects of 'emerging and humanitarian nature'. Thus, Japan joined the Western nations, albeit reluctantly, in a collective venture to censure the generals. Burma began its journey towards isolation, a direction unsuitable for Japan's interests. In this light came the subsequent decision in 1992, the adoption of ODA Charter, which prescribed that, as Bert Edström pointed out, ODA decisions would be taken after factoring in the recipient's record on military spending, democracy, moves towards market economy and human rights.[93] This was seen as Japan's 'bifurcated policy' or the Japanese version of 'a carrot and stick policy'. It promised to be even-handed but, in fact, it was biased in favour of the military over the pro-democracy movement.

Throughout the 1990s and later, Japan appeared to be torn between those who advocated a sanctions-anchored approach like the West, and those who supported constructive engagement, like ASEAN. Tokyo's endeavour was to strike a balance, by keeping the human rights constituency in good humour but, at the same time, taking actions to prevent estrangement in relations with Burma as it could further drive the regime towards China. A Japanese prime minister offered a truly complex explanation in this regard.[94]

As the 'Saffron Uprising' unfolded, Kenji Nagai, a Japanese photographer, was killed on 27 September 2007 when Myanmar soldiers started shooting the protesters. This generated only a mild reaction in Japan although some aid was cancelled. Japanese Prime Minister Yasuo Fukuda requested Chinese Prime Minister Wen Jiabao to take up the matter suitably with the military regime and urge restraint in dealing with the opposition.

It was during the reform era that Japan's Myanmar policy blossomed fully, achieving rapid improvement in bilateral relations. This was evident from the high-level visits from both sides: Deputy Prime Minister and Finance Minister Taro Aso and Prime Minister Shinzo Abe visited Myanmar in January 2013 and May 2013, respectively, whereas Thein Sein and Suu Kyi visited Japan in April 2012 and April 2013, respectively. It is worth recalling that this period was marked particularly by serious tensions in China–Japan relations on territorial claims concerning the East China Sea as well as other issues.

At the conclusion of Prime Minister Abe's visit, a joint statement was issued on 26 May 2013, which reflected the two leaders'

48 Deciphering Myanmar: an Indian perspective

agreement to lay 'a new foundation for taking the relationship . . . to a higher level and establishing a lasting, friendly and cooperative relationship . . .' The four specific areas to be concentrated upon were: support for Myanmar reform, promotion of prosperity, enhancement of people-to-people and cultural exchanges, and strengthening political and security cooperation.[95]

Concerning economic dimensions of the relationship, two notable developments were: Japan's decision to write off past debts amounting to nearly US$2 billion as well as to extend new aid, and the joint decision to make the development of Thilawa Special Economic Zone (SEZ)[96] as a flagship project. In return, Myanmar confirmed its intention to secure further improvement in the country's investment climate. On the political side, particularly noteworthy was the decision to bolster Japan–ASEAN cooperation and continue Japan's assistance to Myanmar towards its role as the ASEAN chair in 2014.

Australia

Before 1988, Burma was a country of peripheral interest to Australia. Following political convulsions in Burma during 1988–90, Australia, in its dual role as a Western and Asian nation, strove to follow a middle-of-the-road policy, adopting limited sanctions and yet maintaining a form of cooperative relationship with the military government. It adopted 'autonomous' travel and financial sanctions and imposed arms embargo, which was instituted in 1991. Concerning trade, its policy permitted neither encouraging nor discouraging trade and investment exchange with Myanmar. Dialogue and restricted cooperation on human rights, labour issues and counternarcotics as part of Australia's regional programme of assistance to ASEAN were maintained. Australia's academic and strategic community took deep interest in studying Myanmar on a sustained basis.

Australia moved swiftly once the reform era began. Foreign Minister Kevin Rudd was among the first foreign dignitaries to visit Myanmar. He went there in June 2011 and this became the first visit from Australia at that level since 2002. He opened discussions with the Thein Sein government when many other governments were still critical or sceptical about the prospects of change. Since that visit, several exchanges followed, which transformed the relationship substantially. The more significant visits were the visit of Australian Foreign Minister Bob Carr to Myanmar in June 2012 and later in July 2013; the visit by Foreign Minister U Wunna Maung Lwin to Australia in October 2012, the first visit by a Myanmar foreign minister since 1984; and the visit of President Thein Sein to Australia in March 2013, the first by a Myanmar head of state since 1974.

Projected as 'a historic visit', Thein Sein's voyage was particularly significant during which the Australian prime minister expressed the view that increased engagement was part of the growing Australian support for the nation in recognition of its progress towards democracy.[97] The visit marked, according to an analyst, 'the increasing international acceptability of the once outcaste state'.[98] In November 2013, Suu Kyi paid the much-awaited visit to Australia. She made a public plea to Australians to understand and appreciate the stakes involved in the next elections and the case for amending the Constitution that would enable her to be a presidential candidate.[99]

Political discussions during the high-level visits contributed to improvement in bilateral relations. The Australian government welcomed the conduct and outcome of by-elections in April 2012 that led to Suu Kyi's entry into the parliament. Immediately the Australian government abandoned its earlier policy and switched to a positive policy to encourage and facilitate trade with and investment flows to Myanmar. In July 2012, Australia lifted travel and financial sanctions in recognition of positive political change, although the arms embargo remained in place. Its development aid touched the level of about US$50 million per year in 2012 and was set to increase to US$100 million by 2015–16. Australian aid was focused on 'education, health, livelihoods and rural development, peace building and democratic governance'.[100] Australian Prime Minister Julia Gillard specifically highlighted possibilities of cooperation in the mining sector.[101] Australia signed a Memorandum of Understanding on Development in January 2013. Among other measures, Canberra decided to extend assistance for conducting census operations, to open an Austrade office in May 2013, and proposed to post a defence attaché in its Embassy in Yangon. Australia also began contributing to the modernisation of Myanmar defence forces, driven by the assumption that transformation of the Myanmar military would be helpful in the nation's march towards democracy.

The shift in Australian policy has been criticised by the advocates of human rights who believed that the situation in Myanmar had not improved much, particularly judging by strife and conflict in the Kachin and Rakhine states. 'The new policy', argued Zetty Brake, the campaign coordinator at Burma Campaign Australia, 'is putting Australia's economic interests ahead of what is in the best interest of the people of Burma, while dismissing human rights as a low priority on the country's foreign policy agenda'.[102]

50 Deciphering Myanmar: an Indian perspective

South Asian neighbours

Myanmar has enjoyed cordial relations, though of varying kind, with its neighbours in South Asia.

SRI LANKA

Among the smaller neighbours, Sri Lanka may be considered as having special ties due to the common bond of Buddhism. The Buddhist faith may have originally reached Burma from India, but its revival many centuries later is traced directly to Sri Lanka. Scriptures that guided and motivated King Anawrahta to spread the faith in his kingdom were brought by the monks who were sent by Sri Lanka's King Vijayabahu. Burma returned the favour by contributing towards the preservation of Buddhism in Sri Lanka when it was under threat due to external invasions. The tradition of exchange of monks and participation in each country's religious conferences by the other's representatives has been a long and established one. Large groups of pilgrims of each country visit the other. Much exchange takes place at the level of religious scholars. The two countries have thus been 'entwined with the golden thread of Theravada Buddhism' for long.[103]

Diplomatic relations were established in 1949. Burma and Sri Lanka, then known as Ceylon, worked as close partners as part of the 'Colombo Powers', together with India, Indonesia and Pakistan. That was the era when Burma looked more towards the West than the East. General Ne Win's visit to Sri Lanka in September 1966 and Prime Minister Sirimavo Bandaranaike's visit to Burma in 1976 helped develop good understanding on several issues. Bilateral ties flourished in the fields of trade, tourism, education and culture. An agreement to establish the joint commission on bilateral cooperation was signed during the visit of Foreign Minister Lakshman Kadirgamar to Myanmar in January–February 1996. Mahinda Rajapaksa visited Myanmar as the prime minister of Sri Lanka in December 2004 when this author had the privilege to meet him briefly at the Sri Lankan high commissioner's residence. The prime minister had come to participate in the World Buddhist Summit. Later, Prime Minister Ratnasiri Wickremanayake visited Myanmar in December 2006.

The second visit by Rajapaksa – this time as the President of Sri Lanka – attracted considerable attention as it took place in June 2009. Myanmar was the first country he visited after inflicting a decisive defeat on the Liberation Tigers of Tamil Eelam (LTTE), a separatist Tamil organisation that engaged in an armed conflict with the

Sri Lankan Army. Sri Lanka projected the appreciation by Myanmar leaders of the bold steps taken by Colombo to defeat terrorism. Foreign Minister Rohitha Bogollagama observed: 'Both countries are linked through political, religious and cultural heritages that have an extended history of over 20 centuries.'[104] Following the eruption of major ethnic and religious strife in the Rakhine state in June 2012 and the spread of Buddhist–Muslim clashes in other parts of Myanmar in March 2013, comparisons were made about the majority–minority relationships in Sri Lanka and Myanmar.[105] It was generally agreed that the equations were more complex and multifaceted in Myanmar than in Sri Lanka.

BHUTAN

Bhutan shares the Himalayan heritage and Buddhism as important bonds with Myanmar. Mutual fascination and appreciation marked these ties that flourished largely at the people's level. Michael Aris, Suu Kyi's husband, was a renowned scholar of Tibetan and Himalayan studies. Bhutan has played an important part in the Suu Kyi's life: this is where Aris proposed to her and, following their marriage in the UK, the couple spent the first year of their marriage in that country. He was the tutor to the royal family and she served as a research officer in the Bhutanese Ministry of Foreign Affairs.

Diplomatic relations between Myanmar and Bhutan were established on 1 February 2012, following the signing of a joint communiqué by their two permanent representatives to the UN. With this agreement in place, Bhutan became the 106th country with which Myanmar maintains diplomatic relations.[106]

NEPAL

Nepal, as the land where Lord Buddha was born, has also held special fascination for the people of Myanmar. Lumbini is one of their favourite pilgrimage destinations. The British connection is another bond that brought Gurkha soldiers into colonial Burma to defend and promote British interests. They and their descendants stayed on. Other Nepalese migrated to Burma in 1950s. Most of them are followers of Hinduism engaged in agriculture, mining and other vocations. The Nepalese origin population was officially estimated to be 'over 200,000' in 2012.[107] Other sources consider it to be a very low figure. Researcher Mrinalini Rai has diligently traced the origin and evolution

52 Deciphering Myanmar: an Indian perspective

of 'the Burmese Nepali', a community of its own that migrated from Nepal to India and then to Burma.[108]

Political and diplomatic relations have been marked by friendship and cordiality, but lacked substance. Among the high-level visits figured King Mahendra's visit to Burma in 1970 and General Ne Win's visit to Nepal in 1966 and 1977. Sujata Koirala, deputy prime minister and foreign minister, visited Myanmar in December 2009. Foreign Minister Nyan Win paid an official visit to Nepal in March 2010 as the two countries celebrated the golden jubilee of the establishment of diplomatic relations.

PAKISTAN

Burma/Myanmar had different neighbours in the east during the twentieth century: British India till 1947, India and Pakistan till 1971 and India and Bangladesh since then. Burma followed the policy to balance India and Pakistan in the first few decades, but the futility and failure of this policy became apparent by the beginning of the twenty-first century when India–Myanmar relations became far closer and more substantive than Myanmar's relations with Pakistan or Bangladesh. Both Pakistan and Bangladesh realised they had little possibilities to match India's Look East Policy that contributed handsomely towards strengthening India–ASEAN ties, especially as the summit dialogue relationship, started in 2002, blossomed into strategic partnership in 2012.

As independent nations, Pakistan and Burma began their exchanges on a note of high hope. Replying to the speech by the first Burmese ambassador to Pakistan at the presentation of credentials on 21 January 1948, Quaid-i-Azam Mohammad Ali Jinnah observed that the attainment of independence by Burma 'gave us in Pakistan the greatest pleasure as it marked the culmination of a process which was initiated in this very subcontinent'. He added: 'I hope these two lands, both ancient in history and both on the road to a new and high destiny, will strive with energy to establish a lasting era of progress and peace.'[109] Simply put, this did not really happen. For much of the post-independence period, both were ruled by the military, a fact that created some mutual empathy, especially in the last decade of SPDC rule.

Beyond the realm of limited intelligence and military exchanges, the bilateral relationship did not get anywhere. Unlike India's extensive contacts with various elements of Myanmar's political class, the Pakistan Embassy contented itself by keeping in touch with the Myanmar people of Pakistan origin and other local Muslims. Two Pakistani scientists reportedly moved to Myanmar in November 2001 when US intelligence was busy investigating their links with the al-Qaeda network.[110] In that year, three Pakistani naval vessels visited Myanmar ports and this was followed by Pakistan President General Pervez Musharraf's visit in May 2001. SPDC's attempt to balance New Delhi and Islamabad came into a sharp focus when in July 2000 Lt. General Khin Nyunt chose to visit Islamabad precisely in the week in which India's Army Chief General V. P. Malik was on a visit to Myanmar at the invitation of General Maung Aye. Concerning Pakistan–Myanmar ties, some in India feared that this linkage could be used adversely for India for the purpose of fomenting trouble in the North East. Besides, the China factor achieved some salience as proximity to China was a common bond between Pakistan and Myanmar. Indian analysts were deeply conscious of its impact. Assessing it in January 2002, one of them observed: 'The growing triangular relationship is not threatening but could become one in the long term.'[111]

Pakistan's return to democracy after Musharraf's rule created fresh hopes, particularly following the commencement of the reform era in Myanmar. This was showcased by President Asif Ali Zardari's sudden visit to Myanmar in January 2012. The visit took place with Naypyitaw extending all due honours to him. Zardari's grand pronouncements about setting up a joint commission, forging new links between business chambers, and exploring possibilities of closer economic and energy cooperation did not lead to many tangible gains. The visit seemed the result of a desire to reach out to Myanmar before India did so at the level of its prime minister. The one photograph that captured a prominent aspect of the visit was Zardari applauding Suu Kyi, surrounded by his children, as she received the Shaheed Benazir Bhutto Award for Democracy. For a while, the similarity in political experience of the two ladies was striking: both had suffered for their cause, had celebrated fathers, and were known for their iron will. But the differences were notable too: one rose to occupy the office of the head of government and was eventually assassinated, whereas the other, as of now, was merely an opposition leader, and about whose security her friends and admirers always remained anxious.

As regards the eruption of Buddhist–Muslim strife in Myanmar, reactions in Pakistan were along the expected lines. The Pakistan government expressed concern and showed support for the cause of Muslims in Myanmar as part of Organisation of the Islamic Conference (OIC) initiatives.[112] But it was the Pakistani Taliban that drew considerable attention through its sharp pronouncements, threatening it would attack Burmese interests to avenge Burmese crimes against Muslims. Its spokesman called on the Pakistani government to sever all relations with Burma and close down its embassy. 'Otherwise we will not only attack Burmese interests anywhere but will also attack the Pakistani fellows of Burma one by one.'[113]

BANGLADESH

Bangladesh, in its previous incarnation as East Pakistan and earlier as part of British India, has been linked to its eastern neighbour through a rich history of interaction. Burma was among the first countries to recognise Bangladesh in January 1972. General Ne Win visited Bangladesh in April 1974; he and Sheikh Mujibur Rahman tried to create the foundation for a new relationship. With a shared land border of about 270 km and their status as developing countries, Bangladesh and Myanmar should normally have had close and cooperative ties, but the fact remains that this has not been so. The relationship has not been smooth and lacks substance. The reasons are not difficult to fathom. While living next to each other, both have paid far greater attention to other neighbours such as India and China in the case of Bangladesh, and China, India and ASEAN in the case of Myanmar than to their own bilateral relations. These, moreover, have been afflicted by a number of contentious issues such as delimitation of maritime boundary, cross-border incidents and exchanges, and the question of Muslims in the Rakhine state, called by different names by the two governments.[114]

The last-mentioned subject became a major bilateral issue in 1977–78 and again in 1991–92. Following the policy of oppression by Myanmar military, a large number of refugees poured into Bangladesh. After protracted dispute and discussions between the two governments, agreements were signed for the repatriation of refugees. Even after the departure of the bulk of refugees, it was noted that 'according to the UNHCR 28,000 refugees remained in UN camps near the border and as many as 200,000 "spontaneously settled" migrants from Arakan state [the old name of the Rakhine state] reside outside the camps'.[115]

While Muslim residents of the Rakhine state sought to flee again to Bangladesh after communal clashes in 2012, the Bangladesh government closed the border firmly and refused them entry. Therefore, on this occasion, the issue did not emerge as a bilateral one but was rather viewed by much of the world as Myanmar's internal problem. Even if the Myanmar argument is conceded that Bangladesh Muslims entered the Rakhine state, using it as a transit point to go off to other ASEAN countries in search of better opportunities, the central point is Myanmar's inability or unwillingness to grant citizenship rights to Muslims of the Rakhine state who have lived there for generations and to insist on treating them as aliens enjoying almost no rights. Of late, however, the government showed some flexibility on this matter.

The highpoint of Bangladesh–Myanmar relations in recent times was the visit of Prime Minister Begum Sheikh Hasina to Naypyitaw and Yangon in December 2011. Her host Thein Sein and she promised, in a joint statement, that relations would 'enter a new phase . . . with a pragmatic and practical approach'. They emphasised 'the need to further accelerate the relations in the best interest of the two peoples'.[116] A number of agreements were signed to foster stronger economic and energy cooperation. Later the maritime boundary dispute was resolved as they accepted the adjudication award by the International Tribunal for the Law of the Sea (ITLOS). Significant scope exists for economic cooperation involving India, Bangladesh and Myanmar. The concept of a potential 'growth triangle' is supported by ADB and UNDP. For its optimal potential to be realised, sincere and sustained endeavours are required at bilateral, trilateral and multilateral levels.

It is thus evident that Myanmar's strategic location, natural wealth, unfolding reform and traditional inclination to be friendly to all as well as the world's need to keep Myanmar engaged would ensure that the country's foreign policy continues to draw much attention in the region and beyond. People in India – government, business, civil society and strategic community – and elsewhere would ignore this certainty at their own peril.

Notes

1 Rabindranath Tagore, *Letters from Java: Rabindranath Tagore's Tour of South-East Asia 1927*, Kolkata: Visva-Bharti Publishing Department, 2010. From the poem, 'To Siam', p. 237.
2 CIA, *the World Factbook* indicates that Myanmar's total coastline is 1,930 km, https://www.cia.gov/library/publications/the-world-factbook/geos/bm.html (accessed on 15 November 2013).
3 Please see CIA, *the World Factbook* for details pertaining to Myanmar's boundaries, https://www.cia.gov/library/publications/the-world-factbook/geos/bm.html
4 Robert H. Taylor, *The State in Myanmar*, London: Hurst Publishers Ltd., 2009, p. 15. The four subperiods mentioned are the classical Bagan period from AD 849 to 1287, a 300-year inter regnum with several rival

56 Deciphering Myanmar: an Indian perspective

state centres, and the founding of the early modern state of the Restored Toungoo (1587–1752) and Konbaung (1752–1885) dynasties.

5 'Summary of the Provisional Results, http://countryoffice.unfpa.org (accessed on 2 October 2014). Some debate is underway about the question of Myanmar's 'missing millions'. Please refer to 'The leftovers', *The Economist*, 4 September 2014.

6 The observation is based on the author's many tours within Myanmar.

7 Chit Oo Nyo, 'The Role of Ramayana in Myanmar Society'. Paper presented at The International Conference on The Artistic, Cultural and Literary Variations on the Ramayana Worldwide, held at Northern Illinois University, 21–23 September 2001.

8 J.S. Furnivall, *Colonial Policy and Practice*, London: Cambridge University Press, 1948, p. 12. 'It is Buddhism that has moulded social Burman life and thought, and to the present day the ordinary Burman regards the terms Burman and Buddhist as practically equivalent and inseparable.'

9 Donald Eugene Smith, *Religion and Politics in Burma*, Princeton, NJ: Princeton University Press, 1965, p. vii.

10 Ibid., p. 296.

11 *Constitution of the Republic of the Union of Myanmar* (2008). Sections: 361–3, www.burmalibrary.org/docs5/Myanmar_Constitution-2008-en.pdf (accessed on 15 November 2013).

12 Bertil Lintner, *Aung San Suu Kyi and Burma's Struggle for Democracy*, Chiang Mai: Silkworm Books, 2011, p. 97.

13 Translated by Pe Maung Tin and G.H. Luce, *The Glass Palace Chronicle of the Kings of Burma*, London: Oxford University Press, 1976.

14 Martin Smith, *Burma: Insurgency and the Politics of Ethnicity*, Bangkok: White Lotus, 1991, p. 29. *CIA, the World Factbook*, estimates of population among ethnic groups is as follows: Burman – 68%, Shan – 9%, Karen – 7%, Rakhine – 4%, Chinese – 3%, Indian – 2%, Mon – 2%, Others –5%, https://www.cia.gov/library/publications/the-world-factbook/geos/bm.html (accessed on 2 October 2014).

15 Bamars are also known as 'Burmans', not 'Burmese', which is a word for all citizens or people of Burma or Myanmar.

16 Shelby Tucker, *Burma: The Curse of Independence*, London: Pluto Press, 2001, p. 11. The author illustrated the point graphically: 'The Mons and Burmans absorbed the Pyus, then mixed with and influenced each other; and, similarly, Burmans and Shans, Shans and Chinese, Burmans and Chinese, Kachins and Shans, Palaungs and Shans, Rakhines and Indians.' His conclusion is: 'Burma thus is a portmanteau of diverse peoples joined artificially by history and politics.'

17 Like Nehru, Aung San negotiated terms of independence with the British; like Patel, he strove to forge national unity; and like Bose, he took Japan's military help in his fight against the British.

18 The Panglong Agreement, 1947. This text is taken from pp. 404–5 of Hugh Tinker's *Burma: The Struggle for Independence 1944–1948* (Vol. II), London: HMSO, 1984. http://www.ibiblio.org/obl/docs/panglong_agreement.htm.

19 F. Tennyson Jesse, *The Story of Burma*, London: Macmillan & Co. Ltd, 1945, p. 88. Jesse, writing in 1946, reported: 'Every Burman knows, as

a good Buddhist, that a woman can never be equal to a man, but every Burmese husband knows also that his wife is the better man of the two.'

20 Jesse, *The Story of Burma*, p. 112.

21 Report by Thein Thein Nyunt, *Rights of Myanmar Women Endowed by Myanmar Customs and Traditions*, Michigan: University Press, 2005.

22 From the author's personal notes.

23 Simon Roughneen, *The Irrawaddy*, 1 June 2012. http://www.irrawaddy.org/archives/5549. Or 'A Conversation with Daw Aung San Suu Kyi', *East Asia 2012*, http://www.livestream.com/worldeconomicforum.

24 The valuable study entitled *Turmoil in Burma* by David Steinberg has the following subtitle: '*Contested Legitimacies in Myanmar*'.

25 Robert H. Taylor, 'Pathways to the Present', in *Myanmar: Beyond Politics to Societal Imperatives*, Kyaw Yin Hlaing, Robert H. Taylor and Tin Maung Maung Than (eds), Singapore: ISEAS, 2005, p. 1.

26 Peter Carey, *Burma: The Challenge of Change in a Divided Society*, New York: St Martin's Press, 1997.

27 P. Sharan, *Government and Politics of Burma*, New Delhi: Metropolitan, 1983, p. 22. 'Although it is true that Western ideas and institutions . . . acted as uniting forces, yet British rule did nothing to foster national unity. On the contrary, both directly and indirectly, it stimulated sectional particularism.'

28 Hugh Tinker, *The Union of Burma*, Oxford University Press, 1959, p. 165: '. . . It is realized by the more clear-sighted that independence did not, of itself, bring Burma nearer to nationhood, it did create the opportunity for fostering the spirit of national unity.'

29 Jan Romein, *The Asian Century*, London: George Allen & Unwin Ltd., 1962, p. 79.

30 Robert Taylor, *The State in Myanmar*, London: Hurst Publishers Ltd., 2009, p. 471: 'The search for political legitimacy has vexed state managers in Myanmar since it became a political issue with the rise of nationalism and the republican state.'

31 For more details read Tinker, *The Union of Burma*, pp. 71–7.

32 It was, of course, common knowledge that the constitution was largely drafted by the strategists of the *Tatmadaw*. Back in 2004–05, many in the diplomatic corps in Yangon were convinced that the draft constitution was essentially ready and would be pushed through when conditions were ripe.

33 Renaud Egreteau and Larry Jagan, *Soldiers and Diplomacy in Burma: Understanding the Foreign Relations of the Burmese Praetorian State*, Singapore: NUS Press, 2013, p. xiii.

34 Many of them returned to Myanmar, following the amnesty granted by the Thein Sein government since 2011.

35 Taylor, 'Pathways to the Present', p. 15. As the author demonstrated, the army 'became more than a pillar of the post-colonial state, it became the state's guarantor and protector'.

36 Myanmar scholars hold divergent views on the *Tatmadaw* as delineated by Shelby Tucker in the last chapter 'Wither Burma?' in his book *Burma: The Curse of Independence*, London: Pluto Press, 2001, p. 202.

37 2008 Constitution's sections 6(f), 14, 40(b), 40(c), 74(a), 74(b), 109(b) and 141(b).

58 Deciphering Myanmar: an Indian perspective

38 Monique Skidmore, *Karaoke Fascism: Burma and the Politics of Fear*, Philadelphia, PA: University of Pennsylvania Press, 2004, p. 59.
39 Myanmar: The Politics of Economic Reform, Asia Report N°231–27 July 2012, p. 1, *International Crisis Group*, http://www.crisisgroup.org/ (accessed on 23 September 2014).
40 *The New Light of Myanmar*, 31 March 2011.
41 Ibid.
42 Ibid.
43 For details, see: 'Myanmar: The Politics of Economic Reform', Asia Report N°231–27 July 2012, *International Crisis Group*, http://www.crisisgroup. org/ (accessed on 23 September 2014).
44 Asian Development Outlook 2014: Fiscal Policy for Inclusive Growth, Asian Development Bank, http://www.adb.org/publications/asian-development-outlook-2014-fiscal-policy-inclusive-growth (accessed on 23 September 2014).
45 'Myanmar Sees Foreign Investment Topping \$5 bln in 2014–15', Reuters, 16 September 2014, http://in.reuters.com/article/2014/09/16/myanmar-investment-idINL3N0RH3EZ20140916 (accessed on 23 September 2014).
46 'Doing Business 2014', *World Bank Group*, http://www.doingbusiness.org/ reports/global-reports/doing-business-2014 (accessed on 23 September 2014).
47 Amitav Ghosh, *Dancing in Cambodia and Other Essays*, New Delhi: Penguin Books India, 2008, p. 57.
48 Please see para three of the article entitled 'Emergence of Foreign Policy' at the website of the Ministry of Foreign Affairs, www.mofa.gov.mm/?page_id=32 (accessed on 15 November 2013).
49 Ibid. Para six.
50 *The New Light of Myanmar*, 31 March 2011.
51 Ibid.
52 Jonathan Head, 'Asean Grapples with Burma Question', BBC News Singapore, 20 November 2007, http://news.bbc.co.uk/2/hi/asia-pacific/7102936. stm (accessed on 11 July 2013).
53 John D. Ciorciari, 'International Politics and the Mess in Myanmar', Japan Policy Research Institute, January 2009, www.jpri.org/publications/ workingpapers/wp114.html (accessed on 12 August 2013).
54 Ibid.
55 Najib Razak, 'The Asean Way Won Burma Over', *The Wall Street Journal*, 3 April 2012, http://www.wsj.com/articles/SB10001424052702303816504577321242628750250 (accessed on 25 April 2015).
56 Kilian Spandler, *Burma's Transformation? Give ASEAN Some Credit*, *IFAIR*, 28 May 2012, http://ifair.eu/en/think/burmas-transformation-give-asean-some-credit (accessed on 25 April 2015).
57 Marie Lall, 'Do the Changes in Myanmar Signify a Real Transition? – A Critique/Response', *Strategic Analysis*, Vol. 37, No 1 (January–February 2013), p. 107.
58 Remarks by the President to the Joint Session of the Indian Parliament in New Delhi, India, The White House, 8 November 2010, http://www.whitehouse.gov/the-press-office/2010/11/08/remarks-president-joint-session-indian-parliament-new-delhi-india (accessed on 14 July 2013).

Deciphering Myanmar: an Indian perspective 59

59 Nehginpao Kipgen, 'US-Burma Relations: Change of Politics under the Bush and Obama Administrations', *Strategic Analysis*, Vol. 37, No. 2 (March–April 2013), p. 204. The article contains an excellent account of US sanctions and the policy shift from Bush to Obama.

60 'U.S. Relations with Burma', http://www.state.gov/r/pa/ei/bgn/35910.htm#relations (accessed on 14 July 2013).

61 'At-a-Glance: "Outposts of Tyranny", BBC News, 19 January 2005, http://news.bbc.co.uk/2/hi/americas/4187361.stm (accessed on 24 October, 2013).

62 Leon T. Hadar, 'U.S. Sanctions against Burma: A Failure on All Fronts', *Trade Policy Analysis*, No. 1 (26 March 1998), http://www.cato.org/publications/trade-policy-analysis/us-sanctions-against-burma-failure-all-fronts (accessed on 14 July 2013).

63 President Barack Obama's Inaugural Address, 20 January 2009, The White House, http://www.whitehouse.gov/blog/inaugural-address (accessed on 24 October 2013).

64 Hillary Rodham Clinton, *Hard Choices*, London: Simon & Schuster, 2014, p. 106. The author recalled having received useful inputs from Indonesian President Susilo Bambang Yudhoyono. 'He told me that he had talked to the Burmese generals and came away convinced that progress was possible. . . . What's more, he reported that the regime might be interested in starting a dialogue with the United States.'

65 Kipgen, 'US–Burma Relations', p. 209.

66 For details of US–Myanmar Relations in 2009, see: http://www.network-myanmar.org/index.php/external-relations/united-states/2009-and-earlier and http://www.bloomberg.com/apps/news?pid=newsarchive&sid=aepdocSWCtmE (accessed on 29 October 2013).

67 Michael Green and Derek Mitchell, 'Asia's Forgotten Crisis: A New Approach to Burma', *Foreign Affairs*, Vol. 86, No. 6 (November–December 2007). Some of the key elements of the new US line could be traced back to this seminal article. Curiously enough, one of them – Mitchell – was appointed later as the US ambassador. www.jstor.org/stable/20032514 (accessed on 15 July 2013).

68 Statement by President Obama on Burma's November 7 Elections, 7 November 2010, http://www.whitehouse.gov/the-press-office/2010/11/07/statement-president-obama-burmas-november-7-elections (accessed on 9 November 2012).

69 For a detailed account of the evolution of Obama's Burma policy, see 'U.S. Policy Towards Burma: Issues for the 113th Congress', 12 March 2013, by Michael F. Martin, www.fas.org/sgp/crs/row/R43035.pdf (accessed on 24 October 2013).

70 Statement by President Obama, 18 November 2011, http://www.whitehouse.gov/the-press-office/2011/11/18/statement-president-obama-burma (accessed on 24 October 2013).

71 Ibid.

72 'Remarks by President Obama at the University of Yangon', 19 November 2012, http://www.whitehouse.gov/the-press-office/2012/11/19/remarks-president-obama-university-yangon (accessed on 10 October 2014).

73 'US President Obama Hails Burma's "Remarkable Journey"', BBC News Asia, 19 November 2012.

60 Deciphering Myanmar: an Indian perspective

74 'Barack Obama, Hillary Clinton Have Emotional Visit with Burma Democracy Activist Aung San Suu Kyi', *The National Post*, 19 November 2012.

75 President Thein Sein's Statement at the General Debate of the Sixty-Seventh Session of the United Nations General Assembly, 27 September 2012, http://gadebate.un.org/sites/default/files/gastatements/67/MM_en.pdf (accessed on 25 April 2015).

76 Hannah Beech, 'Burma's President and Opposition Leader Suu Kyi Visit the US, as Washington Eases Sanctions', *Time World*, http://world.time .com/2012/09/26/charm-offensive-burmas-president-and-opposition-leader-suu-kyi-visit-the-u-s/ (accessed on 9 November 2013).

77 Ibid.

78 Press Availability on the Attended Ministerial Meetings, US Department of State, 10 August 2014, http://www.state.gov/secretary/remarks/2014/08/230478.htm (accessed on 26 September 2014).

79 Comments by Derek Tonkin on 'US Secretary of State John Kerry: Statement to the Press', State Department 10 August 2014, US–Myanmar Relations 2014, http://www.networkmyanmar.org (accessed on 26 September 2014).

80 'The European Union and Burma: The Case for Targeted Sanctions', p. 14, www.ibiblio.org/obl/docs/EU_Sanctions_Report.pdf (accessed on 17 July 2013).

81 www.eu-un.europa.eu/articles/en/article_10339_en.htm (accessed on 17 July 2013).

82 Council of the European Union, 'Press Release', 3082nd Council Meeting, 12 April 2011, pp.15–16, http://www.consilium.europa.eu/uedocs/cms_Data/docs/pressdata/EN/foraff/121506.pdf (accessed on 17 July 2013).

83 Council of the European Union, 'Council conclusions on Burma/Myanmar', 23 April 2012, http://eeas.europa.eu/myanmar/docs/council_conclusions_april_2012_en.pdf (accessed on 17 July 2013).

84 Rajiv Bhatia, 'Travels and Travails of Daw Suu Kyi', *South Asia Monitor*, 7 July 2012, http://southasiamonitor.org/detail.php?type=sl&nid=3339 (accessed on 24 September 2012).

85 Council of the European Union, 'Press Release', 3236th Council Meeting, 22–23 April 2013, p.7, http://www.consilium.europa.eu/uedocs/cms_data/docs/pressdata/EN/foraff/136921.pdf (accessed on 17 July 2013).

86 European Council, The President, 'Building a Lasting EU-Myanmar Partnership', 5 March 2013, http://www.consilium.europa.eu/uedocs/cms_data/docs/pressdata/en/ec/135830.pdf (accessed on 25 April 2015).

87 Andrew Osborn, 'Myanmar Leader Pledges Prisoner Release On UK Visit, *The Irrawaddy*, 16 July 2013, http://www.irrawaddy.org/burma/burma-leader-pledges-prisoner-release-on-uk-visit.html (accessed on 25 April 2015).

88 Please see report by Greg Keller, 'Thein Sein Discusses Widening Ties With France During Visit', 18 July 2013, http://www.irrawaddy.org/burma/thein-sein-discusses-widening-ties-with-france-during-visit.html. (accessed on 26 April 2015).

89 'Aung San Suu Kyi receives Sakharov Prize, finally', CNN.com, edition.cnn.com/2013/10/22/world/Europe/suu-kyi-prize/ (accessed on 9 November 2013).

90 Naftali Bendavid 'Suu Kyi Asks EU to Pressure Myanmar', *The Wall Street Journal*, 21 October 2013, http://www.wsj.com/articles/SB1000 142405270230390240457914935161837 0902 (accessed on 25 April 2015).

91 Aung Zaw, 'On Suu Kyi's Sandhurst Visit, a General Conclusion', *The Irrawaddy*, 30 October 2013, www.irrawaddy.org/commentary/suu-kyi-is-sandhurst-visit-general- (accessed on 9 November 2013).

92 Bert Edström, 'Japan and the Myanmar Conundrum', *Asia Paper*, October 2009, p. 5, http://pwvb.rit-alumni.info/japan_and_the_myanmar_conundrum_-_final.pdf (accessed on 19 July 2013).

93 Ibid.

94 Cited by Bert Edström, 'Japan and the Myanmar Conundrum', *Asia Paper*, p. 51. Japanese Prime Minister Hashimoto Ryutaro said: 'Japan does not feel international isolation is the optimal way for the improvement of (the) domestic situation in Myanmar. Rather, Japan thinks it important to give Myanmar incentives to behave in line with international norms by drawing it out as a member of the international community. From that point of view, Japan appreciates ASEAN's recent agreement to grant official membership to Myanmar sometime in the future. On the other hand, Japan also thinks that ASEAN membership should not provide a smokescreen for oppression in Myanmar. Accordingly, Japan hopes that ASEAN will handle the membership issue in such a manner as to contribute to the improvement of the domestic situation in Myanmar.'

95 Euro-Burma Office Political Monitor 2013, 18–31 May 2013, https://euroburmaoffice.s3.amazonaws.com/filer_public/79/b8/79b802f8-f5e4-453e-9f54-7dd8faa312ce/pm_19_-_05-06-13.pdf (accessed on 17 January 2015).

96 For further details, please see Rahul Mishra, 'Thilawa: Significance of Myanmar's First Special Economic Zone' Viewpoint, ICWA, 30 September 2014, www.icwa.in (accessed on 10 October 2014).

97 Brendan Nicholson, 'Julia Gillard to ease restrictions on Myanmar', *The Australian*, 18 March 2013, www.theaustralian.com.au/national-affairs/foreign-affairs/julia-gillard-to-ease-restrictions-on-myanmar/story-fn59nm2j-1226599791318 (accessed on 27 July 2013).

98 Damien Kingsbury, 'Pariah Myanmar Comes Out As Relations Thaw', http://www.crikey.com.au/2013/03/18/kingsbury-pariah-myanmar-comes-out-as-relations-thaw/?wpmp_switcher=mobile (accessed on 25 April 2015).

99 'Myanmar Opposition Leader Aung San Suu Kyi Pushes Presidential Ambitions during Australia Visit', *Australia Network News*, 28 November 2013, http://www.abc.net.au/news/2013-11-28/an-suu-kyi-in-australia-day-2/5121980 (accessed on 30 November 2013).

100 Myanmar Country Brief, http://dfat.gov.au/geo/burma/Pages/burma-country-brief.aspx (accessed on 25 April 2015).

101 Julia Gillard stated that Australia is 'a great mining nation and we have a competitive advantage when it comes to working with (Myanmar)' Cited in 'Australia signals Myanmar defense links', 19 March 2013, http://www.upi.com/Top_News/Special/2013/03/19/Australia-signals-Myanmar-defense-links/98081363666500/ (accessed on 27 July 2013).

62 Deciphering Myanmar: an Indian perspective

102 Zetty Brake, 'Democratic Voice of Burma: Australia's Pivot on Burma Relations', 11 July 2013, http://www.burmanet.org/news/2013/07/11/democratic-voice-of-burma-australia's-pivot-on-burma-relations--zetty-brake/ (accessed on 27 July 2013).

103 Ministry of Foreign Affairs Sri Lanka, 'SL-Myanmar Relations (download document). . .', http://www.mea.gov.lk/index.php/en/missions/104-myanmar/463-embassy-of-the-democratic-socialist-republic-of-sri-lanka-yangon-myanmar (accessed on 1 August 2013).

104 'Burma–Sri Lanka Connection: Religion and Terrorism', *The Irrawaddy*, 15 June 2009, www.flickr.com/photos/menik/3628686625 (accessed on 1 August 2013).

105 Samir Jeraj, 'The far right in Burma, India and Sri Lanka', *Open Democracy*, 26 June 2013, http://www.opendemocracy.net/samir-jeraj/far-right-in-burma-india-and-sri-lanka (accessed on 1 August 2013).

106 'Establishment of diplomatic relations between the Kingdom of Bhutan and the Republic of the Union of Myanmar', 3 February 2012, http://www.mfa.gov.bt/press-releases/establishment-of-diplomatic-relations-between-the-kingdom-of-bhutan-and-the-republic-of-the-union-of-myanmar.html (accessed on 27 April 2015).

107 'Bilateral Relations (Nepal–Myanmar)', www.mofa.gov.np/en/nepal-myanmar-relations-87.html (accessed on 1 August 2013).

108 'Interrogating Diaspora in Migration: The Burmese Nepalis in Chiang Mai in Northern Thailand', www.icird.org/2012/files/papers/Mrinalini%20Rai .pdf (accessed on 1 August 2013).

109 http://www.quaid.gov.pk/speech17.htm (accessed on 3 August 2013).

110 Prakash Nanda, *Rediscovering Asia: Evolution of India's Look-east Policy*, New Delhi: Lancer Publishers, 2008.

111 C. S. Kuppuswamy, 'China-Pakistan-Myanmar: The Triangular Relationship Needs Careful Watch', South Asia Analysis Group, 29 January 2002, www.southasiaanalysis.org/paper401 (accessed on 3 August 2013).

112 'Anti-Rohingya violence: Pakistan Decries Myanmar Killings', *The Express Tribune*, 27 July 2012. Pakistan Foreign Ministry spokesman stated: 'We are concerned about the situation but there are reports that things have improved there.' www.tribune.com.pk/story/413662/anti-rohingya-violence-pakistan-decries-myanmar-killings/ (accessed on 3 August 2013).

113 'Taliban Calls on Pakistan to Sever Relations with Burma', AFP, 26 July 2012, www.dvb.no/news/taliban-calls-on-pakistan-to-sever-relations-with-burma/23053 (accessed on 3 August 2013).

114 For an excellent analysis, see Kaiser Morshed, 'Bangladesh–Burma Relations', www.idea.int/asia_pacific/burma/upload/chap2.pdf (accessed on 4 August 2013).

115 'Bangladesh–Burma Relations', Arakan Rivers Network, http://www .arakanrivers.net/?page_id=425 (accessed on 4 August 2013).

116 *The New Light of Myanmar*, 8 December 2011, http://www.burmalibrary .org/docs12/NLM2011-12-08.pdf (accessed on 25 April 2015).

Chapter 3

India–Myanmar relations
From antiquity to Raj

> We have said much about India's debt to other cultures, but we must make it clear that she has given as much as or more than she has taken.
>
> – A. L. Basham[1]

To comprehend the true nature, range and depth of relations between India and Myanmar in recent decades and to consider their future trajectory, it is essential to reflect on the broad picture of their evolution through history. Only then can one fully appreciate how diverse and rich these links have been for long. This is the goal of the present chapter. The basic point to stress at the outset is that India–Myanmar relations form part of a larger phenomenon, namely the outflow and spread of Indian influences in the region east of India, stretching from Burma to Bali and beyond.

After pointing out that India and China have 'the oldest continuous cultural traditions in the world',[2] Basham stated categorically in his classic: 'The whole of South-East Asia received most of its culture from India.'[3] The region was a recipient of other influences from China and the Islamic world, but 'the primary impetus to civilization came from India'.[4] This stemmed from a historical process that began long before the Christian era.

Panikkar astutely explained the 'great difference' between India's impact on the Far East, China and Mongolia, on the one hand, and on South-East Asia, on the other; it lay:

> . . . in the fact that in China and in areas where Chinese civilisation was dominant, Indian influence was mainly on religious ideas and not on social or cultural institutions, while in South-East Asia, its influence was more fundamental and led to the creation of a new civilization.

64 From antiquity to Raj

He, however, hastened to add that 'it is the genius of the local people that gives to it its special characteristics and its distinctiveness'.[5]

Eastern adventures

Driven by a mixture of motives – to do trade, experience adventure, share skills and spread faith – Indians of the ancient period including traders, priests, monks, craftsmen and temple builders trekked or sailed to the eastern lands. They braved hazards and dangers, but succeeded in establishing 'colonies'. However, these people were not colonialists in the Western sense; they were different from the Portuguese, Dutch, British and French colonialists who followed much later, riding on the force of superior arms. 'The Indian "colonies" were peaceful ones, and the Indianized kings of the region were indigenous chieftains who had learnt what India had to teach them.'[6] Those who went from India were armed only with a few 'things' to offer – their craftsmanship, religious or spiritual knowledge, and some ideas – along with an intense desire to explore greener pastures or *Suvarnabhumi* as much of the East was known to them at that time. They found in local societies a receptive environment and communities that were willing to welcome, intermingle with new arrivals and absorb 'the goods' they brought with them. As we dig deeper to appreciate the contemporary civilisation of countries such as those of Indo-China or CLMV (viz. Cambodia, Laos, Myanmar and Vietnam), Thailand, Malaysia, Singapore and Indonesia, multiple layers of the impact of Indian thought, art, architecture, culture, philosophy and religion become evident. Whether this linkage is fully acknowledged today or not is a different matter. But, the real inspiration and force behind India's Look East Policy since the early 1990s are embedded in the multisplendoured bonds that were forged during the ancient times.

In this general backdrop, it was perfectly natural that the land adjacent to India came under the sway of its influences in an appreciable manner. People from the erstwhile Bengal (with a part in India and another forming Bangladesh now), Assam and the border region could trek into what was Upper Burma and the Arakan region. Flow of people from Burma to India also took place.[7] Besides, people sailed from the coast of Bengal, Orissa and Andhra Pradesh to the south-eastern and south-western coast of Burma to begin their interaction through trade, culture and religion with the inhabitants of the coastal region and those living in Lower Burma.

In charting the history of human settlement in Burma, anthropologists and historians speak invariably of the flow, in wave after wave, of outsiders from three different directions: China in the north; Cambodia, Malaya and Siam in the east; and India in the west and south. Some of them assert that in the resultant interaction or clash of cultures on the Burmese soil, ancient Indians prevailed over others. As Hall put it:

> The Indo-Chinese peninsula became a battle-ground between the Indian and Chinese civilizations. There was some blending, but in the long run Indian culture triumphed everywhere save in Annam and Tongking. . . . Burma's debt to India is great.[8]

Ancient India viewed parts of the East as *Suvarnabhumi* or *Suvarna-dvipa*, the 'Land of Gold' or the 'Island of Gold', respectively.[9] While it is difficult to determine the exact frontiers of the fabled region, this usage indicates that in the period of antiquity, the region was widely known for its propensity to produce gold, precious minerals and other valuable commodities. Later, historians continued to call Burma as the 'Golden Land', although they advanced at least two additional reasons for this appellation: one, the land was full of gold-covered pagodas, and two, it was blessed with rice plants that turned golden brown as crops ripened.[10] Today's Burma retains its uniqueness as 'the Golden Land'. It is, however, marked by the paradox of people's abject poverty amidst incredible richness of the land's resources.

How old is the relationship between India and Burma forms a subject of considerable debate among scholars. In general, Indian scholars take a really long-term view while assessing the past, whereas others prefer to take a restrictive position, insisting on the need to go by hard, verifiable evidence. The former school's argument probably would be that if the Indian civilisation is at least 5,000 years old, it is wrong to believe that interactions began only 1,500 years ago. They refer to analyses drawn from legends, chronicles, traditions and stories in scriptures, both Hindu and Buddhist, to conclude that links dated back to pre-Christian and even pre-Buddhist eras.[11] Majumdar, a characteristic example of this camp, argued:

> Burma, being the nearest to India and directly accessible both by land and sea, naturally attracted Indian traders, merchants, missionaries and more ardent military spirits from a very early period. There is no doubt that by the first century AD and probably long before that, there were already large Hindu settlements both along the coastal region as well as in the interior of Burma.[12]

He added: 'On the whole we shall be justified, on these grounds alone, in dating the beginning of Hindu colonization in Burma certainly before and probably long before, the beginning of Christian era.'[13]

Harvey presented the contrary view. 'Since, as late as 500 AD writing was rare, the chronicles' accounts of events as far back as 850 BC are invalid.'[14] He believed that history 'cannot be remembered unless it is written', thus debunking portrayals based on oral traditions, which were apparently passed down through succeeding generations. Hence his conclusion is that 'until 1044 AD these accounts are at best containing a substratum of truth'.[15]

Other historians – and even Harvey to an extent – believe that trade and cultural exchanges and movements of people became fairly well established in or around the fifth century AD. 'The earliest archaeological remains, notably at Sri Ksetra and Halingyi in Burma and Mrohaung in Arakan', said Hall, 'show marked Indian influence.'[16]

India's cultural connection was woven into Burma's consciousness. 'Indians from the Coromandel Coast settled in Burma, and it is their 2nd century script which the Burmese learned from the Talaings and use to this day', wrote F. Tennyson Jesse.[17] Excavations in Burma, although limited in terms of the area of coverage, yielded adequate finds such as images, terracotta tablets, gold plates and architectural items that confirmed Indian influence in early centuries after the birth of Christ.[18] They negated the conventional view that the links began later when Burma adopted Theravada Buddhism imported from Sri Lanka. In fact, they presented a more complex and enriching picture of the inflow of Brahmanism, its belief systems and rituals; Sanskrit, Pali and other languages and scripts, both from south and north India; and Buddhism, both Hinayana and Mahayana, to Burmese shores and lands.[19] These rivulets of influences mingled with local values, beliefs and practices (such as Animism) for centuries before producing what eventually became the unique Burmese culture. In the end, Theravada Buddhism no doubt won as the faith that was adopted by the bulk of the population, but it could never set aside the powerful traces of Hinduism from India.

Burma's kings

Throughout the rule by a long series of kings who belonged to three main dynasties – Pagan, Toungoo and Konbaung – Burma retained and developed its connections with India in varying degrees. The royal period began in 1044 with Anawrahta in Pagan and ended with

Thibaw in 1885 in Mandalay, the last king with whom ended the kingdom of Ava and indeed the Burmese monarchy itself. Anawrahta was strongly influenced by Buddhism, which grew in India, whereas the royal rule in Burma was terminated by those who conquered India.

The Buddhist scriptures in the custody of a Mon king caused a great conflict, started by King Anawrahta. His unique decision, taken on the advice of a knowledgeable monk, was to launch a war – not to gain territory or wealth but to capture the holy scriptures. Soldiers were sent to the neighbouring kingdom that possessed 30 complete sets of *Tripitaka* – 'the Three Baskets of Laws'. His conquest of Thaton in 1057 was 'a decisive event in Burmese history'.[20] The defeated king, his family, wealth and scriptures were transported to Pagan, an act that brought 'the Burman into direct contact with the Indian civilizing influences'.[21] Thus,

> . . . the Thaton captives helped to civilise the north of Burma. The clergy taught the art of writing, and since Pali was the language of the sacred writings, so, in the curious way that these things happen, the conquered became the conqueror. The Burmese learned and accepted the Talaing alphabet and started to write the language.[22]

Another great king of this dynasty, Kyanzittha, married a Chola princess. He built the famous Ananda Temple in Bagan, inspired by the inscription given to him by Buddhist monks of the great cave temple of Ananda at Udayagiri in Orissa.[23] Another view is that the temple of Paharanpur in northern Bengal might have served as 'the model'.[24] According to a Mon inscription at Shwehsandaw Pagoda at Prom, Kyanzittha was the first king to undertake the restoration of the Mahabodhi temple at Bodh Gaya in India. In a delicious irony and role reversal, India's offer to help in the restoration of Ananda Temple was accepted by the government of Myanmar in 2011.[25] The work was proceeding satisfactorily at the time of this writing.

History is full of stories of attacks by Burmese kings of the neighbouring lands such as Ayutthaya (in Thailand), Manipur (in India) and Arakan (the present-day Rakhine state), thus demonstrating their military prowess and ambition – but also their propensity to commit atrocities.[26] Arakan turned out to be a vital point of contact between the two countries through centuries. After Anawrahta's assertion of authority over it, Arakan managed to preserve its independence from Burmese kings between the thirteenth and fifteenth centuries. 'Arakan's

68 From antiquity to Raj

contacts with Mohammedan India were probably closer than those with Burma.'[27] Partly river communications with India ensured this. Periodic strife marked the relations between Bengal and Arakan, with one or the other gaining an upper hand. This resulted in the control over Chittagong changing hands between the two (i.e. Bengal and Arakan from time to time). Chittagong remained under the control of Arakan from 1459 to 1666 when it was annexed by the Mughal Empire. In the annals of Arakan the episode of Prince Shuja, the son of Emperor Shah Jahan, figures prominently. Shuja lost his bid for the throne of Delhi and took refuge with the king of Arakan. This earned for the Arakanese king and his partners – Dutch traders – the wrath of Emperor Aurangzeb and his governor of Bengal, Shayista Khan.[28] Much later, King Bodawpaya of Burma attacked Arakan in 1784 and annexed it to his kingdom.

In the quest for trading concessions in Burma, the Portuguese and the Dutch were early winners. But they were gradually displaced by the British who gained ground. Having taken control of India, the East India Company eyed Burma from the west, and France, having made inroads into Indo-China and Siam, lusted for a slice of business and political control of Burma from the east. Burmese kings' tendency to attack the easternmost parts of British India – Assam, Manipur, Cachar – and to pose threat to the security of mainland Bengal provided a strong reason to British colonialists to address seriously 'the Burma problem'. In any case, they were interested in Burma's natural resources purely for commercial reasons. Additionally, there was the pressing temptation to try to open a trade route to China through Burma. Thus by the end of the eighteenth century, a combination of factors, both commercial and geopolitical, had paved the ground for conflict between British India and Burma. It was an uneven fight, the outcome of which became increasingly certain.[29] Astutely charting the prelude to the three wars that were to follow, Frank N. Trager wrote:

> In the 18th century, Britain had achieved supremacy in India by diplomacy where feasible, by war when necessary. During the 19th century, British rule was extended to Burma in the same way. The challenge was one that Konbaung kings were ill-equipped to meet.[30]

In January 1824, Burmese troops again attacked eastern India, particularly Cachar, which was a British-protected state. This triggered the First Anglo-Burmese War in March 1824. The Burmese side was led by a courageous and skilful commander – Maha Bandula – but times had changed. Now valour was no match against superior technology and professionally trained soldiers.[31] The Burmese belief in their invincibility was the first casualty, probably followed by their pride and self-confidence. The war ended with the Treaty of Yandabo in 1826. It resulted in Burma yielding her suzerainty over Manipur and Assam, ceding the provinces of Arakan and Tenasserim, the two important provinces on the southern coast, paying indemnity, and permitting exchange of envoys with the British. The kingdom of Burma was down, but not out yet.

Things settled down for a while, although relations between British India and the Burmese kingdom never really improved. The British complained of the contempt in which the Burmese held them.[32] The Burmese knew that the British lusted for the former's possessions. The Second Anglo-Burmese War followed, resulting in Lower Burma falling like a ripe fruit in the lap of Lord Dalhousie. In December 1852, he proclaimed the annexation of the province of Pegu. The three Burmese provinces (i.e. Arakan, Tenasserim and Pegu) were ruled by Company officials separately until 1862 when, at the end of the Company Raj, they became a single province of British India to be ruled by a Chief Commissioner. Around this time, Colonel Burney, a Company official, successfully strove to restore to Burma the Kabaw Valley that had been given to the Raja of Manipur.[33]

Thirty-three years represented a long gap between the Second and Third (and the last) Anglo-Burmese War. Much of this period was accounted for by the reign of King Mindon and only seven years of rule by Thibaw, the last king. Mindon was a good king, but not Thibaw. Always distressed by the loss of half of his kingdom, Mindon tried to deal with the British with as much dignity as he could muster. He became aware of the wide world through the diplomatic missions he sent to Europe. He sought to approach the British monarch directly rather than through the Viceroy in India. His envoys were received by Queen Victoria who, reciprocating the Burmese royal protocol, which had irritated British envoys immensely, demanded that Mindon's diplomats should prostrate before her.[34] The king's purpose of sending diplomatic missions to London, Paris and Rome was to enlist support for the restoration and preservation of Burma, but it proved futile.[35] He sent the first official message to the President of the USA. Mindon was seen as a caring king, even by the British.[36]

With Mindon's death in 1878, palace intrigue reached its zenith. His favourite son, Nyaung Yan Prince, whom he had not designated as the Crown Prince for fear of the latter's safety, had to flee. Thibaw ascended the throne with much help from the Queen Mother; he remained there with help from Supayalat, his half-sister who became his queen. Thibaw's reign is a long saga of massacre of potential competitors and their families, misrule, Anglo-French competition for business and political interests in Upper Myanmar and eventually the commencement of the Third Anglo-Burmese War. Just before it, Thibaw had opened secret discussions with the French, which made the British feel insecure. The immediate trigger for the war was his attempt to levy a fine on the Bombay Burmah Trading Corporation. The British served an ultimatum, ignored the royal response and sent troops up the Irrawaddy, which faced little resistance. 'The Annexation was not a war but a walk-over.'[37] In January 1886 the British took over Upper Burma, sending Thibaw into exile in Ratnagiri, India, where he stayed until his death in 1916. Burma was annexed to the British Empire. Much earlier, in 1858 they had sent Bahadur Shah Zafar, India's last emperor, into exile in Rangoon where he died in 1862. The two interesting facts – that the last Indian emperor was buried in the Burmese soil and the last Burmese king was buried in the Indian soil – represent a special and unique bond.

In a recent, remarkably readable work, author Sudha Shah traces the life of King Thibaw and his family after his exile to India. The book's 'raison d'être' was 'to provide an insight into . . . how an all-powerful and very wealthy family coped with forced isolation . . . and . . . how the family lived once the exile ended'.[38] The portrayal of Thibaw shows that, unlike the last emperor of India, the last king of Burma was treated quite well by the British government, although Thibaw did not think so. The book relates the story of the visit by the governor of Bombay to Thibaw's new residence in Ratnagiri in January 1911. The ex-king gave to his visitor a memorial or petition, which Sudha Shah rates as 'the most heart-wrenching' of all the memorials submitted by him. In it, Thibaw urged that he should be addressed as 'His Majesty', saying:

> Once I had the same footing as the King of Siam, the Emperor of China, the Emperor of Japan and other Kings. It seems to me rather inconsistent to address such a King as His Highness even if he be an ex-King. . . . Personally any form of address will be acceptable to me. I do not seek for shadow when I know I have lost the substance. But I feel it very much when they address me as His Highness, as it reminds me of my fall. . . .[39]

For Supalayat, the ex-queen, 'the British were anathema: white outside, dark inside, to paraphrase what she once so memorably said'.[40]

As the brief survey demonstrates, apart from trade, three Bs – Brahmanism, Buddhism and British – moulded the relationship between India and Burma. The last B – British rule – had a peculiar and painful outcome. The idea and plan to subjugate Burma, divesting it of its independence and monarchy, which was absolutely pivotal to its socio-political structure, was that of Britain. In its implementation, the leadership role was played by the rulers of British India, but a vast majority of the agents of implementation were Indian soldiers, civil servants, traders, workers, agriculturalists and financiers.

From the Burmese perspective, it was evident that the country had come under the double domination of Britain and India. As the average Burmese grappled with this humiliating reality and as he came into daily contact much more with the Indian rather than the British face of colonialism, he developed hostility towards both, but probably more for the Indian. This perception strengthened over time, although Burmese knew that Indians were victims of the same colonialism in their own homeland. This created some empathy too.

Burmese history since 1886 sheds light on Indians in Burma as both the hunter and the hunted. And it reveals how relations between Burma and India continued to be important but intensely complex too.

Under the Union Jack

The British took over 60 years to secure full control over Burma, from the launch of the first Anglo-Burmese War in 1824 till the end of monarchy in December 1885. Burma Proper, comprising Lower and Upper Burma as well as the provinces in the south-east and the south-west, was governed by the British directly, whereas the Hills – the home of Kachins and Chins – and the Shan States were under indirect control. The Raj lasted 61 years counting from 1886 to 1947 as Burma gained independence in January 1948. Thus, whether one looks at the longer period stretching for 121 years or the shorter period of 61 years, Burma–India relations were inevitably steered by the policy of Great Britain, which ruled over both India and Burma. The nature of linkage of governance in Burma with British India and the influx of Indians into Burma, necessitated by the British policy to develop Burmese economy and modernise administration, were among the key elements shaping the relationship.

The manner in which administrative linkage evolved is interesting – through progressive improvisation. Their earliest gains were the provinces of Arakan and Tennasserim, following the first war. The former was made a part of the Presidency of Bengal and was administered by

72 From antiquity to Raj

a commissioner, whereas Tennasserim was administered by a separate commissioner who was answerable to Penang in Malaya. This arrangement changed in 1834 when both provinces began to be administered from India. The same arrangement was made applicable to Pegu, after the annexation of Lower Burma in 1852. Ten years later, in 1862, the three provinces were merged into a single unit – the Province of Burma – under a single Chief Commissioner who reported to the Governor General of India. The rank of the provincial head was elevated to the Lieutenant Governor in 1897 who was also provided with an appointed advisory body, the Legislative Council.

Subsequently from 1923, the province was ruled by a Governor who was assisted by a partially elected assembly that was created under the dyarchy constitution. This arrangement stipulated a division of powers between the Governor and his ministers, with the latter handling education, health, local government, agriculture and forests, while the former dealt with more important subjects directly. In reality, senior civil servants called the shots under the leadership of the Governor. It was only in 1937 that the Province of Burma was formally separated from British India and made an entity of its own within the British Empire, to be governed directly under the supervision of the British government in London. This also brought, in its wake, an increased role for a fully elected assembly and the ministers responsible to it 'under the supervision and ultimate veto of the governor who remained responsible for defence, foreign affairs, finance and the peripheral regions of the state, now called Frontier Areas and the Shan States'.[41]

Role of Indians

The conquest of Burma was the fruit of British strategy and it was secured with the help of British arms. But the vast majority of troops were Indians. The country was ruled by the British, but the middle and lower positions in the officialdom were manned mostly by Indians. 'The number of European troops in Burma', wrote John L. Christian in 1945, 'was seldom more than 2,000 during the present century and frequently was as low as one battalion'.[42] In the fields of agriculture, industry, police, administration and railways – as in the army – Indians played a pivotal role in Burma through the second half of the nineteenth century and the first half of twentieth century. But it is worth underlining that in the modern era they entered the country riding on the coattails of the British Raj. Naturally, therefore, they were viewed 'as the instruments of foreign domination and certainly not as the torch-bearers of a common civilization'.[43] The net result was that the Burmese had lost their due place in the governance of their own country.[44]

As the British control over Burma expanded in stages, the influx of Indians increased in size, particularly after the second Anglo-Burmese War. After the annexation of Lower Burma in 1852, the British administration faced the challenge of converting Rangoon, which was a mere village in the early decades of nineteenth century, into a modern city with a large international port. This transformation was engineered with the help of 'India's men, money and materials'.[45] The result was that, with the number of Indians reaching 134,000 in the 1901 census out of a quarter million people in Rangoon, the city looked more Indian in appearance. Simultaneously, fuelled by the opening of the Suez Canal in 1869 and the demand for agricultural products of the East, agriculture, especially rice cultivation, was developed in Upper and Lower Burma. For this purpose too, abundant seasonal labour was brought from India, much of which passed through Rangoon, 'the main camp from which Indians filtered all over Burma'.[46] Thus, as Chakravarti wrote:

> Most of its valuable lands, opulent buildings, and shopping centres were owned by Indians, and its trade and commerce remained largely in the hands of Indians. All this became the object of envy.[47]

The driving motivation for a massive influx of Indians in Burma was the British policy, which aimed to use Indian labour to develop a capitalist economy. This was reinforced by other factors, namely 'proximity of two areas' (i.e. India and the Delta in Burma) and the transportation links that were established after the British rule began, as pointed out by Michael Adas who added another factor: 'Burma offered (for the Indian labour) opportunities which far surpassed those of other potential destinations.'[48]

At the end of nineteenth century, the Indian population in the whole of Burma had shot up to almost half a million people, with 'a great majority of them' being 'temporary or seasonal immigrants'.[49] The Indian community's stay in the country was marked by several distinguishing features. The community brought its own regional identities – languages, rituals, cuisine and caste system – from India; it lacked internal unity; and it was unable to mingle with the Burmese with one exception: frequent marriages between Indian men and Burmese women took place, triggering much local resentment. Other causes of negativity towards Indians were the control the Indian businessmen exerted on local economy and the controversial role played by the Chettiars in developing banking and agricultural sectors.

74 From antiquity to Raj

In a recent work named *Fiery Dragons*, Sean Turnell opened its chapter on 'The Chettiars' with two contradictory views, with a Karen witness calling them 'fiery dragons that parch every land that has the misfortune of coming under their wicked creeping' and Sir Spencer Harcourt Butler, Governor of Burma, telling Chettiar representatives in 1927: 'You represent a very important factor indeed in the life of this province. . . .'[50] The author's verdict on whether Chettiars were 'guilty or innocent?' was to rebut 'the notion that the Chettiars charged "usurious" rates of interest with the objective of acquiring land', but he did not conclude 'that all aspects of the Chettiars role in Burma were positive or even benign'.[51] Besides, the Indian face in the army, police and administration was all too visible to the local populace. The cumulative effect of these factors was that the position of Indians became 'politically vulnerable in the latter half of the 19th century'.[52]

In subsequent decades the Indian community, as Tinker explained, had three options: 'throw in their lot with the Burmans', side with 'the British overlords' and support 'explicitly the empire they had implicitly done so much to extend', or demand 'a special position' as Indians 'requiring special safeguards'.[53] As Indians largely adopted the third option, it led to serious problems. 'The insistence upon the Indian identity of Indians in Burma exposed the community to the growing chauvinism of the Burmese nationalists.'[54] Much water had to flow down the Irrawaddy, marked by periods of peace, toil, stability and prosperity (for a few), which were punctuated by opposition, clashes and communal riots in the first four decades of the twentieth century, before the edifice of the Raj was deeply threatened by the arrival of Japanese troops in 1941.

Indian leaders

A brief mention of visits by famous Indian leaders to Burma during the pre-independence period is both interesting and illustrative of the importance Burma enjoyed in India's mind.

Rabindranath Tagore visited Rangoon in 1916 and 1924. While visiting Burma, he wrote evocatively about his visit to the Shwedagon Pagoda, but he prefaced the marvellous description by a veiled reference to the strong presence of Indians. He wrote: 'This is why I say that though I saw Rangoon, in my seeing there was no knowing. I took away from the place recollections of my Bengali friends' hospitality, but did not succeed in receiving any gift from Burmese hands.' However, when Tagore saw the Shwedagon Pagoda, his 'mind was gladdened and responsive'. He added, 'There was no solitude, but there was privacy, no silence, but there was peace.'[55]

Mahatma Gandhi visited Burma on three occasions, in February 1902, March 1915 (for about ten days) and March 1929 (for about two weeks). He went to several towns in addition to Rangoon and met a large number of Indians. He noted the impact of Buddhism on Burma and stated: 'Asia has a message for the whole world if it will only live up to it.'[56] He was happy to see Burmese women enjoy 'a freedom which no other women on earth enjoy elsewhere'. But he was distressed to note that some of them smoked. 'We who come from India are painfully surprised to see beautiful Burmese women disfigure their mouths by cheroots and cigars', he said.[57]

Speaking to Indians in Burma, Gandhi gave valuable advice: 'Since you have come here as foreigners, you should become one with the people here as sugar dissolves in milk.' He also asked them to have due regard for the people of the country. 'The least that the Indians owe to the Burmese', he said, was to learn the Burmese language.[58] Indian settlers followed this advice on a large scale. But relations between Burmese and Indians suffered from considerable tension. While the two influenced each other in the field of dress, cuisine and culture, Indians were seen to be an economic threat. 'They are taking away our lands and jobs' seemed the constant anxiety. Indians were also perceived as having a superiority complex. They made a special effort towards integration, changing their names to Burmese names and adopting the Burmese dress, but this was not enough. Aware of tensions between the two sides, Gandhi urged: 'Indians and Burmese should approach each other not in a spirit of suspicion and distrust but that of amity and goodwill.'[59]

Gandhi reserved his special affection for Mandalay. During a visit to the historic city, he referred to the imprisonment of India's renowned leaders there – Lokmanya Bal Gangadhar Tilak, Lala Lajpat Rai and Subhas Chandra Bose. Hailing Mandalay as 'the place of pilgrimage for us', he said: 'In India, it is a common saying that the way to Swaraj is through Mandalay, and the British Government has taught you too that great lesson, by incarcerating India's great sons here.'[60]

Jawaharlal Nehru visited Burma before its independence. It was 'the summer of 1937' and as he put it, it was 'no holiday as crowds and engagements pursued me everywhere' on the visit to Burma and Malaya. He added that he 'loved to see and meet the flowery and youthful people of Burma, so unlike, in many ways, the people of India with the stamp of long ages passed upon them'.[61] The Burmese women

76 From antiquity to Raj

floored Nehru too. He said that their women were full of charm and activity, and laughter peeped out of the corner of their eyes.

Japan's occupation of Burma created yet another significant dimension relating to India. Subhas Chandra Bose shifted the headquarters of the 'Provisional Government of Free India' and the Indian National Army (INA) from Singapore to Rangoon. Recruitment from among local Indians was stepped up; an INA bank was set up; and considerable donations were raised from the Indian community. With active help from the Japanese Army, INA readied itself to march into battle against the troops of British India, staffed largely by fellow Indians. It succeeded in capturing some territory in India in March 1944 before suffering defeat at the hands of the British. This led to the end of Bose's road to India's freedom.

For Subhas Chandra Bose, Burma was where he had received apprenticeship and prepared himself as a political leader, having gone through imprisonment in Mandalay jail from 1925 to 1927 for his political activities in India. He derived much 'consolation and pride' from the fact that he was following in the footsteps of Lokmanya Bal Gangadhar Tilak who had spent many years in the same jail.[62] Bose used his time in jail to study Burma and the Burmese people. He wrote: 'What struck me greatly was the innate artistic sense which every Burman has. If they have any faults, it is their extreme naiveté and absence of all feeling against foreigners.'[63]

On 24 April 1945, Bose left Rangoon for good, after INA's defeat. In a deeply moving message titled 'India Shall be Free', he said: 'I have always said that the darkest hour precedes the dawn. We are now passing through the darkest hour; therefore, the dawn is not far off.'[64] How right he was! India attained freedom in a little over two years, and it fondly remembered the tremendous contribution of Subhas Chandra Bose and his soldiers to the struggle for freedom.

Bose and Aung San had mutual respect. Speaking at a public reception, given to Sarat Chandra Bose, the elder brother of Subhas, in the City Hall in Rangoon on 24 July 1946, General Aung San said: 'I knew him [Subhas Bose] also as a sincere friend of Burma and Burmese people. Between him and myself, there was complete mutual trust.' He explained that during the war years the stage was not reached for joint action by the INA and the Burma National Army (BNA), but the two leaders were bound by an understanding 'that, in any event, and whatever happened, the I.N.A. and the B.N.A. should never fight each other'. Aung San, moulded by the experience of his interaction with India's great leaders, had the conviction that India and Burma should

From antiquity to Raj 77

be 'not merely good neighbours, but good brothers even, the moment such course should become possible'.[65]

Angle of separation

The Indian connection with colonial Burma may be examined further by recalling the debate on and resolution of the separation issue in the backdrop of the rise of Burmese nationalism.

Following the 'pacification' that took a few years (after the fall of Burmese monarchy), the country became used to the new political dispensation and became relatively peaceful and politically inactive. Burma was called the 'Cinderella of the British Empire'.[66] Burmese nationalism saw initial stirrings only in 1906 when the Young Men's Buddhist Association (YMBA) was established, an organisation started by a handful of educated Burmese who saw it as an instrument of social and religious reform. They focussed attention on 'the shoe question', opposing vehemently the European practice of entering Buddhist pagodas wearing shoes and thus desecrating the holy places. This was an effective way to create pride in Burmans' Buddhist identity, which attracted considerable popular support. YMBA initially had somewhat close connections with the leaders of the Indian community, which worked under the guidance of the Indian National Congress (INC). The party had opposed Burma's annexation, expressing the view, way back in 1885, that 'the country of Burma should be separated from the Indian Vice-royalty and constituted a Crown Colony as distinct from the Government of this country (India) as is Ceylon'.[67] The British government had totally ignored this view and chose to govern Burma as a part of India.

However, many years later, when the British government was ready to move India towards receiving 'self-governing institutions' of a responsible government through Montagu–Chelmsford constitutional reforms, it decided to exclude Burma from their ambit. This caused much concern to the Burmese. YMBA sent a delegation to India in 1917 in order to plead for the cause of Burma – for its separation from India and its desire 'to exist as a separate entity within the Imperial Commonwealth'.[68] By its very nature, the Burmese political movement represented, at the outset, a step away from India, a move against Burma Indians because most of them favoured to retain the administrative link between India and Burma. Nevertheless, Burmese agitation continued against the decision to exclude the application of the dyarchy to Burma. A broader grouping – the General Council of Burma

Association – was established, which sent two delegations to London during 1919–20 with the basic objective of ensuring that in the field of constitutional reforms, Burma kept pace with India. Significantly, the INC, at its Nagpur session in 1920, supported the objectives of political movement in Burma.

Eventually, London veered around to the decision to extend the dyarchy to Burma. The view that prevailed in the British parliament was that 'Burma ought not to be part of the Indian System and made a Separate Government; that there is, in fact, no more reason for making Burma a part of India than there is for making the Malaya States or East Africa or Ceylon part of it'.[69] In the years leading to the dyarchy, opinion in Burma became pronouncedly anti-Indian. As Chakravarti explained:

> Now, the main plank of the Burman political platform was simultaneous separation and self-government; but if both could not be had at once, Burmans would prefer to accept separation first and fight for self-governance next.[70]

The dyarchy became operational on 1 January 1923. It came with separate communal representation and safeguards for the minorities, viz. Indians, Indo-Burmans, Karens and Anglo-Burmans. This issue alone was enough to bedevil relations between the Burmese and Burma Indians – as it had done in India where separate representation was granted to the Muslims on communal grounds. However, the main subject that dominated political discourse and developments during the period of dyarchical constitution (January 1923–March 1937) was separation from India. Generally speaking, the British-led government in Burma favoured it. The Burmese political class was divided between the anti-separationists and separationists who advocated separation along with a Dominion status for Burma. Rich Indians with vested interests were opposed to separation, while a vast majority of about one-million-strong Indian population was probably indifferent and was, in any case, not consulted because only a small portion of them enjoyed voting rights.

Against the backdrop of deteriorating relations between Indians and Burmese, the departing Governor, Sir Harcourt Butler, singled out the Chettiar community by praising its contribution to agricultural development of Burma, in his farewell address in December 1927, as mentioned earlier. He spoke of the role of Burmans and non-Burmans in enhancing the prosperity of Burma, which now boasted the second largest port, bigger than Calcutta, and a record in rice production.

His successor, Sir Charles Innes, however, viewed Burma in the larger geopolitical context, 'a comparatively small land wedged between the two great countries of India and China'. He saw 'evidence' of 'the peaceful penetration of the industrious Chinaman and the no less industrious Indian' everywhere in Burma, raising the question: 'Will the Burmans be able to maintain their individuality as a nation and the distinctive character of their civilization?'[71] This perception had already permeated in the Burmese political circles, thereby strengthening their clamour for separation accompanied by greater autonomy to govern. At the special Roundtable Conference in 1931 with British Prime Minister Ramsay MacDonald, a Burmese delegate, Tharrawaddy Maung Maung, stated:

> No self-respecting nation has ever considered the cost of freedom, but unless separation from India means full Dominion Status *with power of secession*, I do not want separation. We are bound to India by the holy ties of suffering under a foreign yoke, and nothing less than Dominion Status shall cut these ties.[72]

The contrary view indicated that it was 'the mere accident of history that caused Burma to become part of the Indian Empire, to be administered as an Indian province'.[73] The argument, therefore, was that Burma should be separated from India immediately. The INC and other political parties took the line that it was for Burma to decide for itself on the question of separation from India. Meanwhile, Indians, especially those with stakes in Burma, were getting nervous about the prospect of separation.

In a first systematic move, London utilised the visit of the Simon Commission to Burma in January 1929 to deliberate on this matter. The Commission concluded that Burma and India were two completely different countries. It favoured immediate separation, dismissing military, financial and economic objections to separation; but it did not make any recommendation on what kind of constitutional order should be given to a Burma separated from India.

Following the visit of the Commission, Rangoon experienced its first riots targeting Indians in May 1930. Originating from labour trouble pertaining to British firms of stevedores, disturbances grew rapidly in the face of administrative vacuum and incompetence that resulted in 'killing hundreds of Indians and wounding of thousands'.[74] No one was punished for mounting these attacks. An all-time low had been reached. Other attacks on Indians occurred in the countryside, following foreclosures on lands by Chettiar financiers. This was also

80 From antiquity to Raj

the time of 'Burma Rebellion' led by Saya San in parts of Burma such as Pegu, Prom, Tharrawaddy and Shan states.[75] British authorities liberally used Indian troops to control and counter the rebels, a cause for further deepening of Burmese resentment. Nevertheless, INC's political attitude about the inadequacy of constitutional reforms that were on offer to India influenced Burmese leaders.[76]

The Burma Roundtable Conference took place from November 1931 to January 1932. London announced its decision to have the separation issue decided through a general election in Burma. Separation would mean a new constitution, whereas continuation with India would mean permanent stay (short of the Dominion status) within the proposed federation. Elections on this all-important issue took place in November 1932. The verdict was decisively and clearly against separation. Perceptive observers, however, pointed out that Burmese objection was not against separation; it was more against the kind of constitutional offer that was linked to it. As Chakravarti queried and answered: '. . . why were the separationists so badly routed? The reason was that Burmans disliked the constitution attached to separation; they also disliked the unconditional federation, but considered for the time being at least, that federation was the lesser of the two evils.'[77] Regardless of the electoral verdict, subsequent political developments took Burma inexorably towards separation. The British parliament considered the Government of Burma Bill in 1934–35 and the Act that separated Burma from India came into effect on 1 April 1937.

It was observed that 'the period of Dyarchy from 1923 to 1936 not only widened the gulf between Indians and Burmans but also did irreparable damage to Burma's relations with Britain and the Commonwealth'.[78] It was ironical that Burma, which was attached to India through military conquest and remained linked to it, above all, due to military strategy, had to be separated (from India) when the Japanese had entered China and World War II was merely two years away.

After separation

The next decade from 1937 to 1947 may be divided into three subperiods: 1937–42 when the separated Burma functioned under the Raj; 1942–45 when it was 'liberated' but was, in fact, under tight control of Japan; and 1945–47 when the British rule was restored only to bring some normalcy after World War II and then to pave the way for independence.

The years between 1937 and 1942 witnessed continuous deterioration of the position of Indians in Burma. A number of issues commanded the attention of the government, which was now largely in Burmese hands. They were: (a) ending free trade with and free immigration from India; (b) use of Burmese as the major language rather than English in the legislature; (c) increasing the number of Burmese members in Rangoon Municipal Council to enable them to become a majority even though the bulk of residents, especially those paying tax, belonged to the Indian community; (d) measures for Burmanisation of labour as well as easing control over agricultural lands owned by Chettiars with the eventual aim to gain government control, possibly without suitable compensation; and (e) an abortive attempt to change domicile rules in order to treat most Indians as foreigners. Despite clear-cut provisions in the 1935 Constitution for protection of minority interests, Indians continued to lose ground. Further, another series of attacks on the Indian community and their properties in Rangoon took place during July–September 1938 that resulted in 'considerable loss of lives, limb and property'.[79] As a result, the late 1930s proved to be a very difficult period for Indians.

The period of Japanese rule began with the mass exodus of Indians from Burma. Out of about a million Indians present in Burma, most desired to leave or even attempted to leave; about half a million, braving incredible hazards, managed to reach India. They took the following four routes for their perilous journey: Tamu, the Naga Hills, the Hukong Valley and the Maungdaw and Buthidaung in Arakan. To quote Tinker:

> I shall always have a picture in my mind of the trail from Tamu to Palel in the Assam–Burma borderland, and of the bodies which lay where they fell when exhaustion and disease were too much for their enduring spirits.[80]

The essential question to examine is as to why Indians left Burma en masse. 'The amazing flight to India', wrote Ba Maw who served as the prime minister under the 1937 Constitution and later under the Japanese rule, 'was one of the saddest tragedies of the war in Burma'. But his view that there was 'really no adequate explanation for it except mass panic of the most hysterical kind' is hard to accept.[81] Was it the fear of Japanese troops or the belief that without British rulers they would not be welcome in Burma? Perhaps a combination of both factors was behind this tragic phenomenon. They had been brought in large numbers after British conquest, and they left after the British defeat.[82]

The war period was truly transformational, shaped principally by two 'major factors'.[83] First, with the withdrawal of British authority,

82　From antiquity to Raj

those communities and interests dependent on it had to leave the country or seek protection from other sources. Second, a mass movement developed favouring Burma's independence, with the support of Burma Independence Army (BIA), socialists, communists and others assembled under the umbrella of the Anti-Fascist People's Freedom League (AFPFL). In comparison to them, a minority community such as Karens, which preferred the return of the British, was much less influential.[84]

After the war was over, the Burma government, ending its exile in Simla, returned to Rangoon in October 1945. Burma, a major battlefield of the war, had been devastated in the four years of conflict, occupation and liberation. Post-war reconstruction was now its top priority.[85] Apologists of the Raj floated the view that basic reconstruction would need at least six years, thereafter, Burma should be ready for attaining Dominion status within the British Commonwealth. But Burmese were through with foreign rule now. At his historic meeting on 16 May 1945 with General William Slim, Commander of the 14th Army, Aung San was asked as to why he was so keen to get rid of the British. General Slim recalled Aung San's reply: 'He [Aung San] said it was not that he disliked the British, but he did not want British or Japanese or any other foreigners to rule his country.'[86] The British took a while to accept that Aung San was now the most important Burmese leader and that his view would prevail.

Once the British realised that they could not stay on for long, they played a role in the creation of the new state. Burmese scholars may criticise them for creating or deepening disunity, but Taylor argues that 'one of the conditions the British insisted on before granting independence was that the leaders of the Shan States and of the hill tribes had to agree to cede their territories to an independent government in Rangoon'.[87] Aung San stood for building and preserving national unity, for he believed that without it the nation would be weak and vulnerable. But he also encouraged and supported 'local autonomy, diversity, and limited separations among the groups which were ethnically different from the Burmans and wanted to retain their difference'.[88] In regard to the Indian and Chinese, Aung San's position was quite clear. He wanted them 'to choose whether or not to join the people of Burma in creating a new state'. He was particularly cordial to the Indians in conveying that 'we have no axe to grind, we nurture no feeling of racial bitterness and ill-will'.[89]

During the years of negotiations for independence in 1946–47, Aung San enjoyed close relations with Jawaharlal Nehru. The latter 'saw the struggle in Burma as part and parcel of struggle for self expression and political self-determination across the sub-continent'.[90] In January 1947, while on his way to the London conference for negotiations on Burmese independence, Aung San made a transit halt in Delhi to consult Nehru. Nearly half a century later, the Burmese leader's celebrated daughter, Suu Kyi, related the story:

> Pandit Nehru often broke through the barriers of race and generation by his warm humanity. On his way to London for talks on independence for Burma, my father made a stop in Delhi to have talks with Pandit Nehru and other Indian leaders. Panditji immediately showed a fatherly concern for my father, twenty-six years his junior. He cast a critical but kindly eye over the younger mans [sic] shabby, thin cotton uniform and decided it would not do. He arranged for several smart, warm woollen uniforms to be run up hastily by his tailors. Hearing that England was suffering from one of the coldest winters in living memory, Panditji also commandeered a greatcoat: a well-known photograph of my father shows him looking somewhat swamped in this greatcoat which is rather too large for him.[91]

On the tragic assassination of Aung San on 19 July 1947, Nehru stated:

> I mourn for Burma bereft at this critical moment of her chosen leaders, and I mourn for Asia who has lost one of her bravest and most far-seeing sons. . . . To the people of Burma I offer sincerest sympathy on my behalf and on behalf of the people of India. India will stand by them in the difficult days ahead.[92]

In a personal message of condolence to General Aung San's widow, he conveyed: 'I have lost a friend and a comrade and Burma and Asia have lost one to whom everyone looked with hope for the future.'[93]

U Nu, who picked up the baton from Aung San to lead Burma, connected well with Nehru. They were in close touch during the period leading to the attainment of independence by India on 15 August 1947 and by Burma on 4 January 1948.

Notes

1 A. L. Basham, *The Wonder That Was India*, London: Sidgwick & Jackson, 1967, p. 486.
2 Ibid., p. 4.

84 From antiquity to Raj

3 Ibid., p. 487.

4 Ibid.

5 K.M. Panikkar, *Lectures on India's Contact with the World in the Pre-British Period*, Nagpur: Nagpur University, 1963, pp. 54–5.

6 Basham, *The Wonder That Was India*, p. 487.

7 The most remarkable flow of people from Burma to India was that of the Tai/Shan prince Sukaphaa who, along with his followers, marched into the Brahmaputra Valley in 1220 AD and established his rule. His descendants – Ahoms – ruled the region for nearly six centuries and left a deep imprint on Assam. For details, please see Sir Edward Gait, *A History of Assam*, Calcutta: Thacker, Spink & Co, 1926.

8 D.G.E. Hall, *Burma*, London: Hutchinson's Library, 1950, p. 7. The same view has been aptly elaborated in a rare book *The Burmese Empire – A Hundred Years Ago* by Father Sangermano, an Italian priest, who reached Burma in 1783 and returned to Italy in 1808. In the introduction to this book's 1893 edition, John Jardine observed: 'It may therefore be said that the Burman races are indebted to India for their religion, their literature and their law. . . . By these same channels of religion, literature, and law, came also the astronomy, astrology, computation of time, the arts of medicine and divination, and the alphabets known at the present day, all which bear the Indian sign and superscription.' p. XI.

9 R.C. Majumdar, *Hindu Colonies in the Far East*, Calcutta: General Printers & Publishers, 1944, p. 4. He maintained: 'The ancient Hindus designated the country described above, viz. Indo-China and Malay Archipelago, by the general name *Suvarnabhumi* or Land of Gold. They, however, also used the name *Suvarnadvipa* or Island of Gold to denote particularly the islands, including Malay Peninsula. Particular regions in Indo-China (such as Burma and Siam) and Malay Archipelago are also called respectively *Suvarnabhumi* and *Suvarnadvipa*. The names indicate that the Hindus, like the Arabs, believed that this region produced gold in large quantities, or was rich in precious commodities.'

10 John L. Christian, *Burma*, London: Collins, 1945, p. 11. 'In November when the rice fields, a pleasing green from May until October, turn a golden brown over the great delta of the Irrawaddy the countryside is truly golden. In every Burmese village from Bhamo near the Chinese frontier to Victoria Point within 400 miles of Penang are found golden-spired pagodas and monasteries from which go forth each sunrise saffron-robed priests of Buddha on their rounds of the villages.'

11 Myint-U Thant, *Where China Meets India*, London: Faber & Faber Ltd., 2011, p. 9. Perhaps the most popular legend relates to the meeting between two Burmese merchants and the Buddha after the latter attained Enlightenment.

12 Majumdar, *Hindu Colonies in the Far East*, p. 190.

13 Ibid., p. 193.

14 G.E. Harvey, *Outline of Burmese History*, London: Longmans, Greens & Co. Ltd., 1926, p. 9.

15 Ibid., p. 9.

16 Hall, *Burma*, p. 7.

17 Tennyson F. Jesse, *The Story of Burma*, London: Macmillan & Co. Ltd., 1945, p. 13.

From antiquity to Raj 85

18 Majumdar, in *Hindu Colonies in the Far East*, p. 193, pointed out that archaeological finds also prove the existence of important centres of Indian culture at or near Prom, Pegu, Thaton and Pagan.

19 Hall, *Burma*, p. 8. 'Religious remains show both forms of Buddhism, Mahayanism and Hinayanism, together with Vishnu worship. There are large stone Buddhist sculptures in relief in the Gupta style, bronze statuettes of Avalokitesvara, one of the three chief Mahayanist Bodhisattavas, and so many stone sculptures of Vishnu that the city (i.e. Old Prom) was sometimes referred to as "Vishnu City".'

20 Ibid., p. 16.

21 Ibid., p. 18. He further explained: 'Burmese tradition asserts that in AD 403 the Buddhist scriptures were brought to Thaton from Ceylon by the apostle Buddhaghosa. Modern research, however, connects Thaton Buddhism with the important Hinayana School at Conjeveram which flourished under the commentator Dharmmapala in the fifth century'.

22 Jesse, *The Story of Burma*, p. 15.

23 Majumdar, *Hindu Colonies in the Far East*, p. 219. Majumdar cited Duroiselle: 'There is no doubt that the architects who planned and built the Ananda were Indians . . . in this sense, we may take it, therefore, that the Ananda, though built in the Burmese capital, is an Indian temple.'

24 Hall, *Burma*, p. 20.

25 http://mea.gov.in/bilateral-documents.htm?dtl/5326/Joint+Statement+on+the+occasion+of+the+State+Visit+of+the+President+of+the+Republic+of+the+Union+of+Myanmar+to+India (accessed on 22 October 2013).

26 The last-mentioned trait, particularly evident in the attack on Manipur in 1819, became the trigger that heralded the beginning of the end of Burmese monarchy.

27 Hall, *Burma*, p. 57.

28 Ibid. For details, see pp. 60–2.

29 Frank N. Trager, *Burma from Kingdom to Republic*, London: The Pall Mall Press Ltd., 1966, p. 17. He wrote: 'Certainly, the Konbaung kings had failed to understand the significance to Burma of the Indian policy pursued vigorously by the British governors-general from the time of Warren Hastings . . . to Marquess Wellesley.'

30 Ibid., p. 19.

31 Ibid., p. 26. 'He had never even heard of an explosive shell, and when the first one went off near him he remained alone and silent for a whole day.'

32 Jesse, *The Story of Burma*, p. 28. 'In spite of having been beaten, the Burmese continued to treat the English and their representative with the greatest contempt as kalas which means not only foreigners but barbarians, and the Burmans committed acts of violence on British seamen in British ships, to say nothing of treating our envoys with indignity.'

33 This issue became a grievance for the people of Manipur; it remains so even today.

34 Jesse, *The Story of Burma*, p. 38.

35 King Mindon sent the first official message to the president of the USA.

36 Jesse, *The Story of Burma*, p. 43. When the 1857 rebellion or 'the First War of Independence' drove the Raj to the wall, it did not occur to Mindon to take advantage of the situation. He refused to accept the advice that he

too should go after them. Instead, he sent a donation of £1,000 for the relief fund for the sufferers from the Mutiny.

37 Ibid., p. 75.
38 Sudha Shah, *The King in Exile*, Noida: HarperCollins Publishers, India, 2012, p. x.
39 Ibid., p. 149.
40 Ibid., p. 332.
41 Robert H. Taylor, *The State in Myanmar*, London: Hurst Publishers Ltd., 2009, p. 76.
42 Christian, *Burma*, p. 90.
43 Nalini Ranjan Chakravarti, *The Indian Minority in Burma*, London: Oxford University Press, 1971. 'The British Empire in the East', wrote Hugh Tinker in the foreword of the book, 'was largely created and developed by the agency of Indians, as soldiers, policemen, railwaymen, surveyors, and local district officials. In their wake came labourers and traders. All these folk [sic] followed the Union Jack.' Burma was no exception.
44 Shelby Tucker, *The Curse of Independence*, London: Pluto Press, 2001, pp. 38–9. 'The Burman, whose ancestors had fought with Anawrahta and Alaungpaya, but who now were outnumbered 39 to 1 by non-Burmans in the army and the police and by perhaps 20 to 1 in senior positions in industry and commerce, whose position of government was that of a clerk as often as not working under an Indian *babu*, perceived British rule as having deprived him of his right of preeminence in his own country.'
45 Chakravarti, *The Indian Minority in Burma*, p. 7.
46 Ibid., p. 8.
47 Ibid., p. 8.
48 Michael Adas, *The Burma Delta*, Wisconsin: The University of Wisconsin Press, 1974, p. 102. He also pointed out: 'For Indian migrant laborers, the range of economic opportunities was broader in Burma, the potential for mobility greater, and the remuneration better.'
49 Chakravarti, *The Indian Minority in Burma*, p. 11.
50 Sean Turnell, *Fiery Dragons: Banks, Moneylenders and Microfinance in Burma*, Copenhagen: NIAS Press, 2009, p. 13.
51 Ibid., p. 49.
52 Chakravarti, *The Indian Minority in Burma*, p. 11.
53 Ibid. In foreword by Hugh Tinker.
54 Ibid., p. vii.
55 Krishna Dutta and Andrew Robinson (eds), *Rabindranath Tagore: An Anthology*, London: Picador, 1997, pp. 105–6.
56 Information Service of India, *Gandhi in Burma*, Rangoon: Embassy of India, p. 2.
57 Ibid., p. 14.
58 Ibid., p. 17.
59 Ibid., p. 17.
60 Ibid., p. 2.
61 Jawaharlal Nehru, *An Autobiography*, New Delhi: Viking, 2004, p. 626.
62 Information Service of India, *Netaji and Burma*, Rangoon: Embassy of India, 1979, 'In Burmese Prisons', p. 8.
63 Ibid.
64 Ibid., 'India Shall Be Free', p. 20.

From antiquity to Raj 87

65 Ibid., 'General Aung San on Subhas Chandra Bose', p. 24.
66 Christian, *Burma*, p. 11.
67 Chakravarti, *The Indian Minority in Burma*, p. 97.
68 Ibid., p. 101. 'The Burma nation is as dissimilar from the Indian peoples as any two nations can possibly be', and 'the dissimilarity is not merely one of religion, but also of race, language, tradition, art, ideas, laws and the whole fabric of social system.'
69 Ibid., p. 105.
70 Ibid., pp. 115–16. Furthermore, Chakravarti explained: 'Before Dyarchy was finally extended . . ., Burma nationalists had resolved to turn their back on India, Burman nationalism had taken a new direction, and anti-Indian agitation had become the daily occupation of a section of the nationalist Press and politicians.'
71 Ibid., p. 127.
72 Jesse, *The Story of Burma*, p. 166.
73 Ibid., p. 162.
74 Chakravarti, *The Indian Minority in Burma*, p. 133.
75 Hall, *Burma*, p. 138. According to Hall, it was 'an anti-foreign movement, due largely to economic discontent arising out of the great slum'.
76 Trager, *Burma from Kingdom to Republic*, p. 49. 'This understanding conditioned and determined Burmese political responses throughout the period from the enactment of the Montagu-Chelmsford reforms to the establishment of a new Constitution in 1937.'
77 Chakravarti, *The Indian Minority in Burma*, p. 143.
78 Ibid., p. 149.
79 Chakravarti, *The Indian Minority in Burma*, p 158: 'The verified causalities included about 200 killed, about 1,000 injured, but the unofficial estimates of killed and wounded ran into several thousands.'
80 Ibid., p. viii.
81 Ba Maw, *Breakthrough in Burma*, London: Yale University Press, 1968, p. 198.
82 Chakravarti, *The Indian Minority in Burma*, p. 170. Explaining their motives, Chakravarti wrote: 'General apathy of the local people, if not hatred and envy consistently encouraged by a section of Burmans, fear for their life, or of molestation, and the enemy threat to remove Indians from their key positions to dislocate business, transport and communications to prepare grounds for invasion, all combined to compel the Indians to leave their homes and properties in Burma and to start the journey to the unknown.'
83 Taylor, *The State in Myanmar*, p. 223.
84 Tucker, *Burma: The Curse of Independence*, p. 39. Karens apart, other minority groups from the mountainous region looked at colonial rule quite differently from the broader mass movement of resistance. While colonial rule had left the minorities relatively free to go on with their own style of living in an undisturbed manner, the prospects of self-rule, as Tucker stated, 'effectively portended Burman rule, or at best, Burman domination . . . if British rule exacerbated divisions already present in Burmese society, the Resistance intensified them'.
85 Hall, *Burma*, p. 172. 'Burma suffered more from the war than any other Asiatic country save possibly Japan herself.'

88 From antiquity to Raj

86 Maung Maung (ed.), *Aung San of Burma*, The Hague: Yale University, Southeast Asian Studies, 1962, p. 84.
87 Taylor, *The State in Myanmar*, p. 228. For details concerning the British role, this is a useful source.
88 Josef Silverstein, *Burma: Military Rule and the Politics of Stagnation*, New York: Cornell University Press, 1977, p. 11.
89 Ibid.
90 Shashi Tharoor, 'An Optimistic Approach To Democratization Process in Burma', India–Burma Relations: Trends and Developments, Burma Centre Delhi, 2011, p. 9.
91 Aung San Suu Kyi's speech at Nehru Prize Address on the occasion of the presentation of the 1993 Nehru Memorial Prize for International Understanding, 14 November 1995, http://www.burmalibrary.org/reg.burma/archives/199511/msg00096.html (accessed on 12 November 2013).
92 Jawaharlal Nehru, *Selected Works of Jawaharlal Nehru Second Series – Volume – 3*, New Delhi Jawaharlal Nehru Memorial Fund, 1985, p. 398.
93 Ibid., p. 399.

Chapter 4

India–Myanmar relations
From independence to military rule

> As in the past, so in the future, the people of India will stand shoulder to shoulder with the people of Burma, and whether we have to share good fortune or ill fortune, we shall share it together.
> – Jawaharlal Nehru[1]

To trace the story of development of relations between India and Burma/Myanmar since the attainment of independence by the latter is the aim of this chapter. When the period under discussion began is clear – 4 January 1948. It ended in November 2010 when the elections were held, or perhaps it concluded more formally in March 2011 when the State Peace and Development Council (SPDC) was replaced by a new 'civilian' government.

Four phases

The period of multiparty democracy lasted from 1948 to 1962. For a little over 17 months, from 28 October 1958 to 4 April 1960, the country was under the army rule with Army Chief Ne Win serving as the caretaker prime minister, the result of what came to be known as a coup by invitation. Democratic rule was restored, but barely for two more years. The era of democracy was remembered later as a golden period, but it had its flaws. It was marked by disunity, instability, ethnic rebellion and divisive politics. Despite its failures, the constitutional period was rated to be remarkable in Burma's politics. This positive perception continues in many circles till the present day.

On 2 March 1962 Ne Win staged a real army coup, removing Prime Minister U Nu and suspending the 1947 Constitution. The country was placed under martial law. With the announcement of the Burmese Way to Socialism in April 1964, the nation was put on the road to

90   From independence to military rule

political oppression and economic disaster. A little later, in July 1964, the Burma Socialist Programme Party (BSPP) was established. A significant constitutional milestone was reached when Ne Win introduced a new Constitution in 1974 and proclaimed 'the Socialist Republic of the Union of Burma'. The new Constitution paved way for the legalisation of one-party rule, but it was viewed widely as a political camouflage. Burma had an elected parliament, but only one candidate could contest from each constituency and the candidate needed the approval of BSPP. Ne Win and the military continued to rule the country, but under a different garb. It lasted till 1988.

The years 1988–90 are generally considered as the period of transition. The country went through complex changes, characterised by turbulence and violence. Its evolution will be presented a little later. The next phase truly began in April 1992 when Lieutenant General Than Shwe took over as the new chairman of the State Law and Order Restoration Council (SLORC), which was eventually replaced by SPDC in November 1997. From April 1992 to March 2011, Than Shwe was the highest ranking leader of the military regime that ruled Myanmar.

In this backdrop, we may consider the main trends and principal features of the India–Myanmar relationship as it traversed through four phases: (i) the U Nu era, (ii) the Ne Win years, (iii) the transition period and (iv) the Than Shwe rule.

The U Nu era

Burma attained its independence a little over four months after India. The two nations thus stood at the same point in their political history. As they looked back, they were acutely conscious of their colonial past and the British connection that moulded their present. As they looked ahead, they knew they would face many common problems concerning domestic and foreign realms: the challenges of preserving national unity, addressing poverty and underdevelopment and securing international peace and cooperation. They were not strangers to each other, having seen their destinies intertwined for long, even before the colonial times. Therefore, they appeared set to unveil a new chapter in their centuries-old interaction.

In U Nu and Jawaharlal Nehru, respectively, the first prime ministers of Burma and India, the two nations found leaders who were both democrats and had a similar outlook on politics, in addition to a socialist orientation, a shared worldview and a common sense of history. They were driven by a commitment to foster Asian unity and to ensure that Asia – and the developing countries in general – played their due role in a world riven by the Cold War that had already begun. Above all, they belonged to a generation that had a vivid memory and personal experience of close association of their peoples – Burmese and Indian – at the level of grassroots as well as front-ranking political leaders such as Aung San and Mahatma Gandhi. In the background of such a rich legacy, the two men laid the foundation of a cooperative relationship in the formative years.

The presence in Rangoon of Rajendra Prasad, president of India's Constituent Assembly, at Burma's first Independence Day, was a clear indicator of how India viewed the new nation.[2] Prasad brought with him a sapling of the sacred tree of Bodh Gaya from his native state of Bihar and helped to plant it in the complex of Shwedagon Pagoda.[3] Nehru hailed Burma's independence as 'an event of significance to the whole of Asia, and to India particularly'. He went on to add:

> India and Burma have been so closely associated in the past that anything that happens in either country affects the other. In the future I have no doubt that our association will be even closer.[4]

One may highlight a few key issues pertaining to India–Burma relations, their relations with other neighbours, and burning international questions of the time in order to demonstrate how the two nations learnt to deal with each other in the post-independence era.

Right from the beginning, New Delhi and Rangoon strove to develop cordial and friendly relations. In April 1949, the new Burmese government faced an existentialist crisis as communist rebels and a few ethnic minorities (particularly the Karens) closed in on it. An overthrow of the government by violence was a distinct possibility. The Burmese authorities needed arms on top priority. Nehru's government recognised the urgency and acted swiftly to supply rifles and ammunition that made a crucial contribution to the government gaining an upper hand. U Nu observed:

> Without the prompt support in arms and ammunition from India, Burma might have suffered the worst fate imaginable. As it turned out, from the middle of 1949 when Mr. Nehru's rifles began arriving, the enemy's threat was first contained, and then eliminated.[5]

In July 1951, the two countries signed the Treaty of Peace and Friendship, which spoke of 'everlasting peace and unalterable friendship between two states'.[6] Economic cooperation received constant attention, particularly such practical issues as purchase of Burmese rice by India, disposal of Burma's debts going back to the country's separation from India in 1937 and extension of financial assistance. These matters were important to both sides. Under Nehru's guidance, the Indian government adopted a positive and generous approach, evoking much appreciation from Burma. In March 1950, India's efforts lay behind the crafting of a package of loans by five Commonwealth countries for Burma. Of the six-million pound package, one million pounds was contributed by India. On a separate plane, border security and insurgency in the Naga region generated its own complications. The response of the two prime ministers was unique. They undertook a joint visit to the border region in March/April 1953 to obtain a direct appreciation from the field and then agreed to take cooperative measures.

In the backdrop of Burma Indians' controversial role before independence, the Burmese government took steps to nationalise property through the Land Nationalisation Act of 1948. This largely affected Indian landlords, triggering huge resentment and anger in parts of India. This translated into pressure on New Delhi, which was urged to counter the adverse impact of Burmese measures of land acquisition. Official discussions helped in ameliorating the situation somewhat as the Burmese side was persuaded to agree to offer reasonable compensation. Later, another grievance appeared for Indians as the Burmese government amended the Burma Immigration and Foreigners' Registration Act of 1957. Nehru refused to let these matters affect bilateral relations, partly due to his firm conviction that Indians in foreign countries should assimilate locally or return to India, and partly owing to the line that his government took, namely India could really do very little on the internal matters of a foreign country. 'The personal friendship of U Nu and Jawaharlal Nehru allowed no disputes to disturb the good relationship between Burma and India.'[7]

As regards regional subjects, China figured prominently in India–Burma exchanges from the outset. At U Nu's request, the Nehru government agreed to delay its recognition of the People's Republic of China so that Burma could become the first country outside the Communist bloc to recognise it.[8] The problems created by the presence and nefarious activities of Kuomintang troops in northern Burma caused immense worry to Rangoon. The troops' presence was supported by the US, a combination, it was feared, which could attract invasion of Burma by Communist China.[9] The Burmese consulted New Delhi. Burma took the matter to the United Nations (UN) in 1953. India played an active role in drafting and eventual adoption of a resolution in the General Assembly, which called for removal of troops from the Burmese soil. Speaking in the General Assembly debate, India's representative V. K. Krishna Menon stated:

> As I have said before, what hurts Burma hurts us. Burma is our immediate neighbour. Its people have been linked to us by centuries of civilisation. A country that has recently emerged from colonial rule has its own difficulties and problems. That it should be harassed by foreign invaders of this type and should have to fight on yet another front, is indeed a very sad fact.[10]

On the Sino-Burma boundary question, a critical look at developments in 1950s and beyond shows that the situation took a full circle, from the time when U Nu sought and obtained Nehru's help in opening Sino-Burmese discussions[11] to the stage when, after the successful conclusion of negotiations with China in 1956, Burma cited their agreement as a model for Sino-Indian border dispute, causing much annoyance in India.[12] In terms of ideology and political thinking, U Nu was far closer to Nehru (whom he visited frequently, staying at the prime minister's residence as his personal guest), than the Chinese leaders he dealt with. Yet, U Nu handled the relationship with China with utmost care and caution. It may be underlined that, once out of power, he sought refuge in Thailand and India, not China.[13]

It is on the larger international themes of the age – the questions of Asian unity, Cold War, UN's role in peace and conflict – that Burma and India worked closely together. Along with Ceylon, Pakistan and Indonesia, they formed a new grouping called the 'Colombo Powers'. Their two meetings, held in Colombo in April 1954 and in Bogor in December 1954, paved the way for convening of the Bandung Conference in April 1955. The latter event, in turn, became the precursor for the launch of the Non-Aligned Movement.

Three observations need to be made here. First, the idea that newly independent countries should have a choice beyond joining the US-led Western bloc or the Soviet Union-led communist camp was developed by Nehru and U Nu separately as well as jointly. As Frank N. Trager pointed out, there was an attempt by Burma during the two years starting before independence 'towards achieving security through a system of beneficial alliances and through whatever additional protection the UN might offer its members'.[14] The failure of this policy eventually led U Nu to neutralism.[15] Second, despite striking similarity in the theory and practice of neutralism or non-alignment by Burma and India, there were shades of difference. Besides, there were real

94 From independence to military rule

differences between the two countries on several international issues such as Hungary, Korea and threats to world peace.[16] India considered colonialism as the main threat, whereas Burma regarded international communism as serious a threat as colonialism.[17] Third, despite their differences and difficulties in managing bilateral relations, the two leaders enjoyed a personal bond of the kind that no subsequent leaders of India and Burma/Myanmar could replicate. The admiration and consideration they displayed for each other created a widespread perception that India and Burma enjoyed a special relationship for 14 years after Burma's independence.[18]

Myanmar's military rulers made it a point to paint U Nu's years in office, in the darkest possible colours. But the verdict of history may be a little different, a little more nuanced. Burmese were often asked in the decade after independence whether democracy could take firm roots in Burma. U Nu's answer always was to stress that 'there was no reason why it should not'.[19]

Concerning the years of exile spent in India, U Nu was deeply appreciative of India's hospitality and assistance. Later, his daughter Than Than Nu worked in the Burmese language unit of All India Radio for 20 years from 1980 to 2000. Her husband also worked there. She observed:

> I too came to know many kind and good-hearted people, far too numerous to count, who helped me overcome several obstacles through their kindness and generosity. My family and I cherish the years we spent in India, and remember her people and places with great fondness.[20]

The Ne Win years

The original strongman of Burma, General Ne Win, ruled the country for over quarter of a century. Like Aung San, he was a member of the 'Thirty Comrades' who received military training abroad from the Japanese and returned home to find the Burma Independence Army (BIA). Aung San emerged as virtually the father of the nation; Ne Win resented the fact and the man. Later, he worked with U Nu, coming forward as the saviour of the latter's government, and eventually became the architect of the coup d'état against it. No ordinary military dictator, he developed an ideology of his own – 'the Burmese Way to Socialism'.[21] He held various important posts at different times but his power came from unquestioned hold on the army. When in July 1988 he resigned as the party chairman, he was still regarded as the master puppeteer of the military coup of September 1988. The generals took their time to move out of his shadows.

Within months of this author's arrival in Yangon, Ne Win, aged 91, died on 5 December 2002. He played a vital role in holding the country together more than once, but he ruined the nation's economy and institutionalised military dictatorship.[22] No wonder that he died unsung. Ne Win left a political legacy of questionable value. The army, which assumed the responsibility to rule the country after 1988 disturbances, was his creation. But as the years passed, his successors disowned him. They opened up the economy and began reconnecting Myanmar with the world, but they continued his authoritarian model of governance.

Recalling Ne Win's role in Burma's governance should help us to appreciate that he held the unique record of having dealt with five prime ministers of India from Nehru to Rajiv Gandhi. Military coups were in fashion in the 1960s. Ne Win's coup in 1962 had been preceded by the emergence of General Ayub Khan as the dictator in Pakistan. Jawaharlal Nehru was nevertheless deeply unhappy over the ouster from power of his friend U Nu. Coldness in relations at the highest levels was, therefore, inevitable, but there was no question of shunning the new government. Normal dealings with it were ensured. The year of coup in Burma was also the time of rising Sino-Indian tensions, resulting in the border war in October. Decisive defeat inflicted on India caused a serious setback to the country's diplomatic standing in the region and around the world. The Burmese government took note of changing power equations and acted accordingly, staying neutral on the India–China conflict and participating in a diplomatic initiative to bring the two sides to the negotiating table.[23] After helping to convene the Colombo Summit of the six non-aligned nations[24] in order to mediate in the conflict, Ne Win visited New Delhi to enquire about Nehru's failing health. This enabled the Burmese and Indian authorities to discuss the post-conflict situation and other issues. Clearly bilateral relations needed to be rebuilt.

Before long, they suffered a major blow by Ne Win's decision to nationalise small businesses through the Enterprise Nationalisation Law in October 1963. It caused havoc among the Indian community in Burma. Another exodus was triggered off. Between then and September 1964, an estimated 100,000 people of Indian origin left for India, embittered and impoverished, having been paid little by way of compensation for their properties. Rounds of official discussions followed before and during the visits of Ne Win to India and of Prime Minister Lal Bahadur Shastri to Burma during 1965. These

96   From independence to military rule

endeavours produced little comfort for the deprived Indians. What, however, they did was to achieve a degree of normalcy and correctness in the relationship. The Burmese were much concerned over the India–Pakistan conflict in 1965. Shastri assured his interlocutors that he planned to visit Tashkent to hold discussions with the president of Pakistan under the good offices of the Soviet Union. Before a peaceful settlement could be reached, Shastri died in harness.

During Indira Gandhi's first innings as prime minister (1966–77), relations with Burma improved and became stable. This has been attributed by experts to realpolitik associated with her political style. She dealt with Ne Win as he was. Besides, there was lingering affection of the Nehru-Gandhi family for Burma. The tradition of frequent visits at the highest level returned. General Ne Win became a frequent visitor to India; he paid at least 11 official and other visits between 1959 and 1984.[25] Indira Gandhi visited Burma in March 1969, besides a stopover in Rangoon in June 1968.[26] The land boundary agreement was signed in March in 1967, although the two countries had to wait longer for the maritime border agreement, which came in 1986. Relations were managed from the top, with very limited institutional underpinnings. The Burmese had misgivings about developments in East Pakistan and India's role in the liberation and creation of Bangladesh in 1971, but this did not prevent Burma from recognising its new neighbour immediately.

The decade under discussion was a difficult one for Ne Win's government, the consistent recipient of Maoist China's ideological onslaught through support to the Burmese Communist Party. This created considerable synergy between Burma and India. The latter too suffered from China-supported insurgency in the border region as Indian Insurgent Groups (IIGs), especially Nagas and Mizos, received Chinese arms as well as support from their comrades on the Burmese soil. As a result, India–Burma cooperation to address this serious issue increased, with security of the two countries linked together through a common threat perception.[27]

During the Janata Party government, the Minister of External Affairs, Atal Bihari Vajpayee, visited Burma in August 1977. He laid special emphasis on ties between the two non-aligned countries, reaffirming India's commitment to the policy of non-alignment despite New Delhi's close relations with the USSR. However, Burma chose to deepen its isolation further by withdrawing from the Non-Aligned Movement in September 1979.

The decade of 1980s is remembered for two major developments. First, India was engaged in the mid-1980s in efforts to establish the

South Asian Association for Regional Cooperation (SAARC). During the visit of Burmese Foreign Minister Chit Hlaing in May 1984, the question of Burma joining the grouping was brought up by the Indian side, but the Burmese response was negative.[28] Second, Prime Minister Rajiv Gandhi undertook an official visit to Burma in December 1987. The official view about the outcome of the visit was reflected in the annual report of Ministry of External Affairs (MEA):

> The talks centered on ways and means of expansion and further consolidation of the existing friendly relations between the two countries. A number of decisions were taken to give a fillip to bilateral relations between India and Burma.[29]

However, the reality was different. Despite positive atmospherics, Ne Win displayed utter negativism towards Indian proposals as Natwar Singh, minister of state for external affairs who had accompanied Rajiv Gandhi, disclosed later.[30] Discontent against Ne Win's government had begun to manifest itself before Rajiv Gandhi's visit. Few, however, sensed that Burma's history was about to take a major adverse turn and, with it, India–Burma relations would enter the most difficult phase.

The transition

A narrow view may suggest the years 1988–90 as the time of transition, but it may be more realistic to treat the nearly five-long year period from late 1987 to mid-1992 as the real transitional period in the political history of modern Burma. In September 1987, the first student protests began, triggered by Ne Win's strange decision, apparently guided by astrology, to demonetise all currency notes (of 100, 75, 35, 25), except those of 45 and 90. Marked by a prolonged and violent turbulence, frequent changes of leadership and even changes in the country's name, the transition finally culminated in the arrival of Than Shwe as the new chairman of SLORC in April 1992.

The year 1988 witnessed historic developments. Under pressure from student protests and demonstrations that tuned into a mass movement against the government, Ne Win announced his resignation as chairman of the ruling party BSPP on 23 July. He was replaced by Sein Lwin and then Maung Maung. Countrywide protests led by people reached their zenith on 8 August, giving the struggle its name and identity – 8888 Rising. Security forces took harsh countermeasures. They acted against the government of Maung Maung, ousting

98 From independence to military rule

it through a coup on 18 September (which was led by General Saw Maung, a confidant and henchman of Ne Win).[31] Thereafter they proceeded to subject the protestors and people in general to a brutal crackdown. By October protests began to die down. Thousands of people were dead or injured; many more fled across the Thai and Indian borders. Burma's prospects for transition to democracy had darkened. In order to calm down the nation, the military announced its four goals: 'ensuring law and order; facilitating transport and communications; alleviating the shortage of food, clothing, and shelter; and holding general multiparty elections'.[32]

The following year, 1989, brought hope as the army took a few significant steps to break away from the Ne Win model of governance. Political parties were allowed to be formed. Changes in the economic policy were introduced. On 10 November, the Union Election Commission announced the date of first multiparty elections since 1960: 27 May 1990. The next year, 1990, registered a glorious triumph of democratic forces as the National League for Democracy (NLD) won over 80 per cent of the seats in the National Assembly, 392 out of 492, even though Chairman Tin U and Secretary General Suu Kyi were out of action. (The former was in prison and the latter was under house arrest.) This outcome came as a complete shock to the military leadership and especially to the National Unity Party (NUP), the reincarnation of Ne Win's BSPP, which secured only ten seats.[33] Initially SLORC seemed inclined to respect the people's verdict. General Saw Maung stated: 'Our duties will not be over until a government has been formed in accordance with the law.'[34] Later the military changed its mind and worked on other plans, which included neither transferring power to NLD nor convening the newly elected MPs as a constituent assembly. It simply proceeded to subject Myanmar to military rule, which would last until March 2011.

This brief backdrop should help us to appreciate the trajectory of India–Burma/Myanmar relations during the transition period. Two more points are relevant here concerning the context. First, a new era was beginning, with the end of the Cold War. 'Winds of change' blew in East Europe; the USSR disintegrated and the US emerged as the only superpower. China went through its share of turbulence as the Tiananmen Square episode took place in June 1989. Second, India went through a transition of its own as the Rajiv Gandhi–led Congress government was succeeded by Prime Minister V. P. Singh and his team, following the general elections in November 1989. When Singh's term ended abruptly in November 1990, India had a new prime minister, Chandra Shekhar, who was in office briefly from November 1990 to

June 1991. Elections in May–June 1991 brought the Congress-led coalition government headed by Prime Minister P. V. Narasimha Rao.

Burma's journey through the tragic stages of its transition was watched in India with a blend of deep concern and close interest. The crushing of the people's movement by the army, the imprisonment and forced exile of pro-democracy leaders, and the house arrest of Suu Kyi were all condemned roundly by the government and civil society. NLD's landslide victory was hailed warmly, whereas the army's refusal to transfer power was criticised severely. Through a series of statements and reports issued by the MEA during this period, India followed a clear, courageous and principled policy line.[35] Its critical elements were admiration for the Burmese people's resolve to secure their rights and liberty, a call for respecting the people's will and for restoration of democracy, and a firm appeal for the release of Suu Kyi from house arrest and of other prisoners. India did all this, while affirming its adherence to the principle of noninterference in internal affairs of a foreign country. Its leaders and officials made it clear that when human rights and democratic values were being violated so openly, silence could not be an option. A similar approach was adopted in India's pro-active multilateral diplomacy through UN channels.

Diplomatic and political support was backed by practical action on the ground. The Indian Embassy in Rangoon/Yangon provided medical assistance to students injured during violent actions by security forces. When Burmese refugees reached the Indian border, they were allowed in. Special camps were set up in Manipur and Mizoram to provide shelter to them. The United Nations High Commissioner for Refugees (UNHCR) acted to grant them refugee status. Indian authorities kept in close touch with various constituents of the democracy movement in Thailand, UK and US to discuss their situation and understand their views, problems and needs.[36] Heading the division in charge of Myanmar (among other countries) in the MEA, this author dealt with complex issues.[37] An important facet of India's policy was the use of All India Radio (AIR); its broadcasts were popular with audiences in Burma. A specific programme presented in the Burmese language by Than Than Nu, daughter of U Nu, former prime minister, was utilised to voice and convey India's ideological support for the democracy movement.

Two Rangoon University students hijacked the Thai International Airways flight TG 304 on 10 November 1990. They were arrested, but they received valuable support from the People's Union for Civil Liberties (PUCL) of India. After spending three months in jail, they were released on bail. 'Many called for their release, and thirty-eight

Members of Parliament signed the letter requesting the prime minister of India to give them political asylum in India.'[38] When Suu Kyi was awarded the Nobel Prize in October 1991, India was among the first countries to congratulate her. Prime Minister Rao observed:

> The news has been greeted with joy and pride throughout India. It is a most timely and an apt recognition of the non-violent struggle launched by the people of Myanmar for democracy and respect for human rights under the able leadership of Mrs. Suu Kyi.[39]

At a function to facilitate Suu Kyi organised by the India–Myanmar Friendship Society on 6 November 1992, Natwar Singh, former minister of state for external affairs, said that if the Burmese government continued to debar the elected representatives from running the country, the Indian government should recall its ambassador from Myanmar.[40]

Predictably the reaction of the SLORC government was negative and hostile to India's pro-democracy line. The post of Indian ambassador in Yangon had been kept vacant for over a year. When Preet Malik arrived as the ambassador-designate, he received a cold reception and was kept waiting for several weeks for the presentation of credentials.[41] It was thus evident that during Burma's transition, India was in the forefront to support its democratic aspirations, even at the cost of damage to government-to-government relations. Thant Myint-U noted:

> In the years immediately following the failed 1988 uprising in Burma, the Indian government took a very hard-line position against the Burmese military government, perhaps the hardest line anywhere in the world.[42]

The Than Shwe rule

Than Shwe became the chairman of SLORC in April 1992, as mentioned earlier. In November 1997, SLORC was replaced by SPDC. Throughout the 1990s and later, a few other generals were important too, particularly secretary-1 of SLORC and SPDC, General Khin Nyunt, who was the chief of military intelligence during a part of the Ne Win era and later, and who served as the prime minister from August 2003 to October 2004. But the hallmark of the period from mid-1992 to early 2011 was the stewardship of Than Shwe as the topmost leader whose authority and influence increased progressively

From independence to military rule   101

and whose steady hand at the helm provided stability and continuity to army rule.

Policy review

Reverting to the story of the evolution of India's Myanmar policy, it is noteworthy that Prime Minister Rajiv Gandhi and his two successors, V. P. Singh and Chandra Shekhar, did what they could to support the cause of democracy in Burma. Rajiv Gandhi's cabinet included P. V. Narasimha Rao who, in various capacities, fully supported and actively implemented this policy.[43] However, when he returned in his new avatar as the prime minister in June 1991, his government was faced with a changed and (further) changing situation. Insurgency in the North East was becoming a serious challenge once again. Experts believed that it could not be tackled without cooperation from Myanmar's security forces. Moreover, with India and the West riding on the democracy bandwagon, the field had been left open for China to make headway in strengthening and deepening its relations with SLORC, and the Chinese were making full use of this rare opportunity.[44] Besides, Prime Minister Rao was in the process of developing his own vision of a new relationship with Southeast Asia, which would eventually be translated into India's Look East Policy in which Myanmar would have a vital place. The strategic community was beginning to raise its voice, arguing that for the sake of democratic values, India's hard national interests should not be sacrificed.[45]

At the official level in MEA, a significant convergence of views and coordination emerged. In the early part of my tenure as joint secretary in charge of Myanmar, I visited Yangon on a familiarisation tour. Detailed discussions with senior officials in the Ministry of Foreign Affairs, leaders of the Indian community, and Ambassador G. Parthasarathy and his team provided valuable inputs for the preparation of an up-to-date assessment of the evolving situation and its implications for India. This was read with interest at the higher levels. Soon afterwards, a policy review exercise was undertaken. Consultations with Foreign Secretary Dixit, Special Secretary Malik who had served as the ambassador in Yangon from 1990 to 1992, Parthasarathy who was the ambassador from 1992 to 1995 and others followed, and our policy paper was finalised. Discussions based on it then moved to the Prime Minister's Office (PMO) and political direction was obtained. Eventually it was decided that India would now adopt 'a two-track policy', that is, it would continue to extend moral and political support to the democratic forces and leaders, and it would also engage

102 From independence to military rule

military government in order to improve and upgrade government-to-government relations. It was a calibrated and complex initiative to balance principles, values, interests and geopolitical realities.

Why did the change in policy become necessary? 'There were many reasons for this, but perhaps the most important was a very simple one: the old policy had failed.'[46] In 1988, democracy seemed likely to descend on Burma; in 1992, the army rule was assessed to be well entrenched. India had to return to its traditional policy to do business with whosoever wielded power. Answering a question, Shyam Saran, former foreign secretary and former ambassador to Myanmar, observed:

> India assumed that the longevity of the military regime was limited which did not prove to be true. . . . When it realized that this regime was here to stay, New Delhi started its constructive engagement policy with Yangon.[47]

In subsequent years, the new policy received considerable criticism from elements of the strategic community in India as well as the liberal lobby and supporters of democracy based in India, Myanmar and elsewhere. But this author has been a consistent advocate of engagement since the beginning. Two decades later, one still believes that the course correction in 1992 was both essential and desirable.

Within a short period of two years from August 1992 to September 1994, a total of six important visits took place: two from the Myanmar side and four from the Indian side. The visit in August 1992 of U Aye, director general in the Ministry of Foreign Affairs, was followed by that of a delegation led by Foreign Secretary Dixit to Yangon in March 1993. This paved the way for the return visit by his counterpart U Nyunt Swe, deputy foreign minister, in January 1994. These three interactions at high diplomatic levels helped in removing many misunderstandings and in creating a solid foundation for rapprochement between the two governments. Yangon got a clear signal that, while India would continue to press for restoration of democracy and release of political prisoners, it was willing to build a fresh government-level relationship that helped to enhance security and commercial cooperation. In turn, Myanmar sent a clear message that, while China would remain its close and vital partner, Yangon had no desire to set up permanent foreign bases on its soil and that it was willing to extend some cooperation to India in dealing with insurgent activity in the border region.

The three other visits from the Indian side in 1994 were by Home Secretary N. N. Vohra (February), Chief of Army Staff General B. C. Joshi (May) and Commerce Secretary Tejendra Khanna (June). This productive and fascinating period was marked by the conclusion of two important agreements in January 1994, namely (i) Agreement on Border Trade and (ii) Agreement on Cooperation between Civilian Border Authorities.

During the period 1992–94, the role of ambassadors Malik and Parthasarathy, foreign secretaries Dixit and K. Srinivasan, and the PMO headed by Principal Secretary A. N. Verma was commendable. As the point man in MEA, this author had a ringside view as well as a rare opportunity to contribute to rebuilding ties with a neighbour whom our earlier policy had turned into a bitter adversary.[48]

Subsequent years in the decade witnessed a series of visits and a gradual strengthening of relations.[49] However, the relationship was marked by ups and downs because the two-track policy was subjected to pressures and counter pressures. Liberals still clamoured for breaking contact and engagement with the junta, whereas realists pressed for giving up the pro-democracy track. A peculiar episode happened in November 1995. Just when Indian and Myanmar security forces were engaged in cooperating on 'Operation Golden Bird' aimed at anti-India insurgents, Jawaharlal Nehru Prize for International Understanding was awarded to Suu Kyi. The decision on the award was believed to result from the advice of Vice President K. R. Narayanan.[50] The timing of the announcement caused embarrassment to the Indian government and considerable annoyance to the government of Myanmar, which promptly withdrew its forces from the joint operation.[51] As Suu Kyi was unable to leave Myanmar in order to receive the award, it was collected on her behalf by Daw Than E at a ceremony on 14 November 1995 in New Delhi.[52] Narayanan paid a rich tribute to Suu Kyi in a well-crafted speech.[53]

The new phase

Before the decade ended, a new phase was beginning in India–Myanmar relations, triggered by a combination of three factors. Firstly, a new non-Congress coalition government, National Democratic Alliance (NDA), took office in Delhi in May 1998. Despite the personal preference of its senior figure Defence Minister George Fernandes to support the cause of democracy in Myanmar, the new national security and foreign affairs team, under the leadership of Prime Minister Atal

Bihari Vajpayee, planned to adopt a hard-headed strategic approach. It had no fascination for the past pro-democracy line on Myanmar and wished to emphasise the engagement segment of the two-track policy of the Narasimha Rao government. Secondly, in Myanmar's top leadership circles discontent was rising on the country's growing dependency on China, thereby strengthening the case, advocated by the No. 2 of the regime, SPDC Vice Chairman Maung Aye, that the Indian option needed to be explored more vigorously. Thirdly, in Shyam Saran, India's ambassador in Yangon from 1997 to 2001, an exceptionally gifted diplomat was operating on the ground. Through his visionary thinking, key contacts in the SPDC set-up, flair for energetic follow-up action and easy access to the leadership in MEA and PMO, he was able to make a substantial difference.[54]

The story of how it all unfolded must come from the principal actors themselves. Two of them – Shyam Saran and General V. P. Malik, former chief of army staff – shared their versions with this author under different circumstances.[55] As Malik explained, the situation at the decade's end was marked by (a) India's inability to eliminate insurgent activity, despite heavy deployment of regular and paramilitary troops in all the four border states and (b) lack of progress on a number of proposals for cooperation with Myanmar due to the absence of political level communication and contact between New Delhi and Yangon. This was the stage when messages from the Indian Embassy began to receive close attention in Delhi. 'The Prime Minister, Vajpayee, and National Security Advisor (NSA) Brajesh Mishra then decided to utilise military diplomacy to supplement India's foreign policy.'[56] This resulted in an unprecedented flurry of high-level visits, including two visits by Malik to Myanmar in January and July 2000, two visits by Maung Aye – the first to Shillong in January 2000 to meet Malik as well as an inter-ministerial delegation led by Union Minister of Commerce and Industry Murasoli Maran and the second to Delhi in November 2000, and two visits to Myanmar by Minister of External Affairs Jaswant Singh in February 2001 and April 2002. Referring to his discussions during the January 2000 visit, Malik wrote:

> During our meetings, right at the beginning, Maung Aye assured me that Myanmar would not allow any country or organization to pose a threat to its neighbours, now or in the future. It would not accord military bases to any country, or allow any Indian insurgent group to operate from Myanmar.[57]

Subsequent conversations with Maung Aye led to Myanmar extending solid cooperation to India on countering insurgency.[58] The Myanmar side, in return, was given credible assurances about India's readiness to support various infrastructure projects. Evidently the China factor influenced the dialogue. Malik's recommendation to the government was clear-cut, favouring a closer cooperation with Yangon.[59]

Maung Aye's second visit to India at the invitation of India's Vice President Krishna Kant was the highest-level visit after a long hiatus. It was imbued with deep political significance.[60] Within months Jaswant Singh was at the India–Myanmar border to inaugurate the Tamu-Kale-Kalewa highway. This project was conceived in October 1993; its implementation commenced in July 1997. The Myanmar side conveyed 'their deep appreciation' for the road project and they 'underlined the role the highway would play in promoting economic development in the region as also providing valuable cross-border link between India and Myanmar'.[61] Later, Jaswant Singh, while visiting Yangon, called on Than Shwe and Khin Nyunt, secretary-1 of SPDC, and held detailed discussions with them and Foreign Minister Win Aung.[62] His second visit in April 2002 was for the India–Myanmar–Thailand Ministerial Meeting on Transport Linkages. Thus, by mid-2002, the two countries were enjoying a phase of exceptional warmth and cooperation.

My tenure as ambassador

Serving as India's high commissioner in Kenya, I watched from afar the significant developments relating to India and Myanmar with much interest and some envy. Shyam Saran had been succeeded by a colleague, Vivek Katju, as ambassador to Myanmar. With this, the possibility of my serving in Yangon seemed to be over. However, al-Qaeda's decision to destroy the twin towers in New York and stage other tragic 9/11 incidents unleashed a train of events that led to the ouster of the Taliban government in Afghanistan. To represent India in Kabul in the new era, New Delhi selected our foremost Afghanistan expert Katju who had barely spent a few months in Yangon. The post fell vacant again. Fortunately the government remembered my previous service as joint secretary in charge of BSM division and selected me to be the next ambassador. It was a privilege for me to return to a country that I had known before and studied closely for over a decade.

Prior to my departure for Myanmar, I called on Prime Minister Vajpayee in Delhi who gave me some advice and instructions, underlining the importance of Myanmar for India's interests. I was a little anxious about my meeting with George Fernandes, the defence minister, considering the fact that a group of pro-democracy activists operated from his official residence. The minister lost little time in putting me at ease, by making a distinction between his personal views and the official government policy.

Arriving in Yangon in June 2002, I hit the ground running. My endeavour was two-fold: to bring previous initiatives to fruition and to devise new measures and programmes for bringing further expansion of bilateral cooperation – and, while doing so, to try to remain fully supportive of those who were committed to the cause of democracy in Myanmar.

The Indian consulate general in Mandalay was re-established and inaugurated at a special ceremony in November 2002. For this purpose Kanwal Sibal, foreign secretary, and his counterpart Khin Maung Win, deputy foreign minister, flew to Mandalay after their official discussions in Yangon. The consulate's reopening symbolised the broadening of India's footprint in the country, and it served as a morale booster for the Indian origin community. It set the stage for 2003, which turned out to be a most productive year for the relationship. By the time it ended, a series of high-level visits had taken place and several new agreements had been signed.[63] Undoubtedly, the most significant development was the visit of Vice President Bhairon Singh Shekhawat to Myanmar in November 2003. He was the highest-level visitor from India since Prime Minister Rajiv Gandhi's visit in 1987. The SPDC government went out of its way to extend a warm reception and the highest protocol billing to him. Discussions were rated to be fruitful by both sides. Shekhawat expressed satisfaction with the 'multi-faceted relationship . . .'[64] His host Maung Aye observed: 'Myanmar remains grateful to India for the cooperation extended in education, science and technology and other fields. . . .'[65] The significance of Shekhawat's visit lay in the fact that it generated hopes of both sides for a higher-level bilateral interaction in the future.

The NDA government was replaced by the Congress-led UPA government in May 2004. Natwar Singh became the new minister of external affairs. Given his close association with Suu Kyi and NLD, his appointment caused some concern in political circles in Myanmar. I met him in Delhi to brief him about various matters. Evincing great interest, he inquired if he could send some books for Suu Kyi, then under house arrest. This was promptly arranged. As subsequent developments demonstrated, India's Myanmar policy was backed by political consensus, reflecting convergence of views between the two principal parties, the BJP and the Congress, if not national consensus in the fullest sense. This enabled us, the day-to-day managers of the relationship, to continue and consolidate our efforts to nurture it.

The high point was the state visit of Chairman Than Shwe to India in October 2004. The previous visit at the head of state level was by Ne Win in November 1980.[66] Despite severe criticism by the liberal lobby in India and the refusal of UPA Chairperson Sonia Gandhi to meet Than Shwe, the visit went off smoothly. It was successful, judging by the range of discussions, the number of agreements signed and the kind of mutual understanding reached at the highest levels. The Myanmar side left us with a clear impression that they were much pleased with the outcome. So was the Indian side. Two paragraphs in the joint statement were of particular significance in this context. Para seven conveyed India's interest in democracy as well as the implication that it was for Myanmar to bring it.[67] Para eleven signalled Myanmar's willingness to help India cope with security challenges in the border region.[68] The discussions, 'enabled better understanding and appreciation of each other's concerns and perspectives and enhanced closer understanding at the political level'.[69]

In relating the story of the evolution of India–Myanmar relations, I have restricted myself to the interaction involving the highest-level political leaders. But ministerial visits too played a useful role. In this author's time, four visits stood out, that is, those by two NDA ministers – Arun Shourie (communications, information technology and disinvestment) and Arun Jaitley (commerce and industry) and visits by two UPA ministers – Mani Shankar Aiyar (petroleum and natural gas) and Natwar Singh (external affairs). Each visit involved interesting experiences pertaining to the dialogue between the two countries, and each contributed to advancing the bilateral relationship. Besides, the Embassy showed much activism and creativity in promoting cultural, economic and people-to-people exchanges.[70] Notably Shyam Benegal's film *Netaji Subhas Chandra Bose: The Forgotten Hero* was shot during this period, with the Myanmar authorities providing valuable assistance.

Myanmar personages

In order to provide a little more flavour of my time in Myanmar, a brief account of the more important interactions with political leaders and others is presented here.

Travelling with Than Shwe on his tour of India, this author held several conversations with him. At Rajghat, he mentioned that, as a schoolboy, he had studied India's history and geography in an era when Burma being a part of India was not too distant a memory. He

108 From independence to military rule

added that he was now in India in order to build a closer relationship so that both countries could benefit from stronger cooperation. At Bodh Gaya, he stated, pointing a finger towards his teenaged grandson Ne Shwe Thway Aung: 'This boy was only three years old when he had visited Bodh Gaya with his grandmother.' The Embassy knew that Than Shwe had desired for long to visit Buddhism's holiest place. At Kolkata, he expressed immense curiosity about Motilal Nehru and Jawaharlal Nehru, Abul Kalam Azad and the 'Frontier Gandhi', as I explained about their portraits displayed at Victoria Memorial Hall, a prestigious museum. Statues of Queen Victoria as also of Clive, Curzon and Dalhousie triggered in Than Shwe a train of memories of colonial times. During our farewell call on the chairman and the first lady, my wife Kumkum told them that the short rains, which had preceded their departure for home, carried 'blessings from the gods'. Than Shwe observed that in Myanmar too they had a similar belief.

This author had the rare privilege to have an exclusive, one-to-one meeting with Aung San Suu Kyi at her historic residence, No. 54–56 University Avenue, Yangon. It was on 30 January 2003. I was ushered into the sitting room by an old man. There was a small round table in the centre, with four chairs. Furnishings were austere, but the room was a picture of elegance. Suu Kyi gave me a cup of tea and her undivided attention. She heard my initial presentation with rapt attention, with her eyes totally fixed on my face and ears glued to every word spoken. She believed in total communication and giving to her interlocutor the feeling that he was important to her. I referred to the importance of the date and timing of our meeting, the precise hour when the people of India observed silence to remember the Father of the Nation, Mahatma Gandhi. She recalled the Tees January Marg, the road near which was located the official residence of her mother who served as Burma's ambassador to India. At this meeting we discussed several subjects relating to Myanmar and its external relations, including ties with India. Always a picture of grace and courtesy, she came out to the driveway to bid goodbye.

It is worth recalling that Daw Khin Kyi, Aung San's wife and Suu Kyi's mother, served as the Burmese ambassador to India from 1960 to 1967. Prime Minister Nehru took special interest in her welfare. This left a strong enough impression on Suu Kyi in her teen years for her to recall it in her acceptance speech during the presentation of the 1993 Nehru Memorial Prize for International Understanding:

> When my mother was appointed Burmese ambassador to India in 1960, Pandit Nehru cast over her the warm protection of his

friendship, always making a point of singling her out at public occasions to enquire after her well-being. It was with such gestures of human warmth that Pandit Nehru won the hearts of peoples of all races and creeds.[71]

Khin Nyunt was part of the power troika for much of my tenure in Myanmar. One saw the transformation of his image from that of the much-dreaded chief of Military Intelligence into a reform-minded, internationalist prime minister. He was the darling of the media, the most visible and friendly face of the regime. UN special envoy Razali Ismail saw him as a promising interlocutor, interested in bringing a transition to democracy. Even the US was dealing with him, increasing cooperation on a range of issues such as narcotics and counterterrorism. Towards India too, Khin Nyunt began to display new realism and friendliness.

A leader with modern temper, Khin Nyunt worked tirelessly to bring information technology (IT) to Myanmar. The country entered the IT age on his watch. Spotting potential synergy between this trend and India's achievements and expertise in the field, our Embassy worked pro-actively to craft cooperation from scratch. These efforts led to the visit of India's IT Minister Arun Shourie in August 2003. On a major Buddhist holiday and immediately on return from a foreign tour, Khin Nyunt, now prime minister, received Shourie as a special gesture. Their discussions contributed to enhancing bilateral cooperation. When Vice President Shekhawat visited Myanmar in November 2003, Khin Nyunt attended the state banquet. The prime minister's presence was unusual, meant perhaps to underline the high importance attached to India and also reflecting his role in the government. Khin Nyunt's interest in India was increasing as also his desire to pray at Bodh Gaya.

In order to cultivate ties with Khin Nyunt, the Embassy persuaded him to be our special guest at the CII's 'Made in India Exhibition' that was arranged in February 2004. In the half-hour he spent with us, he was given a detailed briefing about India's industrial progress. When Foreign Secretary Shyam Saran called on Khin Nyunt in early October 2004, there was a mutually shared sentiment that the relationship between India and Myanmar had strengthened significantly in recent years. As the meeting ended, the prime minister inquired about the welfare of Mrs. Saran and invited him to visit Myanmar again. The foreign secretary was delighted. 'Khin Nyunt is a changed man,' he remarked later. A very reserved leader determined to maintain his distance from diplomats in the past, the prime minister was now going out of his way to woo India.

From independence to military rule

My last meeting with Khin Nyunt was in mid-October 2004 in the National Theatre when he inaugurated the national dance and music competition. We shook hands, and I observed that the prime minister was maintaining a very busy schedule. He nodded and smiled. Four days later, he was ousted from power. He was placed under house arrest, along with his wife Dr Khin Win Shwe and other family members.[72]

Indian community

A brief reference to the Indian community in Myanmar is indispensable here, considering its important role and the time we spent with it in various parts of the country.[73] Fellow diplomats often asked us about the size and status of the Indian community, for along with the Chinese community, it was one of the two largest communities of foreign origin in Myanmar. It was not possible to give an accurate figure about the size, mainly because no census had taken place in Myanmar for a very long time.

According to the official figures supplied by the government of Myanmar, a total of 353,400 people of Indian origin lived in Myanmar in 2004. On the other hand, the L.M. Singhvi Committee on the Indian Diaspora estimated, in its report released in December 2000, that the total size was 2.5 million. After extensive consultations with community organisations, the Indian Embassy concluded that the number of Persons of Indian Origin (PIOs) in Myanmar was about 1 million in 2005. As to the number of Non-Resident Indians (NRIs), that is, expatriate Indians, it was quite small, perhaps less than 2000. Community associations were playing a useful role in serving as an interface with India's diplomats and political, business and cultural personalities visiting from India.

During our first visit to Mandalay in August 2002, this author had an opportunity to interact with Indians in Upper Myanmar, whose forefathers had come from India over a century back. At a round-table discussion with Consul General Pramod Bhutiani and this author, select leaders of the Indian community in Mandalay spoke of the problems faced by them. The biggest problem was the lack of suitable documentation in respect of their citizenship status, governing their stay and work conditions in the country. Due to a restrictive policy followed by the government and harassment meted out by lower level officials, nearly 50 per cent of Indians, it was claimed, were yet to become Myanmar citizens, despite having been born and lived all their lives in Myanmar. This largely reflected the situation of the community

From independence to military rule   111

in the whole of Myanmar. At this meeting, Dr Mohan Lal, a respected community leader, provided a balanced analysis of the prevailing situation. He asserted that, given the long and painful history of Indians in Myanmar, they had been much better off during the military rule since 1988 than in the Ne Win era and that they were well rooted in the Myanmar soil now.[74]

We also travelled to other near and far off places such as Bago near Yangon, Mogok and Mytikyina in the north, Mawlamyine in the south-east and Pathein in the Irrawaddy division. One always made it a point to meet representatives of the local Indian community and enjoyed doing so. They never failed to impress us with their warmth, hospitality, willingness to exchange views and the desire to share the glory of a resurgent India. But our most memorable meetings with the Indian community took place in Zeyawaddy, Kyauktaga and in Taungoo in the Bago division, the places we visited twice in February 2003 and February 2005.

Later developments

In March 2006, Dr A.P.J. Abdul Kalam, president of India, paid a three-day state visit to Myanmar, 19 years after Rajiv Gandhi. Kalam's discussions with Myanmar leaders were wide-ranging but candid. In an exclusive conversation with Than Shwe, he conveyed India's clear view that the military government should work hard to restore democracy in accordance with its own declarations and that the opposition leader, Suu Kyi, should have a suitable role in it.[75] In course of briefing the media prior to the visit, Foreign Secretary Shyam Saran gave some clues about India's thinking. New Delhi, he recalled, had welcomed the National Convention process, 'but we have also said that . . . it needs to be as inclusive as possible'.[76] Answering a question on Suu Kyi's role, he said '. . . we do believe that her welfare and her release would be very helpful in terms of the process of democratization that Myanmar itself is engaged in.'[77] Tackling a question on India–China rivalry concerning Myanmar, he stated:

> I do not think it is accurate to look at India–China rivalry in Myanmar just as I think it is not appropriate to look for India–China rivalry at every nook and corner of Asia. . . . The fact is that this is a very important neighbour to India.[78]

A special feature of Kalam's visit was its public diplomacy dimension. Ample interaction with students, monks, civil society leaders, Indian community and business leaders was built into the programme, in order to leverage Kalam's celebrity status as a rocket scientist and a secular Indian Muslim deeply steeped in the country's liberal ethos. While talking to monks at Kuthodaw Pagoda on 10 March, he spoke about the need for establishing an 'Enlightened Society'.[79] Speaking to the students of Yangon University, he observed: 'Thoughts and actions of renowned professionals of the Universities are intertwined with the history and progress of Myanmar.'[80] Addressing a meeting hosted by the Union of Myanmar Federation of Chamber of Commerce and Industry, he said:

> I visualize a great future for Myanmar towards development and economic prosperity. India will be very happy to be a partner in the development of agriculture, manufacturing and services sector of Myanmar. Let us remember youth force is the most powerful resource, both our countries cherish.[81]

The visit resulted in a joint statement and conclusion of four new agreements. It was truly impactful.

'Saffron Uprising' was the name given by media to a series of anti-government protests and demonstrations that took place in Yangon and other towns in August–September 2007. They represented the largest manifestation of popular discontent against SPDC caused by the authorities' decision to raise fuel prices. They were reminiscent of the anti-regime movement of 1988–89. Students, monks, women and other activists participated in protests. The government's response was the same – crackdown, but on this occasion violence was on a smaller scale than in the past. Thousands were arrested, but the number of deaths through action by security forces was small. Nevertheless the uprising showed that governance was basically flawed and that a transition to a better, more accountable system was essential, perhaps even inevitable.

The crackdown on protests triggered adverse reactions around the world. The US and other Western countries tightened economic sanctions, announcing additional measures. Earlier in the year – in January 2007 – the UN Security Council (UNSC) had considered a resolution calling for the cessation of grave violations of human rights, but its adoption was blocked by a double veto by Russia and China. In October 2007, the UNSC agreed on a Presidential Statement, which strongly deplored 'the use of violence against peaceful demonstrations' and called 'on the Government of Myanmar and all other parties concerned to work together towards a de-escalation of the situation and a peaceful solution'.[82] The United Nations Human Rights Council (UNHRC) convened a special session on Burma on 2 October and adopted a resolution urging the government of Myanmar 'to ensure full respect for human rights and fundamental freedoms and to investigate and bring to justice perpetrators of human rights violations . . .'[83] There was mounting pressure on countries such as China, ASEAN member states and India to intercede with the government of Myanmar and help in facilitating the mission of Ibrahim Gambari, special envoy of the UN secretary general.

Gambari paid two visits to India in July and October 2007 to hold discussions with the Indian government. There were several other meetings between Indian and UN officials in Delhi, New York and Geneva. On a separate track, the prime minister and the external affairs minister of India met with their Myanmar counterparts on different occasions. India decided to support the consensus resolution adopted by UNHRC after giving an Explanation of Vote (EOV).[84] In essence, India articulated its concern at the situation in Myanmar, suggested an enquiry into 'current incidents and the use of force'[85] and expressed hope for the process of national reconciliation and political reform to move forward expeditiously and that it should be 'broad-based, including Daw Aung San Suu Kyi and the various ethnic nationalities'.[86] Indian representatives reiterated support for the Gambari initiative and UN endeavours in this context. What the Indian government sought to do was to adapt carefully its pragmatic policy on Myanmar with the 'Saffron Uprising' and the pressures generated by it, both nationally and internationally.

In May 2008 Myanmar was struck by a massive natural disaster, Cyclone Nargis. The cyclone made landfall on 2 May, causing immense havoc to the Ayeyarwady Delta. 'According to official figures, 84,500 people were killed and 53,800 went missing. A total 37 townships were significantly affected by the cyclone. The UN estimates that as many as 2.4 million people were affected.'[87] India's assistance at this grim hour was both 'spontaneous and immediate' in keeping with its 'close and friendly neighbourly relations with Myanmar'. Two Indian Navy ships and five Indian aircraft carried relief and medical supplies as well as food items to Myanmar. Minister of External Affairs Pranab Mukherjee telephoned Foreign Minister U Nyan Win to convey India's 'deep sorrow' at the loss of lives and widespread damage suffered by the country. The latter expressed Myanmar's 'gratitude for the prompt and generous assistance'. In view of reports that Myanmar was reluctant to receive relief supplies by the Western countries, and the US request to India, among other nations, to intercede with the Myanmar authorities, the Indian government 'urged Myanmar to accept international relief supplies to supplement their efforts'.[88]

The decade ended with another cycle of VVIP visits, namely of Vice Chairman Maung Aye in 2008, Vice President M. Hamid Ansari in 2009 and Chairman Than Shwe in 2010. The period of rapprochement had begun in 1992, but consolidation and expansion of the relationship began with Maung Aye's two visits in 2000. His visit in April 2008 was the occasion to take stock of the distance the two countries had travelled together in the quest of mutually beneficial cooperation. Vice President Ansari, while visiting Myanmar in February 2009, observed that India had made 'great strides' in building bilateral relations. He recognised Maung Aye's contribution by recalling that the latter's visit (as SPDC vice chairman) in 2000 had 'marked the beginning of a series of initiatives designed to bring our peoples together'.[89]

Chairman Than Shwe's tour of India in July 2010 was an unspoken valedictory visit. It took place just a few months before the elections in Myanmar. At official discussions, the two countries renewed their commitment to further strengthen and broaden their 'multi-dimensional relationship'. The joint statement issued during the visit reflected India's stress on comprehensively broad basing the national reconciliation process and democratic changes being introduced in Myanmar. But, much of its other contents related to deepening political understanding and, more importantly, advancing the cause of bilateral economic and development cooperation. This author analysed the state of relationship in light of the visit.[90] Satish Chandra, former deputy national security adviser, interpreted the visit as leading to 'newer heights'.[91]

The stage had thus been set for the next phase in the development of India–Myanmar relations, the theme for the following chapter.

Notes

1 Jawaharlal Nehru, *Selected Works of Jawaharlal Nehru Second Series, Volume V*, New Delhi: Jawaharlal Nehru Memorial Fund, 1987, p. 536.
2 Dr Rajendra Prasad later became the first president of the Republic of India.
3 Dr Rajendra Prasad, *Correspondence and Select Documents, Vol. 10.* Allied Publishers, 1988, http://books.google.co.in/books?id=FpGsCSxQ MXUC&pg=PA333&lpg=PA333&dq=Rajendra+Prasad+and+Bodhi+tre e+and+Burma&source (accessed on 10 May 2012).
4 *India News Annual 2001*, Indian Embassy in Yangon.
5 U Nu, *U Nu Saturday's Son*, London: Yale University Press, 1975, p. 227.

From independence to military rule 115

6 Chi-shad Liang, *Burma's Foreign Relations: Neutralism in Theory and Practice*, New York: Praeger Publishers, 1990, p. 128.
7 Ibid., p. 132.
8 K. M. Panikkar, *In Two Chinas: Memoirs of a Diplomat*, London: George Allen & Unwin Ltd, 1955, p. 68. Relating the factual story, the author wrote: 'In due course, Burma announced its recognition and we followed in a few days.'
9 Uma Shankar Singh, *Burma and India 1948–1962*, New Delhi: Oxford & IBH Publishing Co., 1979. For details, please refer to 'The Issue of Kuomintang Troops', pp. 167–172.
10 Statement by Head of Indian Delegation, V. K. Krishna Menon at United Nations General assembly at the 8th Session, 448th Plenary Meeting, 28 September 1953, Permanent Mission of India to the UN, New York, https://www.pminewyork.org/landmark.php?id=6 (accessed on 5 October 2014).
11 Chi-shad Liang, *Burma's Foreign Relations: Neutralism in Theory and Practice*, New York: Praeger Publishers, 1990, p. 131.
12 David I. Steinberg and Honguei Fan, *Modern China–Myanmar Relations: Dilemmas of Mutual Dependence*, Copenhagen: NIAS Press, 2012. For a crisp analysis of other aspects of the Burma–China boundary settlement, readers may refer to the relevant section on pp. 55–68.
13 During his eleven-year long exile, he spent five years in Thailand and six years in India from 1974 to 1980.
14 Frank N. Trager, *Burma from Kingdom to Republic*, London: The Pall Mall Press Ltd., 1966, p. 218.
15 Ibid. Please refer to the analysis of a speech by U Nu in December 1949 on p. 219.
16 Chi-shad Liang, Burma's *Foreign Relations: Neutralism in Theory and Practice*, p. 130. 'According to Nehru, however, U Nu "was not a follower in international meetings in which I participated with him. He had definite ideas of his own and pursued them."'
17 Frank N. Trager, *Burma from Kingdom to Republic*, p. 257. 'But on such key issues as Korea and Hungary, and on the degree to which they condemn all varieties of imperialism, the cleavage between India and Burma is as strong as is their agreement on other questions. The varieties of neutralist policy are as numerous as those of Western democratic policy.'
18 Chi-shad Liang, *Burma's Foreign Relations: Neutralism in Theory and Practice*, p. 130.
19 Ibid., p. 220.
20 Her email dated 14 October 2014 to the author.
21 His advocates and apologists, of course, had a different take. For example, in *Burma and General Ne Win*, Rangoon: Religious Affairs Department, Press, 1969, biographer and later a successor, Maung Maung, wrote: 'The Burmese way to Socialism is thus an act of faith, a definition of the goals, and a chart of the path to the goals.' p. 296.
22 Maung Maung, *Burma and General Ne Win*. Ironically towards the end of his tenure as caretaker prime minister, Ne Win had said in December 1959 regarding the forthcoming elections: 'Let the people make their choice in freedom. The country will get the government it deserves.' p. 270.
23 For details, please see: 'The Foreign Policy of Sirimavo Bandaranaike – The Colombo Powers and the Sino-Indian War of 1962', InfoLanka.

asia, http://infolanka.asia/sri-lanka/people/the-foreign-policy-of-sirimavo-bandaranaike/the-colombo-powers-and-the-sino-indian-war-of-1962 (accessed on 11 October 2014).

24 The six nations were Egypt, Burma, Cambodia, Sri Lanka, Ghana and Indonesia. They were selected as they were all acceptable to both India and China. They met in Colombo on 10 December 1962.

25 MEA Records.

26 Ibid.

27 For details, please see MEA reports for 1966–67 and 1969–70.

28 This was tried again at the official bilateral discussions during 1992–94, but it too proved futile due to Yangon's caution and disinterest.

29 MEA Report 1987–88, http://mealib.nic.in/?2516?000#India%27s%20 Neighbours (accessed on 28 April 2015).

30 K. Natwar Singh, *Walking with Lions: Tales from a Diplomatic Past*, Noida: HarperCollins Publishers India, 2013, pp. 125–26. He gave an interesting account of the meeting between Rajiv Gandhi and Ne Win: 'From the word go, General Ne Win adopted an avuncular tone. Every proposal the Prime Minister made was brushed aside. Tourism. "I dislike tourists. They give wrong ideas to our people. I made a big mistake by allowing Germany to open a tourist office. I am going to have it closed," the General announced. Before the Prime Minister could make a proposal to increase trade, the General lapsed into nostalgia. . . . Rajiv Gandhi kept his cool. I could see he was driven to controlled indignation . . . Later, there was a meeting with Burmese PM and several ministers. Each proposal made by Rajiv Gandhi was joyfully accepted. What a contrast! What fruitful discussions! Our joy was short-lived. General Ne Win would have none of it. He overruled his prime minister.'

31 Martin Smith, *Burma: Insurgency and the Politics of Ethnicity*, Bangkok: White Lotus, 1991, p. 15. 'Though widely described in the foreign media as a "coup", it was more obviously a change of faces or, as one as diplomat put it, "a reshuffling of the pack."'

32 Liang, *Burma's Foreign Relations*, p. 237.

33 Myanmar Parliamentary Chamber: Pyithu Hluttaw. Elections held in 1990, http://www.ipu.org/parline-e/reports/arc/2388_90.htm (accessed on 14 November 2013).

34 Liang, *Burma's Foreign Relations*, p. 239.

35 A select sampling is given below from Ministry of External Affairs (MEA) Records and Reports:

(i) Official Spokesman of the MEA on 10 September 1988: '. . . We have noted the undaunted resolve of the Burmese people to establish a fully democratic structure in their country. This aspiration fully accords with India's firm commitment to democracy. . . .' http://mealib.nic. in/?999834 (accessed on 31 October 2013).

(ii) Official Spokesman of MEA on 5 October 1988, responding to a query from the press, stated: 'We have given clear instructions to our border authorities that no genuine refugees from Burma are to be sent back.' http://mealib.nic.in/?999834 (accessed on 31 October 2013).

(iii) MEA Annual Report 1991–1992: 'India views with regret that political power yet remains untransferred, to the people's representatives after the general elections in Myanmar in May 1990. India is equally distressed at the continued house detention of Ms Aung San Suu Kyi. Despite its policy of non-interference in the affairs of other countries, India cannot ignore the democratic aspirations of the people of Myanmar. . . .' http://mealib.nic.in/?2021 (accessed on 31 October 2013).

(iv) MEA Annual Report 1992–1993: 'Despite some tentative steps taken by the Myanmar Government recently towards addressing the issue, Myanmar's suppression of the democratic movement continued to be a factor in India's relations with that country. India continued to press for the early restoration of democracy in Myanmar.' http://mealib.nic.in/?2013 (accessed on 31 October 2013).

36 Thant Myint-U, *Where China Meets India*, London: Faber and Faber Limited, 2011, p. 269. 'The West was then just starting to impose sanctions, but India was already actively financing Burmese opposition groups, including exiles and militant groups based along the Thailand–Burma border.'

37 I served as joint secretary in MEA's Bangladesh and Myanmar (BM) division and later in Bangladesh, Sri Lanka, Maldives and Myanmar (BSM) division from June 1991 to August 1994.

38 Thin Thin Aung & Soe Myint, 'India–Burma Relations', in Challenges to Democratization in Burma, International IDEA, p. 513, http://www.idea.int/asia_pacific/burma/upload/chap4.pdf (accessed on 4 November 2013).

39 '1991 Nobel Peace Prize for Daw Aung San Suu Kyi', Burma Alert No. 10 Volume 2, October 1991, http://www.burmalibrary.org/docsBA/BA1991-V02-N10.pdf (accessed on 3 November 2013).

40 Thin Thin Aung & Soe Myint, 'India–Burma Relations', p. 514.

41 From my discussions with Ambassador Preet Malik.

42 Thant Myint-U, *Where China Meets India*, p. 268.

43 P.V. Narasimha Rao was the tenth prime minster of India from June 1991 to May 1996.

44 Ranjit Gupta, 'China, Myanmar and India: A Strategic Perspective', *Indian Foreign Affairs Journal*, Vol. 8, No. 1, (January–March 2013), p. 86. 'In a sharp departure from what had been a standard Indian foreign policy norm since independence of normal interaction with all countries irrespective of the nature of their regimes, India exhibited uncharacteristic hostility to Myanmar's new military junta during 1988–91, thus giving China an open field to play.'

45 For example, numerous research products of IDSA bear testimony to this observation.

46 Thant Myint-U, *Where China Meets India*, p. 269.

47 'India's Strategic Interest in Myanmar: An Interview with Shyam Saran', IPCS Special report 98, February 2011 by Medha Chaturvedi, www.ipcs.org/pdf_file/issue/SR98-ShyamSaranInterview.pdf (accessed on 3 November 2013).

48 Renaud Egreteau, *Wooing the Generals: India's New Burmese Policy*, Delhi: Authors Press, 2003, p. 3. 'India realised it must not ignore such a strategic neighbour – for several geopolitical, military and even economic reasons. "Wooing" the Burmese Generals, with a velvet glove policy, made

India enter the game and conduct another Realpolitk towards another military regime.'

49 For details, please refer to the paper by Thin Thin Aung and Soe Myint, 'India–Burma Relations'.

50 His wife of Burmese origin, Usha, was a staunch advocate of the cause of democracy in Burma.

51 Dr Vijay Sakhuja, 'India and Myanmar: Choices for Military Cooperation', Issue Brief, ICWA, 11 September 2012, http://www.icwa.in/issue_briefs.html (accessed on 3 November 2013).

52 Daw Than E, 'honourary aunt' of Suu Kyi and democracy activist, read out a statement on this occasion on behalf of Suu Kyi, http://www.burmalibrary.org/reg.burma/archives/199511/msg00096.html (accessed on 12 November 2013).

53 K.S. Narayanan, 'Governance and Democracy', http://www.krnarayanan.in/html/speeches/others/democracy_14nov1995.htm (accessed on 12 November 2013).

54 Shyam Saran served as joint secretary in MEA and PMO from 1989 to 1992. After his stint in Myanmar, he served as India's ambassador in Indonesia and later in Nepal. He was then elevated as foreign secretary and, in this capacity, he oversaw the growth of India–Myanmar relations. Handling numerous post-retirement assignments, he was chairman of the National Security Advisory Board and continued his interest in Myanmar.

55 During a long car drive from Naypyitaw to Mandalay on 8 March 2013, Shyam Saran narrated to me a detailed story of his years in Myanmar. Earlier, at a seminar co-hosted by Asia Centre Bangalore and India Council of World Affairs (ICWA) on 9 June 2012 and on its sidelines, Malik recounted his story and analysed it, drawing suitable lessons for future.

56 V.P. Malik, 'Past, Present and Future of Indo-Myanmar Relations from the Perspective of India's National Security', India's Security Environment: Proceedings of Select Seminars held by Asia Centre Bangalore, New Delhi: Asia Centre Bangalore, 2013, p. 104.

57 General V.P. Malik, *India's Military Conflicts and Diplomacy: An Inside View of Decision Making*, Noida: HarperCollins Publishers India, 2013, p. 221.

58 Ibid., p. 224. After giving a brief account of a specific episode, the author added: 'The prompt and effective response to my request for an important security mission came as a big surprise to the Prime Minister's Office and the Ministry of External Affairs.'

59 'India–Myanmar Relations' India's Security Environment, Proceedings of Select Seminars held by Asia Centre, Bangalore, p. 105. 'China had gained marked socio-economic influence, particularly in North and North-East Myanmar. Unless we made efforts, this influence would extend to the West of Irrawaddy River and in the South. The Myanmar Government was keen to improve relations with India in the fields of economic development and technology, which ought to be reciprocated.'

60 MEA Annual Report 2000–2001, p.7.

61 India News 2001, Special Annual Issue, p. 22.

62 MEA Annual Report 2000–2001, p. 7. 'These discussions and the talks with the Myanmar Foreign Minister and other Ministers covered all aspects of bilateral relations including border trade and infrastructure project.'

From independence to military rule 119

63 Rahul Kulshreshth, 'India–Myanmar Relations: An Overview', Focus on India-Myanmar Relations, Special Booklet, Embassy of India: Yangon, November 2003, p. 13.
64 Bhairon Singh Shekhawat, 'Message', Focus on India–Myanmar Relations, November 2003, p. 4.
65 Ibid. Vice Senior General Maung Aye, 'Message', p. 5.
66 According to MEA Records, Ne Win also made a private visit to India in November 1984 and met Prime Minister Rajiv Gandhi to personally convey his condolences for Indira Gandhi's assassination.
67 Joint statement issued on the occasion of the state visit of Senior General Than Shwe, Chairman of the State Peace and Development Council of the Union of Myanmar to India (25–29 October 2004). October 29, 2004. Para seven: '. . . The Indian side stressed that it wished to see a stable, peaceful, prosperous and democratic Myanmar and was ready to assist the Government and people of Myanmar on their path to further political and economic progress.' www.mea.gov.in/bilateral-documents.htm?dtl/7468/Joint+Statement (accessed on 9 November 2013).
68 Ibid., para eleven: '. . . The Myanmar side reiterated that it would not allow insurgent activities against India from its soil. The Indian side thanked the Myanmar side for the assurance. Both sides agreed to take necessary steps to prevent cross border crimes, including drug trafficking and arms smuggling, and to upgrade substantially bilateral cooperation in this context.'
69 Ibid., para five.
70 For relevant details, please see Kriti, India–Myanmar Relations, published-forscholar, 18 December 2006, https://publishedforscholar.wordpress.com/2006/12/18/india-myanmar-relations/ (accessed on 11 October 2014).
71 Aung San Suu Kyi's speech at Nehru Prize. Address on the Occasion of the Presentation of the 1993 Nehru Memorial Prize for International Understanding, 14 November 1995, http://www.burmalibrary.org/reg.burma/archives/199511/msg00096.html (accessed on 12 November 2013).
72 Prime Minister Khin Nyunt was ousted from power on 18 October 2004 and was arrested immediately. Later he was tried and sentenced to 44 years in prison, which was converted into house arrest or protective custody. He was released from it on 12 January 2012. A favourite of interviewers, he drew much attention both for his past role and present views. For details, please refer to, 'In New Myanmar, Junta's "Evil Prince" Wants to Offer His Help', 9 November 2013, http://www.newrebound88.com/Articles/Details/1624 (accessed on 13 November 2013).
73 From the author's personal notes.
74 Ibid.
75 From my personal discussions with a top official of the Indian government.
76 Ministry of External Affairs, Visit of President Dr A.P.J. Abdul Kalam to Myanmar and Mauritius: 8–13 March 2006, New Delhi: Ministry of External Affairs, 2006, p. 135.
77 Ibid., p. 136.
78 Ibid., p. 137.
79 Ibid., p. 16.
80 Ibid., p. 20.
81 Ibid., p. 50.

82 Security Council SC/9139, 11 October 2007, www.un.org/News/Press/docs/2007/sc9139.doc.htm (accessed on 14 November 2013).

83 Human Rights Council Resolution S-5/1: Situation of human rights in Myanmar 2 October 2007, www.refworld.org/pdfid/470b4e912.pdf (accessed on 14 November 2013).

84 Text of EOV is available at http://www.mea.gov.in/in-focus-article.htm?1970/Statement+by+Mr+Swashpawan+Singh+Ambassador+amp+Permanent+Representative+of+India+at+the+Fifth+Special+Session+of+the+Human+Rights+Council+on+the+Human+Rights+Situation+in+Myanmar (accessed on 12 November 2013).

85 'Statement by Mr. Swashpawan Singh, Ambassador & Permanent Representative of India at the Fifth Special Session of the Human Rights Council on the Human Rights Situation in Myanmar', 2 October 2007, http://www.mea.gov.in/in-focus-article.htm?1970/Statement+by+Mr+Swashpawan+Singh+Ambassador+amp+Permanent+Representative+of+India+at+the+Fifth+Special+Session+of+the+Human+Rights+Council+on+the+Human+Rights+Situation+in+Myanmar (accessed on 12 November 2013).

86 'Briefing points on Prime Minister's meeting with Prime Minister of Myanmar, Singapore, 21 November 2007', http://www.mea.gov.in/media-briefings.htm?dtl/3755/Briefing_points_on_Prime_Ministers_meeting_with_Prime_Minister_of_Myanmar (accessed on 12 November 2013).

87 Myanmar: Cyclone Nargis 2008 Facts and Figures, International Federation of Red Cross and Red Crescent Societies, http://www.ifrc.org/en/news-and-media/news-stories/asia-pacific/myanmar/myanmar-cyclone-nargis-2008-facts-and-figures/ (accessed on 9 November 2013).

88 On India's assistance for the cyclone in Myanmar, see http://www.mea.gov.in/press-releases.htm?dtl/2053/OntIndias+assistance+tfo . . . (accessed on 9 November 2013).

89 http://vicepresidentofindia.nic.in/contents.asp?id=202 (accessed on 9 November 2013).

90 Rajiv Bhatia, 'Crafting a Richer India–Myanmar Partnership', *The Hindu*, 10 August 2010.

91 Satish Chandra, 'Senior General Than Shwe's Visit: A Grand Success'. He wrote: 'Quite clearly Than Shwe's visit to India has been useful in further consolidating ties between the two countries. If we continue to nurture this relationship in a similarly workmanlike fashion uninfluenced by third parties, India–Myanmar ties are bound to attain newer heights which will rebound to the benefit of both countries.' Vivekananda International Foundation, www.vifindia.org/SENIOR-GENERAL-THAN-SHWE-VISIT (accessed on 9 November 2013).

Chapter 5

India–Myanmar relations
During reform period

> Burma has still not reached the goal of democracy and in this last, I hope, and most difficult phase, India will stand by us and walk by us as we proceed on the path that they were able to proceed upon many years before us.
>
> – Aung San Suu Kyi[1]

As we noted earlier, India's Myanmar policy sought to deepen cooperation in all relevant fields with the government and people of Myanmar, especially during the last decade of the State Peace and Development Council (SPDC) rule. But there were red lines in place beyond which the relationship could not progress as long as the country's democratic aspirations were trampled upon by the generals. This was both understandable and unavoidable, given the public opinion in India and the restrictive policy line key stakeholders in the international community had adopted. South Block simply could not be immune to these two powerful influences.

However, following the elections in November 2010, the political situation in Myanmar began to unfreeze. On 13 November 2010, Aung San Suu Kyi was released from house arrest, a development that was welcomed by New Delhi, as mentioned earlier. S.M. Krishna, India's external affairs minister, visited Myanmar in June 2011 in order to 'take stock of our broad-based engagement with Myanmar' and 'to get a better feel of the priorities and the outlook of the new government', as an Indian official put it.[2] Contours and directions of the transition in Myanmar were still unclear. This was perhaps the reason why Krishna decided to skip meeting Suu Kyi. Caution was still the ruling sentiment. But in a finely calibrated move, Foreign Secretary Nirupama Rao called on the NLD leader to initiate a substantive conversation. It was the highest level contact with her from the government side in over two decades.

122 During reform period

Krishna's visit to Myanmar helped in preparing the ground for several high-level visits that were to follow in the future. This chapter presents a critical analysis of the high-level visits as a medium to present the unfolding story of bilateral relations during 2011–14.

President Thein Sein's visit

With the exception of Prime Minister U Nu and General Ne Win, the Myanmar leader who visited India the maximum number of times was Thein Sein. He accompanied SPDC chairman Than Shwe on his historic visit in 2004, visited India as the prime minister in November 2008 to participate in the Bay of Bengal Initiative for Multi-Sectoral Technical and Economic Cooperation (BIMSTEC) Summit, and undertook two visits as the president in 2011 and 2012.

President Thein Sein's visit in October 2011 had a clear aim to move forward the bilateral relationship to a higher level even as he was engaged in steering major changes in Myanmar's internal and external policies. The joint statement issued at the conclusion of the visit portrayed bilateral ties as 'a multi-faceted relationship' that was set to grow.[3] *The New Light of Myanmar* stated subsequently in an editorial that the visit opened 'a new chapter' for cementing relations with 'high momentum'.[4] This was a justified conclusion because of three reasons. First, the two governments reached agreement on 'enhancing effective cooperation and coordination' between their security forces in tackling 'the deadly menace of insurgency and terrorism'.[5] Second, recognising new realities, India decided to offer a generous Line of Credit amounting to US$500 million for various development projects. This was an indication of the recognition that Myanmar's importance as India's neighbour was on the rise. Third, the degree of convergence between the two countries on a host of regional and international issues was a special feature of the deliberations.

At the state banquet, President Pratibha Devisingh Patil stated: 'When we look eastwards, we first see Myanmar', stressing that the country enjoyed 'a central place in our vision and approach of rebuilding our Eastern connections'.[6] Thein Sein reciprocated by expressing Myanmar's high appreciation for India's Look East Policy.[7]

Prime Minister Manmohan Singh's voyage

During the 1950s the prime ministers of India and Burma met frequently, demonstrating not only their personal friendship but also the proximity of their governments. In 1954–55, Prime Ministers Nehru and U Nu met at least eight times. Three subsequent prime ministers – Lal Bahadur Shastri, Indira Gandhi and Rajiv Gandhi – paid only a visit each to Burma. Rajiv Gandhi's visit in 1987 was a bold but failed attempt to revitalise the relationship. Twenty-five years would pass before Manmohan Singh became the fifth prime minister to visit the country in May 2012.[8]

The context

Singh had received invitations twice – in 2004 and 2010 – to visit Myanmar from SPDC Chairman Than Shwe personally. All concerned on the two sides were aware that a prime ministerial visit was not feasible. Between Than Shwe's two visits, the Indian government had felt courageous enough to send President A. P. J. Abdul Kalam on a state visit in 2006. But in 2011, Myanmar stood at the cusp of transition, marked by elections, dissolution of SPDC, launch of the reform agenda by the new president and Thein Sein–Suu Kyi reconciliation in August 2011. The president of Myanmar paid a state visit to India in October 2011. Singh now received his third invitation. The chances of his visit still looked dim, but discussions with Thein Sein showed promise.

This is where the BIMSTEC Summit entered into diplomatic calculations. South Block worked on the plan that Singh should attend the summit and then stay on for a brief bilateral visit. But agreement eluded the planners on the dates acceptable to all summit participants. Meanwhile, Thein Sein's reform train was gaining traction and attracting unprecedented international attention. US Secretary of State Hillary Clinton visited the country in December 2011, the first trip at this level since 1955. Her meetings with the president and Suu Kyi and her announcing measures to improve US–Myanmar relations underlined dramatically the nature of change unfolding in Myanmar and the readiness of the international community to open a new chapter with Myanmar. This visit unleashed an avalanche of VIP visits from Europe and Asia. Apart from numerous foreign ministers, the other high-ranking visitors were the president of Pakistan, prime ministers of Bangladesh, Thailand and UK as well as the UN secretary general and the president of South Korea.

The only country that seemed to stay aloof was China. Its relations with Myanmar, though very strong in the previous two decades, suffered a major setback in September 2011 when the Myanmar government, bowing to the 'will of the people', suspended the US$3.6 billion Myitsone hydropower project without consulting or even informing Beijing in advance.[9] Clearly, the diplomatic landscape in Myanmar was changing rapidly.

124 During reform period

Monitoring all this closely, South Block seemed close to taking a bold decision. There were unambiguous signals from the insiders in March that Dr Singh was inclined to visit Myanmar – with or without the BIMSTEC Summit. In this specific context came the decision that, even though the summit had been deferred beyond May 2012, Singh's visit would take place as an exclusively bilateral diplomatic initiative. A few weeks before the formal announcement was made, Singh himself confirmed this while visiting Assam.

Reactions within India were positive. Experts emphasised Myanmar's multi-dimensional importance for India, agreeing generally that the visit should help in strengthening the relationship. A few pessimists and sceptics made dissenting noises, arguing that, due to political difficulties faced by the UPA government and challenges facing the country's economy, a beleaguered prime minister was unlikely to achieve much. An academic based in Delhi maintained that India lacked the 'strategic vision of a future Asia-Pacific, especially in the case of Myanmar that can inform its policies and actions'.[10] A business leader engaged in promoting India's relations with Myanmar asserted that 'all elements are in place for a turnaround . . .' He believed that India's policy since the 1990s could now pay 'rich dividends' as 'India is on the winning side of both' – the military establishment and the opposition leader, Suu Kyi.[11]

Several commentators interpreted that the visit after a 25-year gap was an indicator of India's neglect of Myanmar. This was an unfair assessment. If dialogue at the highest political level is a key parameter of friendly relations, the two countries had already ensured it. During the period 2000–11, a total of 9 VVIP level visits had taken place, giving an average of one visit in nearly every 14 months. Besides, having followed a carefully calibrated policy of engaging the military government but also extending political support to the cause of democracy, India could hardly have gone ahead with a prime ministerial visit so long as Suu Kyi was under house arrest and in an opposition mode vis-à-vis the government. As soon as conditions changed materially, decks were cleared for the visit by Prime Minister Singh. Once the decision was taken, it was also evident that he would travel with a rich basket of programmes and proposals to deepen bilateral cooperation. Therefore, some optimism was justified.

Key highlights

Scheduled for 27–29 May, Singh's visit to Myanmar in a generation caused considerable excitement within the strategic community in Delhi. A large number of intellectual activities had already taken place, following developments in Myanmar since November 2010. In the specific context of the visit, a few think tanks such as the Aspen Institute India and the Indian Council of World Affairs hosted special brainstorming meetings to develop recommendations for the government's consideration.

Briefing media persons in New Delhi on 25 May, Foreign Secretary Ranjan Mathai emphasised that the visit would be an opportunity 'to review [previous] progress and to discuss new initiatives . . . in the furtherance of our relations'. Significantly he observed: 'The new political environment in Myanmar also provides fresh opportunities to take our bilateral relationship to a new phase.'[12]

In a pre-departure statement on 27 May, Prime Minister Manmohan Singh said: 'India attaches the highest importance to its relations with Myanmar, which is a close friend and neighbour.' He spoke of India's commitment to 'a close, cooperative and mutually beneficial partnership with the Government and people of Myanmar'. Adding that India welcomed Myanmar's transition to democratic governance and a more broad-based, inclusive reconciliation process, he expressed readiness to share India's democratic experiences with Myanmar.[13]

Singh was accompanied by the minister for external affairs, senior officials, a media team and a business delegation. It was probably on the cards that the chief ministers of four Northeast states bordering on Myanmar, namely Arunachal Pradesh, Nagaland, Manipur and Mizoram, would be part of the prime minister's delegation. Their inclusion would have highlighted India's plan to establish new links of communication and cooperation. The prime minister had been accompanied by the chief ministers of Assam, Tripura, Mizoram and Meghalaya on his visit to Bangladesh in 2011, but the last minute decision of the chief minister of West Bengal to drop out and to oppose the signing of the India–Bangladesh agreement on sharing of Teesta River water had caused considerable embarrassment. This experience perhaps made Dr Singh more cautious. After the visit, a journalist asked him whether taking chief ministers would not have produced 'greater dividends'. He responded that he first wanted to discuss the 'basic principles and modalities' regarding the problems of border management where after visits by chief ministers would take place 'sooner or later'.[14]

Protocol experts worked hard to craft a suitable programme. Singh and his official delegation spent both nights of his two-day trip in Naypyitaw. Singh was received by Foreign Minister Wunna Maung Lwin on his arrival. The next day he was accorded a ceremonial welcome. This was followed by discussions with President Thein Sein, first in a restricted format with only a few officials in attendance and then in the formal setting of delegation-level talks. Other calls and meetings were arranged, including an official banquet in the evening of 28 May.

Although media persons accompanying Dr Singh covered official talks and ceremonies, many of them had ample time and curiosity to explore and comment on the new capital. Under Than Shwe's leadership, the government had shifted the capital from Yangon to Naypyitaw in 2006. Indian journalists told their viewers and readers for the first time about the strange nature of a city that was new and filled with grand structures, but it was also 'strikingly un-peopled'.[15] In contrast, Yangon was an old, dilapidated city with 4.5 million inhabitants. One city was dominated by the government's presence, the other by the people where also lived the pro-democracy icon Suu Kyi.

On the last day of his visit, the prime minister and party travelled to Yangon where his programme included a meeting with Suu Kyi, his second most important meeting; a policy speech at a public forum; a separate meeting with the Indian community; and visits to the Shwedagon Pagoda and the Mausoleum of Bahadur Shah Zafar, the last emperor of India.

As the visit progressed, on several occasions, Singh articulated India's views on the relationship with Myanmar – its past, present and future. Therefore, a brief analysis of at least two of his speeches and a statement would help in appreciating India's position. He delivered a succinct but meaningful banquet speech.[16] Calling India and Myanmar as 'natural partners, linked by geography and history', he recalled: 'Since time immemorial, trade, people and ideas have flowed between our two lands.' He referred to Lord Buddha whose teachings had inspired 'generations of scholars, monks, pilgrims and common people in both our countries for almost two millennia'. He drew upon Nehru to reinforce the message of proximity, citing the latter's comment made on the occasion of Burma's independence in January 1948. Singh made a special reference to 'a journey of national reconciliation and transition' embarked by the country. Singh voiced India's readiness to support the creation of 'a democratic, stable and prosperous Myanmar'.[17]

Speaking at the banquet, Thein Sein too placed the relationship in a historical perspective.

> Our two countries have enjoyed diplomatic relations for 64 years only. But historically people-to-people contact between our two countries has stood [for] thousands of years already. . . . Myanmar attaches great importance to promote friendly relations with India in the same way India does in its relations with Myanmar.[18]

The second speech was delivered by Singh before a mixed academic and business community, at an event hosted by the Myanmar Federation of Chambers of Commerce and Industry and the Myanmar Resource Institute.[19] He spoke on an aptly chosen subject – 'India and Myanmar: A Partnership for Progress and Regional Development'. The two countries, he began, shared age-old cultural and civilisational ties. 'Merchants, monks and maritime traders carried influences and traditions from one to the other.' The story of rich cooperation and ties in the past was helpful and relevant as the two countries now had an opportunity to work as 'equal partners to revive ancient links' and to 'rediscover the immense possibilities of cooperation'. He stressed Myanmar's importance for India and the region in unambiguous terms:

> Myanmar is a critical partner in India's 'Look East' policy and is perfectly suited to play the role of an economic bridge between India and China and between South and South-East Asia.[20]

Singh advocated the need for the two countries to work together as well as with other countries in order 'to create a regional economy that can become a hub for trade, investment and communication in the region'.[21] He elaborated on agreements reached with the government of Myanmar.

Soon after a 45-minute meeting with Suu Kyi, Singh told media persons it was his 'great honour and great privilege' to meet the NLD leader. Her life, struggle and determination had 'inspired millions of people all over the world'. He invited her to visit India, hoping sincerely that she would do so soon. The letter of invitation to deliver the prestigious Jawaharlal Nehru Memorial Lecture, addressed by Sonia Gandhi as the chairperson of the Nehru Memorial Fund, was handed over to the Burmese leader. He also added that it was India's 'sincere belief' that in the national reconciliation process launched by the president, she would play 'a defining role'.[22]

Speaking immediately after Singh, Suu Kyi recalled that India and Burma had been particularly close over the years 'not just because of our geographical positions' but because they shared 'deep ties of friendship'. 'My parents', she stressed, 'were great admirers of Pandit Jawaharlal Nehru and other Indian leaders'. She expressed happiness 'at the prospect of closer ties with India' because the two countries had much to learn from each other and to contribute to the region's peace and stability. Noting the growing bilateral exchanges, she said she had conveyed to the prime minister that 'true friendship between the

128 During reform period

countries can be based only on friendship between our two peoples, and this is what I hope we will be able to achieve'.[23]

While interacting with media representatives on his return flight, Singh disclosed a little more about his meeting with Suu Kyi. Their discussion was concentrated on national reconciliation and making development more inclusive, transparent and people-friendly. She talked about the difficulties Myanmar people faced in accessing various services provided by government agencies. As India faced similar problems but did not have all the answers, he suggested engaging the government and civil society of Myanmar with a view to devising 'common pathways to find productive, mutually acceptable solutions to these difficult problems of development and inclusion'.[24]

Concerning this meeting, a pre-visit report in an Indian national daily claimed that New Delhi was uncertain whether to arrange the prime minister's call on Suu Kyi at her famous lake-side residence (where she spent 15 of past 22 years under house arrest) as several world leaders had done earlier or whether she should come to meet Singh at his hotel.[25] The report was speculative. Protocol authorities of the two sides had already decided through mutual agreement to make the Sedona Hotel (where Singh was to stay) as the venue for this meeting. But, the report got much play, with critics of South Block and champions of 'The Lady' assailing the Indian government for its insensitivity. Later, a leading weekly asserted: 'Protocol scored a petty point. India lost a major opportunity.'[26] But it proved to be a non-issue. An interesting sidelight was that a private meeting between Suu Kyi and Gursharan Kaur, the prime minister's wife, also took place. This came from the latter's personal request, and it helped to underline that the Indian side was willing to go an extra mile to establish a personal rapport with the democracy icon.[27]

Singh's itinerary in Yangon included a visit to the famed Shwedagon Pagoda. Visiting it in 1852, Lord Dalhousie, the governor general, called it the best historical monument that he had visited in British India, with the exception of the Taj Mahal.[28] For Prime Minister Singh, this was not a tourist site. The importance of visiting Burma's holiest shrine and the unquestionable symbol of cultural nationalism was evident to all. What Singh wrote in the visitors' book revealed his thoughts.[29] In addition to a substantial cash donation, he promised to gift a 16-foot tall sandstone replica of Sarnath Buddha, and handed over its smaller version during his visit to the pagoda.

Like other Indian VIPs in the past, Singh visited the *Mazar* of India's last emperor, Bahadur Shah Zafar. He gifted a chador brought especially from the famous Sufi shrine in Ajmer. His comments in the visitors' book stressed the importance of this monument as the historical bond between India and Myanmar.[30] As an aside, one may refer to a question posed by a journalist at the pre-visit briefing hosted by the ministry of external affairs. The journalist asked an official if the prime minister would take up the question of bringing back the emperor's remains to India and placing them in the Red Fort in Delhi. Clearly the questioner did not know that the issue had been considered in the early years of independence, by Nehru and U Nu. They decided that the remains of the last Mughal emperor and of the last Burmese king should be left where they were – in Yangon and Ratnagiri, respectively. This piece of history, they believed, served as a unique and unbreakable bond between the two countries.

Joint statement

The most important achievement of the visit was the release of a very substantive joint statement.[31] This document also lists the agreements and memoranda of understanding (MoUs) signed during the visit. All agreements signed since Myanmar's independence are given in Appendix I.

The joint statement was a well-crafted and balanced depiction of various facets of the relationship as it stood in May 2012. It also spelt out mutual understanding on specific areas of collaboration in future. An analysis of its main elements is necessary here.

On political and security dimensions, a number of points should be noted. First, after undertaking 'a comprehensive review', the two leaders expressed 'satisfaction' with the ongoing official exchanges and the growing economic, trade and cultural ties and people-to-people contacts. Second, in Nehruvian terms, they articulated a vision for 'the pursuit of the common good – bilaterally, regionally and globally'. This vision was based on the need for peace and stability in the region that was a pre-requisite for development and well-being of the people. In this broad context, they laid emphasis on the importance of India–Myanmar cooperation. Third, the Indian prime minister congratulated President Thein Sein on 'the path breaking reform measures' for greater democratisation and national reconciliation, commending him for having secured preliminary peace agreements with several ethnic groups and dialogue with various political parties, including the NLD. Singh reiterated India's readiness to extend 'all necessary assistance in accelerating the country's democratic transition and developing the capacity of democratic institutions such as the Parliament, National Human Rights Commission and the Media'.

Fourth, having noted that India–Myanmar relations were 'rooted in shared history and geography, culture and civilization', the two leaders decided that the frequency and range of engagement would be further enhanced 'so as to take bilateral cooperation to a higher level'.

Fifth, they resolved to fight 'the scourge of terrorism and insurgent activity in all its forms and manifestations'. It was reiteration of an old commitment. Having drawn suitable lessons from the past experience of cooperation – both its strengths and weaknesses, the two governments set up a new mechanism, the (bilateral) Regional Border Committee. Deliberations at its first meeting were judged to be 'useful in promoting . . . cooperation and understanding for better border management'. The joint statement went on to add:

> Both leaders reiterated the assurance that territories of either countries would not be allowed to be used for activities inimical to the other, including for training, sanctuary, and other operations by terrorists and insurgent organizations and their operatives.

Sixth, the two sides shared the view that sound border management was essential for maintaining border security. Seventh, the leaders discussed several issues of regional and international nature. The discussion ended with an agreement to continue 'their coordination' on issues of common interest on the international agenda. Seasoned observers noted the absence of a traditional reference to Myanmar's support for India's candidature for permanent membership of the UN Security Council. Myanmar's position had not changed, but it was perhaps felt that a mechanical repetition of known and well-established positions was unnecessary. In particular, they stressed the significance of close coordination to promote regional cooperation. Noting Myanmar's role as the present chair of BIMSTEC and future chair of ASEAN (in 2014), Dr Singh emphasised that it 'holds a significant place both in India's Look East policy and in its collaboration with ASEAN countries under the Initiative for ASEAN Integration (IAI)'. The two leaders also agreed to cooperate closely on activities, to be held for the ASEAN–India Commemorative Summit.

The joint statement also identified five other areas of cooperation, namely connectivity, development cooperation, trade and investment, power and energy, and cultural and people-to-people exchanges.

Connectivity was viewed as 'a means of promoting commercial, cultural, touristic and other exchanges'. Progress in implementing the Kaladan multi-modal transport project was reviewed. New Delhi had received much criticism within India about its slow progress, although the two governments still managed to express satisfaction at 'the steady progress', presumably due to diplomatic reasons. The port and river development as well as construction of the road connecting the Rakhine state with Mizoram were expected to be completed in the near future. Concerning the Trilateral Highway project, a new formula was agreed. Of its three segments, the Tamu–Kalewa–Kalemyo road would receive further assistance from India for upgradation and reconstruction of its 71 bridges. The second 120-km-long section, running from Kalewa to Yargyi, would be constructed and upgraded by India. The third section from Yargyi to Monywa would be taken up for construction by Myanmar. The two sides agreed to complete the entire road project by 2016.

Other measures were taken to enhance connectivity. There was an in-principle agreement to launch a transborder bus service from Imphal in India to Mandalay; the proposal received much play in the media, but its implementation was not imminent because the bus service was unlikely to become operational until the Trilateral Highway was ready. A new Air Services Agreement was signed, providing for expansion of air connectivity to cover more carriers, flights and destinations. It also provided the fifth freedom rights that would enable Indian carriers to combine their flights to Myanmar with other destinations eastwards. The decision to set up a joint working group to examine technical and commercial feasibility of cross-border rail links and commercial feasibility of direct shipping links seemed, at best, a symbolic gesture, as these ideas had been under consideration for many years. Of the agreements signed, only one agreement related to the area of connectivity.

Turning to development cooperation, it was noted that many projects in the field of infrastructure, agriculture, human resource development, industrial development, power and health were executed or were in the process of implementation, with Indian assistance comprising grants and concessional loans 'amounting to $1.2 billion' till May 2012. By any reckoning, it was judged as a substantial commitment, the proof of India's prudent magnanimity towards Myanmar. Looking at the potential, the two leaders cleared the signing of a new MoU on the $500 million Line of Credit (LOC) extended by India. This LOC had been announced at the conclusion of Thein Sein's visit to India, but after subsequent discussions, New Delhi decided to relax the terms and conditions, thereby making the LOC more attractive to Myanmar. Another important decision was to undertake both infrastructure development and microeconomic projects, including upgradation of roads and construction of schools and health centres, among others, in the border region of Sagaing division and Chin state.

132 During reform period

India decided to create three new institutions to expand cooperation in the field of human resource development, namely Myanmar Institute of Information Technology, Advanced Centre for Agriculture Research and Education and Rice Bio Park to demonstrate available techniques of sustainable rice biomass utilisation. The latter two institutions were expected to represent a qualitative increase in agricultural cooperation. Of the agreements signed, five related to the field of development cooperation.

Regarding trade and investment, the target set earlier of doubling, by 2015, the existing level of bilateral trade at $1.5 billion was endorsed. Indian companies were encouraged to invest in areas such as ports, highways, oil and gas, plantation, manufacturing, hospitality and information and communication technology. As a means to promote dialogue leading to new business linkages, it was decided to set up a bilateral Trade and Investment Forum. This forum was tasked with monitoring and reviewing the existing mechanisms for expanding and diversifying bilateral trade, for encouraging further measures to secure the trade target and for undertaking trade facilitation in a proactive manner. India's banking sector was encouraged to contribute to the removal of impediments to economic cooperation. Three Indian banks – the Reserve Bank of India, the State Bank of India and the United Bank of India – were expected to play a pivotal role. Other decisions included the setting up of 'border *haats*', upgrading of banking infrastructure at border trade points and establishing 'Border Trade Committee' to hold discussions involving officials and business persons at Tamu–Moreh and Rhi–Zowkhathar. Of the twelve agreements signed, two related to this field.

Concerning power and energy, it was evident that progress was slow and inadequate. India's proposal to build two hydropower projects – Tamanthi and Shwezaye – had been on the bilateral agenda for many years. After much internal deliberations, the Indian side was now ready with detailed project reports, but all that the two leaders agreed was to direct officials 'to study' and 'finalise' the future course of action. Not even a single word indicating urgency was added. These two projects were, therefore, unlikely to be pursued further. On the other hand, in the field of energy, India was happy to note that another of its companies had been awarded a production-sharing contract for an onshore oil block. Three of its companies had already been engaged in exploration and production of natural gas.[32] All this, however, amounted to very little in comparison with China's strong economic presence. Indian and Myanmar leaders reached agreement 'to encourage' investments by Indian companies in downstream areas of the petroleum industry. Singh publicly stressed that the energy sector was 'an area of great potential for cooperation', suggesting that the two countries should elevate their cooperation to 'a comprehensive energy partnership'.

The fifth area of cooperation related to culture, human resource development, science and technology and people-to-people exchanges. The joint statement referred to 'the centrality of culture' for deepening close bonds between the two peoples. Signing of the cultural exchange programme for 2012–15 and India's assistance for an ongoing project for construction and restoration of the Ananda Temple in Bagan evoked much satisfaction. The two leaders strongly supported the idea of expanding exchanges between academic and strategic communities. Concerning human resource development, numerous measures were agreed, in particular on increasing training fellowships under the Indian Technical and Economic Cooperation (ITEC) programme from 250 to 500 annually, upgrading the existing India–Myanmar centre for enhancement of IT skills, a specially designed training programme for members and officials of the new parliament, a training programme for Myanmar diplomats in conference management and awarding of ten additional fellowships for Myanmar researchers in Indian universities and research institutions. Of the agreements, four related to this field. Singh emphasised the desirability to 'promote more exchanges among our parliamentarians, academics, scientists, artists and intellectuals'.

Evaluation

In assessing the visit's outcome, we should factor in what the two governments, media pundits and others stated on the subject.

Commenting on the visit, the Myanmar president said it paved the way 'to further consolidate the existing bonds of friendship, mutual understanding and cooperation between our two countries'.[33]

In a comment prior to the visit, Dr Khin Zaw Win, director of Tampadipa Institute, a private think tank in Yangon, expressed the hope that Singh's visit 'in the first stages of democratic revival will usher a new era of not only cooperation with geostrategic overtones but also of democratic co-development in a true sense'.[34] Following the visit, the *New Light of Myanmar*, the government's mouthpiece, articulated, in an editorial, its belief that the visit was '. . . a herald of greater cooperation between the two friendly neighbours that may even contribute to regional peace, stability and progress'. It went on to highlight a notion that is central to Myanmar's policy towards

134 During reform period

India: 'In fact, India needs Myanmar and Myanmar also needs India, and that is the common ground.'[35] Asked to voice his overall assessment, Foreign Secretary Mathai observed: 'We are more than satisfied with the outcome of the visit.'[36]

In a perceptive editorial, *The Hindu* brought out the constraints of policy that India had followed in the past two decades, portraying it as a tightrope walk between 'the need to build relations with an important neighbour' and 'its conscience'. It added:

> In the struggle to keep a balance between the two, New Delhi could neither go full steam ahead with the military regime that had kept Ms. Suu Kyi under arrest, nor go all out to support the pro-democracy movement she led.

Its assessment of the visit was that India had 'signalled' that 'it wants nothing other than a full normalisation of relations, and quickly'. It appreciated the prime minister underlining Suu Kyi's 'defining role' in the political process, though the daily was clear about its bottom line: 'But New Delhi still has a lot of catching up to do on this front.'[37]

The Indian Express stated in an editorial that history was being made by Myanmar's military and political leaders while Singh was 'merely adapting to this historic change'. It explained that India's prime minister faced 'three challenges': 'a newly competitive diplomatic environment'; the need to calibrate carefully so that India enjoys good equation with the government 'while engaging all the political forces in the current phase of transition'; and the imperative to 'bring a measure of credibility to India's economic partnership with Myanmar'.[38] Ranjit Gupta presented his take stating: 'India's policies since 1992 stand vindicated as a bright new dawn grows visible over the horizon.'[39] Pramit Pal Chaudhuri, diplomatic editor of *The Hindustan Times*, who was part of Dr Singh's media delegation, wrote: 'With gifts for Myanmar's economy, people and its physical links with India, Prime Minister Manmohan Singh sought to make up for 15 years of stunted relations.'[40]

In its editorial, *The Times of India* evaluated the visit to be 'of substantial significance'. Pointing out the complexities involved, it stated:

> In pushing India's interests Singh will need to balance President Thein Sein and the military-dominated government on the one hand, and Aung San Suu Kyi on the other. Both the military and Suu Kyi are potent forces in today's Myanmar; neither can be written off.[41]

The daily also carried an op-ed by this author, which stressed the following:

> The visit's significance stems from what they [the two leaders] have achieved and what they have promised, together. By actively assisting it [Myanmar] to secure its goals – democratization and economic development, India will promote its own interests.[42]

Other assessments were also noteworthy. Renaud Egreteau interpreted the visit as an attempt to realign policy. 'India is trying', he said 'not to miss the bus in Myanmar as it opens to the world'. He added that the 'obstacles are always the same for India', including delays with its infrastructure projects and a lack of political confidence between the two countries.[43] A former Indian diplomat opined:

> Thus, the most important part of the visit was to gently let the controversial chapter of the two-decades-old Indian apathy towards Myanmar's democratic aspirations drift away and craft a contemporaneous approach.[44]

In a seemingly biased article, *The Irrawaddy* concluded that the visit indicated India's 'lack of success in gaining a firm foothold in Burma', claiming that 'both political and business relations have been uncertain and sluggish for years'.[45]

Having analysed media reactions and interacted with members of strategic and academic communities in India, one had a clear impression that both divergences and convergences persisted. Opinion remained divided on whether India's policy to engage the military government was wise and right or unwise and wrong; whether New Delhi should have continued to support the pro-democracy movement optimally through the 1990s and later; whether the change in Myanmar necessitated a modified policy or validated the old policy; whether there was an India–China competition in Myanmar; and whether the Indian and Myanmar governments had the political will, institutional capacity and stamina to implement mutually agreed programmes. On the other hand, scholars and analysts agreed on the need and desirability of enhancing connectivity and economic links between India's North East and Myanmar, especially its western region; on the imperative of expanding and diversifying India's trade, economic, technical and cultural cooperation with Myanmar; and on the basic notion that South Block should accord a higher (than before) priority to this country in its foreign policy perspective. Besides, much attention was focused on

136 During reform period

the likely impact of changing US–China equations in Asia-Pacific on the future of India–Myanmar relations.

Suu Kyi's visit

If the year 2012 was exceptionally good for India–Myanmar relations, a part of the credit should go to Suu Kyi's visit to India, for it increased significantly the public awareness about stakes in the relationship as well as the unfolding complex transition in Myanmar.

At her historic meeting with Prime Minister Singh in Yangon, Suu Kyi had received the invitation to visit India. But an early visit seemed difficult. Subsequently she travelled to Thailand, several West European capitals and the US, while her admirers and supporters in India seemed resigned to waiting for her for many more months. Some believed that NLD officials were probably in contact with interlocutors in Beijing and Delhi in order to plan a grand tour, which might take her to India and China on one combined visit. But, in retrospect, it seemed that the Indian Embassy's wise endeavour to keep in close touch with Suu Kyi paid off. As soon as a window in her hectic calendar became available, Delhi moved quickly to finalise dates of the visit. That is how she came visiting India from 13 to 18 November 2012.

Programme

Although the main purpose of her visit was to deliver the Jawaharlal Nehru Memorial Lecture, Suu Kyi's was a full-fledged visit as the guest of the Indian government. She was received at the airport by the foreign secretary. In terms of protocol, the visit was pitched a little below the level of a visiting prime minister, but from the viewpoint of public exposure and media coverage, Suu Kyi was given the treatment very few heads of state or government can hope to receive in India. A close look at the programme showed that interaction with both government leaders and non-governmental role players was given ample space in her schedule.

The NLD chairperson was taken to the *samadhis* of Mahatma Gandhi and Jawaharlal Nehru to lay wreaths, a task she must have found important and emotionally fulfilling, considering her close intellectual association with both of them. Suu Kyi held a meeting with Dr Singh 'without aides', whereafter he hosted a lunch for her. UPA Chairperson Sonia Gandhi hosted a dinner in her honour. Special attention was paid to her role as a member of parliament; she met Vice President of India M. Hamid Ansari, who was also the Chairman of the

Rajya Sabha as well as Meira Kumar, Speaker of the Lok Sabha, who too hosted a lunch for her. Separately she held 'a restricted meeting' with Salman Khurshid, the minister of external affairs. This was followed by an 'interactive meeting' involving a cross-section of eminent persons from various walks of life prior to the minister's banquet at Hyderabad House on 15 November. Earlier, on 14 November, she delivered the Nehru Memorial Lecture before a packed house at Vigyan Bhawan.

An important motivation of the planners was to sensitise Suu Kyi about India's progress in those sectors of economy that had direct relevance to Myanmar. She visited The Energy and Resources Institute (TERI) and its various facilities near Delhi, where she was hosted by Dr R.K. Pachauri, its director general. Later, while in Bengaluru, she visited the Indian Institute of Science and Infosys, India's premier institutions in their respective fields. She also visited an Indian village – Papasanipalli in Madaksira Mandal of Anantpur district in Andhra Pradesh to see for herself a few rural development projects and meet women activists involved in the women's self-help group movement.

Suu Kyi's programme in Delhi gave her two opportunities to meet with members of the Burmese community. She visited Prospect Burma's English language teaching school in Janakpuri and the Oxford senior secondary school in Vikaspuri. The visit to her alma mater, Lady Sri Ram College for Women (LSR), where she had obtained a bachelor's degree in 1964, was an emotional homecoming. She paid a brief visit to the Burmese Embassy in Delhi. Besides, she spent some quality time with her personal friends, especially on the first day of the visit, with a walk in Lodhi Garden squeezed in. Considerable time was also devoted to giving interviews to several top media organisations of the country.

The lecture

The Nehru Memorial Lecture, a key element in Suu Kyi's visit, went off without a hitch. On the podium she was flanked by Vice President Ansari, Sonia Gandhi who introduced the speaker and Karan Singh, a senior Congress leader, who presented the vote of thanks, ending it with a long Sanskrit *shloka* in praise of Goddess Laxmi.

Suu Kyi's lecture, a rich intellectual homage to Nehru, was extremely well-crafted and thoughtful. It presented the story of her life and how it had been influenced by Nehru – his actions, struggles and thoughts. Suu Kyi had won the Jawaharlal Nehru Award for International Understanding for 1993.[46] 'The thoughts and actions of

138 During reform period

leaders of the Indian independence movement', she said, 'provided me with ideas and inspiration'. She stressed that her own movement for democracy and human rights in Burma was rooted in the principle of non-violence 'that Gandhi made into an effective political force even against the most powerful opponents'.

Then she added: 'His influence on my political thinking is widely recognised. The influence of Jawaharlal Nehru on my life in politics is less well known.' Her description of a scene at Delhi railway station where her mother, as the Burmese ambassador to India, and Prime Minister Nehru waited for the train that was to bring Prime Minister U Nu from Calcutta was vivid and moving. 'His aristocratic disdain for public approbation filled me with both astonishment and admiration.' This reminded her of her own father, 'notorious for his stern, almost scowling expression and for his lack of social graces'. The Burmese loved him, she said, 'for these very defects, which they saw as proof of his honest, open nature'.

Suu Kyi noted that the year 1964 in which she left India to join Oxford University was also the year when Nehru died, recalling the public grief as well as the news of the poem by Robert Frost, which was found on his desk. The year of his birth centenary, 1989, was the year when she was placed under house arrest by the military junta, thus making it 'the year of my political coming of age'. To chart the course of her life in her long years of imprisonment, she needed to figure her way. She stated: 'Among the "maps" I used to see me through, the years that headed into the unknown, were Nehru's autobiography and *Discovery of India*.'

She was deeply impressed by the 'fortitude and dedication' shown by Kamala, Nehru's wife, in supporting her husband and India's freedom struggle. 'The ones who make real sacrifices', said Suu Kyi, 'are those who let us go free to keep our secret trysts with destiny'. She stressed that the 'lesson Nehru learnt' and imparted to others was that one's goals could be achieved only 'through hard work and perseverance'. She observed that the 'two Indian leaders' she felt 'closest are undoubtedly Gandhi and Nehru' and she took the opportunity to express her 'deep appreciation' for them 'who became my most precious friends because they helped me to find my way through unchartered terrain'. She gave to her lecture the title – 'Discovery of Nehru' and remarked poignantly in conclusion: 'The discovery of Nehru was also a discovery of myself.'[47]

Speaking on the occasion, Sonia Gandhi depicted Suu Kyi as a synthesis of the 'best of East and West, but rooted in her own country and its culture, just like Nehru'. 'She exemplifies all qualities he [Nehru]

During reform period   139

most admired – fearlessness, integrity, moral and intellectual courage, perseverance, freedom from anger and bitterness and unqualified devotion to betterment of the life of her people through the path of dialogue and national reconciliation.' Vice President Ansari released a new edition of *Burma and India: Some Aspects of Intellectual Life under Colonialism*, which Suu Kyi had authored as a fellow at the Institute of Advanced Study in Shimla during 1987–89.

The story of her memorial lecture would not be complete without bringing in the critical, though calibrated, reference she made to India's Myanmar policy, after concluding the main lecture itself. She remarked:

> I was saddened to see that we had drawn away from India, or rather that India had drawn away from us during our very difficult days, but I always had faith in the lasting friendship between our two countries based on lasting friendships between our two peoples . . . Governments come and go, and this is what democracy is all about, but people remain. . . . Burma has still not reached the goal of democracy and in this last, I hope, and most difficult phase, India will stand by us and walk by us as we proceed on the path that they were able to proceed upon many years before us.[48]

These remarks revealed her deep *sadness* over New Delhi's decision in early 1990s to dilute its pro-democracy policy by engagement with the military government, which was necessitated by India's national interests, and her *hope* of obtaining India's support for her struggle in future.

She was accorded a standing ovation by the audience. Discussing the impact of Suu Kyi's lecture, one found that people differed: one section felt that it influenced the audience deeply, whereas another section believed that it failed to connect her to her listeners. This author's assessment was that Nehru was hardly an effective instrument for Suu Kyi to connect with changing perceptions in India; he had become, however unfairly, a maligned figure at a time when the country was introspecting about the 50th anniversary of the 1962 India–China border conflict. Nevertheless, Indians were beginning to get to know the real Suu Kyi.

Her discussions

Suu Kyi's discussions with government leaders were less about the past than about the present and future. With Dr Manmohan Singh, she probably resumed the conversation they had begun in May. The focus

140 During reform period

was on the complexity and future evolution of Myanmar's democratic transition, the weaknesses inherent in institutions after half a century of military rule and the direction that India–Myanmar cooperation should take in strengthening the parliament and judiciary of her country. The need to enhance people-to-people relations through education, cultural exchanges and tourism might have been emphasised. Singh lauded her indomitable courage and conveyed India's good wishes to her in the continuing struggle for democracy.

What she might have discussed with the minister of external affairs came through clearly at the interactive meeting that followed immediately after the official level discussions. This author had the privilege to moderate the dialogue involving Suu Kyi, the minister and about 75 select guests from the realm of scholarship, media, business, diplomacy, politics and government. In her initial remarks and while answering questions, she stressed that democracy meant effecting 'a healthy balance between security and freedom', pointing out that Burma today was not a democracy because people enjoyed neither freedom nor security. What the country lacked was 'the rule of law'. She noted that Burma was a country of diversity that needed decentralisation of power; this existed on paper only at present. She questioned the military's view that it alone could hold the country together. Referring to the absence of ethnic reconciliation, she underlined that the military had not succeeded in its mission to bring internal peace. Only through the rule of law and independent judiciary could the governance be improved. 'We sorely lack courageous judges', she said.[49]

At the banquet that followed, guests kept approaching her with requests for photographs, autographs or just a word or two with her. This continued even after the food was served, which made it difficult for her to eat. But she took celebrity adulation and its hassles in her stride, obliging everyone smilingly. Suu Kyi's 'only comment, made in appreciative jest' as Karan Thapar wrote later, was: 'I've never been to such a wonderfully informal formal dinner!'[50] Speaking at her alma mater, Suu Kyi said she felt herself to be 'partly a citizen of India – a citizen of love and honour'. 'Coming back to LSR', she added, 'is not just coming back home, it is coming back to a place where I know my aspirations have not been wrong'.[51] Spelling out her vision of democracy in Burma, she said her people were trying to achieve it. 'We need you to help us in our progression towards democracy.' She urged the students 'not to take their democratic rights for granted', adding:

> Democratic rights are very precious. Students in India are fortunate to have a life outside the classroom and to walk through their

campus freely. Students in Burma are struggling for these rights. Always cherish these rights, for only when you don't have them you realise what you lack.[52]

Her interviews

Indian media, dominated by liberal elements that consistently supported Burma's pro-democracy movement and opposed the Indian government's policy shift towards the generals since the early 1990s, showed immense interest in Suu Kyi's visit. This was entirely expected, but the noteworthy point was that planners of the visit were able to allocate adequate time in her hectic schedule to media in order to enable her to reach out to the people at large. This was secured through a careful and wise selection of media organisations and their well-known representatives. A close look at five major interviews Suu Kyi granted to *The Hindu*, *India Today*, *The Outlook*, CNN-IBN and NDTV revealed her views on important issues and her personal style as a communicator and leader.

A critical analysis of her interviews showed that Suu Kyi was clear, consistent and forthright in articulating her views. Regarding the Indian government's shift from supporting the pro-democracy movement to also engaging with the military junta, she said she was 'saddened' by it; however, the sadness was momentary and then it went away due to her essential pragmatism as she knew that governments sometimes took positions in their own interest rather than the interests of others. Efforts by interviewers to get her to say that she felt 'disappointed', 'betrayed', 'let down' or 'surprised' were gently but firmly rebuffed. The only interesting addition she made was to state that she thought 'Mahatma Gandhi would have been very vocal about his disapproval. . . . I think he would have insisted that India try to stand by us because this is the kind of man he was'.[53] She pointed out that she looked upon India 'as a friend'. India could help, first of all, through a correct appreciation of the present situation in Burma – that it was not yet a democracy, but she hoped that once Burma became one, her country and India 'as a practicing democracy' would get closer. She reiterated the importance of people-to-people relationship as compared to mere government-to-government ties. Her visit was meant to improve and strengthen relations. When asked in what specific way India could help Myanmar, she observed: 'It is to be able to take a hard look at what is really happening. Not to be over-optimistic, at the same time, to be encouraging of what needs to be encouraged . . .'[54]

142 During reform period

On the situation in Burma following the introduction of reforms, she declined to term it as 'irreversible', empathising that hard work must continue to ensure that 'things keep moving in the right direction'.[55] She added another nuance by conveying that a test of irreversibility would be the government's 'preparedness to consider changing the sections of the Constitution that are not democratic'.[56] She argued that instead of focusing on pace and reversibility or irreversibility of reform, it should be appreciated that the reform process was without a proper structure, that it was 'ad hoc'. Highlighting the centrality of constitutional reform, she brought up three of its critical aspects. First, provisions should be made for decentralisation of power, given ethnic insurgencies in the country. She stressed that 'the regional governments do not actually have real power. It's still a very centralised system and such a centralised system is not going to promote democratic values, but more important than that, it's not going to promote ethnic harmony'.[57]

Second, the 2008 Constitution had given 'too much power' to the military, which needed to be reduced. She did not believe in 'a political army', favouring one which played a role consistent with the needs of a democracy. 'The legitimate role of any army would be to defend the people and the constitution that is voluntarily accepted by the people'.[58]

Third, restrictions on an individual to contest the presidency should be removed. On her wish to be the president, she said flatly:

> I would be prepared to take over the position of President . . . Not so much because I want to be President of a country but because I want the President of the country to be elected through the will of the people.[59]

She added another reason: 'Oh, we need power for the sake of making change.'[60]

Suu Kyi told Karan Thapar that those sections of the Constitution that prevented Burma from being a working democracy should be removed in order to make the elections in 2015 'free and fair'. She added, 'The elections may be free but unless there are the necessary amendments made, I don't think we could say that they would be fair.'[61]

On President Thein Sein, she was quite guarded, pointing out that she did not know him well. On his contribution to the reform process, she gave a calibrated response: 'I think he needs to be given credit, but I don't think he's the only one who brought it about.'[62]

During reform period 143

Interviewers asked her, with one of them describing her as 'the poster girl for the human rights activism everywhere in the world', about her 'ambivalence' on the age-old strife and recent clashes involving Muslim and Buddhist communities in the Rakhine state and the role of government authorities in it. In response, she brought out the complexities of the issue, placing the responsibility squarely on the government. As to her own perspective on it, she observed:

> I am not ambivalent about my views on violence. Violence is something I am appalled by completely and condemn completely, but don't forget that violence has been committed by both sides. This is why I prefer not to take sides and I also want to work to [sic] reconciliation between these two communities. I am not being able to do that if I am going to take sides.[63]

Talking to other journalists, she rejected that an ethnic cleansing of the Muslims took place, thus defending her own Buddhist community. She also called it a huge international tragedy, thus implying that, together with Burma, Bangladesh was part of the problem and should, therefore, be made a part of the solution too.

On Burma's equation vis-à-vis India and China, the NLD leader expressed little anxiety and abundant realism. Noting that every country needed to have good relations with its neighbours, she recalled that Burma had managed, especially when it was a democracy and China was a communist nation, to enjoy cordial relations with its two giant neighbours. She was confident that this would happen again even when Burma emerged as a true democracy.

The Nobel Laureate handled questions about her personality and her political style with adroitness. She was not 'a saint' but a politician who was 'always prepared to compromise' and was committed to negotiations involving give and take. She readily conceded that she had made 'a lot of mistakes' in her life. 'To begin with, I think I have a bit of temper, I think I have to learn to keep that under control.'[64] She also showed her quiet sense of humour. Talking of the army captain who, in that famous incident, had threatened to shoot her if she walked on the street, she recalled that she decided to move to the side of the street, 'and then he said he can shoot me anytime, anywhere, which was rather unreasonable'.[65] Ending her interview with Karan Thapar on IBN-CNN, she teased the interviewer: 'I wanted to tell everybody that you were a roly-poly, little five-year old when I first met you.'[66]

In evaluating the outcome of the visit, media pundits expressed divergent views. The visit was 'a homecoming as well as reconciliation'.[67]

144 During reform period

Calling her 'Burma's iconic democracy leader', an editorial column noted: 'She wins hearts wherever she goes. She did that in New Delhi as well this week . . .'[68] Asserting that few leaders 'today have as much global heft and credibility as Aung San Suu Kyi', another editorial argued:

> The reality is that Myanmar needs India now, as much as India needs Myanmar. If opening closed borders and reviving historical connections that had been obscured by recent geopolitics drives India's 'look east' policy, then closer relations with Myanmar play a critical role in that policy.[69]

Sreeram Chaulia, an academic-columnist, opined that it was 'time to make up for lost ground'. He suggested: 'Our efforts must be more political and larger in ambition and size, matching the grand and noble vision of the Nobel Laureate . . .'[70] *The Indian Express* was convinced that her 'rich and varied itinerary' gave 'ample indication of the deepening of India–Myanmar ties'. It suggested: 'India must keep pushing the envelope to hasten the economic integration on its eastern borders.'[71] Baladas Ghoshal highlighted 'the absence of institutions' in Burma, identifying it as the long-term challenge of which Suu Kyi was fully conscious.[72] Writing immediately after the conclusion of the visit, this author expressed the view that 'despite some lingering bitterness of the past', she was 'fully conscious of India's role as a key player in the region; she expects it to play an active role in helping Myanmar's transition to democracy'.[73]

Visit by Salman Khurshid

External Affairs Minister Salman Khurshid visited Myanmar from 14 to 16 December 2012, with MEA portraying the visit as 'an opportunity to review the entire gamut of the bilateral relationship and build further upon the momentum in bilateral relationships'.[74] While in Myanmar, Khurshid undertook the customary activities, meeting the president, the foreign minister, others in the government and the NLD chairperson. He also visited the *Mazar* of Bahadur Shah Zafar[75] and the Shwedagon Pagoda where the 16-ft statue of Sarnath-style Buddha, gifted by the people of India, was consecrated in his presence.

But Khurshid also performed an act of exceptional importance by inaugurating on 15 December, together with Myanmar Vice President Dr Sai Mauk Kham, the international conference on Buddhist cultural heritage in Yangon. This was jointly organised by the Indian Council of

Cultural Relations (ICCR) and Sitagu International Buddhist Academy. The sight of a Muslim dignitary from India gracing the inaugural ceremony of a conference on Buddhism in Myanmar conveyed a perfect message of secularism and religious tolerance, broadly practiced in India. In a country that was riven by Muslim–Buddhist strife in the Rakhine state with its nationwide repercussions, the irony may not have been lost on many.[76]

In his inaugural address, the Myanmar vice president expressed his belief that the conference would immensely strengthen the friendly relationship between Myanmar and India. Referring to the latter as 'the birth-place of Lord Buddha and the seat of Buddhist culture', he appreciated that India was leading efforts to preserve the teachings of Lord Buddha and the Buddhist heritage by organising conferences and other events all around the globe. Dr Ashin Nyanissara, Sitagu Sayadaw, observed that the conference not only celebrated the 2,600 years of Buddha *sasana* but was also a landmark in Indo–Myanmar relations.[77]

External Affairs Minister Khurshid spoke about Buddha's teachings, the impact of Buddhism and various facets of relations linking India and Myanmar. Talking about the imprint of Buddhism in Myanmar, he stated:

> The people of Myanmar, influenced by profound Buddhist philosophy, have over a long period, created beautiful art, built splendid pagodas and monasteries, crafted elegant sculptures, drawn magnificent mural paintings and developed classic literature and poetry.[78]

Khurshid pointed out that the 'shared traditions of Buddhism' formed 'the bedrock of our early contacts', which led to the movement of people and trade, creating 'a continuum of complex exchange'. Referring to Myanmar's march on the path of reform, he noted that the country today was 'reinventing itself and its relationship with the global community'. At this 'fascinating point in its history' when it had 'an ambitious agenda' of achieving good governance, rule of law, economic reform, environmental conservation and political dialogue, he assured it of India's optimal support by conveying:

> We in India stand ready to assist, in whatever way desired by the government and the people of Myanmar, in this transition to what I would believe would create a democratic polity and lead to economic prosperity and well-being of the people of Myanmar.

146 During reform period

He cited India's initiatives in the fields of connectivity, border road development, information technology, agriculture and capacity building as 'a demonstration of our resolve to create a bright future. . .'[79]

Thein Sein's second visit

This visit enabled the president of Myanmar to participate in the India–ASEAN Commemorative Summit, held in Delhi from 20 to 21 December 2012 to mark the 20th anniversary of a fruitful dialogue partnership. Of the ten ASEAN leaders who attended the summit, Thein Sein was the only one who stayed on to hold discussions with the Indian prime minister and to visit a few cities other than the capital. Myanmar figured prominently in India's endeavours to develop and expand connectivity with ASEAN. Manmohan Singh made a special mention of the trilateral highway, the completion of which would greatly help increasing trade and travel between India and the regional grouping.

Speaking at the summit, Thein Sein noted: 'Myanmar valued the friendly ties that have long existed between ASEAN and India as Myanmar is a neighbour of India and a member of ASEAN.' He added that Myanmar viewed India as an important dialogue partner of ASEAN, which was playing a crucial role in regional peace and security. 'Myanmar reaffirms the pledge to boost ASEAN–India ties.'[80]

Noting that even after 20 months of reform, the situation in Myanmar was fragile (as reflected particularly in the brutal crackdown on protesters including monks at Monywa in the Sagaing division), a five-day protest rally was organised in Delhi during Thein Sein's visit. In a statement issued by 'Burmese Democratic Forces in India', it was asserted that the release of political prisoners 'alone' did not 'signify Burma's transition to democracy', and that other rights – land rights, rights to have assembly and form association, etc. – must also be respected if the government 'genuinely' wished to establish democracy. The statement requested ASEAN member nations 'to review its approval' of Burma chairing ASEAN in 2014. It also made several demands on the Indian government.[81]

During his sojourn in Mumbai, Thein Sein concentrated on persuading a select group of leaders of India Inc. to deepen economic ties with his country. At a closed door discussion, he invited them to invest in infrastructure, power and energy projects and encouraged them to explore cooperation in the field of agriculture. In response, Adi Godrej, president of the Confederation of Indian Industry (CII), proposed 'a five-point agenda to strengthen bilateral economic relations'. He observed:

> I propose enhancing connectivity in culture and commerce between the two countries; promoting integration and synergy in power and railway sectors; appropriate banking arrangements to foster trade and investment; enhancing bilateral engagement in trade protection, cooperation and collaboration in industries like tourism and software; and inviting managers from Myanmar to Indian industry's centres of excellence.[82]

On 22 December, Thein Sein visited the tomb of King Thibaw, Burma's last king buried at Ratnagiri.[83] The president laid a wreath there, met five descendants of the late king and provided cash assistance. He undertook a tour of the royal residence where the king's portrait, furniture and other items were on display and he signed the visitors' book. While meeting local Indian officials, he thanked and urged them to conserve the tomb well. On his visit, the president was accompanied by a few royal relatives from Myanmar. Thein Sein became 'the first-ever Myanmar leader' to visit the royal tomb at Ratnagiri.[84] Commenting on the visit, Thant Myint U said it was symbolically significant. 'The King was the very centre of the old state. (His defeat) was the overthrow of a 1,000-year old monarchy but also the complete destruction of the old system of governance and aristocracy.'[85]

Other visits

It is noteworthy that during 2012 all the three Service Chiefs of India, including the Chief of Air Force and Chairman, Chiefs of Staff Committee (CoSC) visited Myanmar.

One may mention that diplomacy conducted through high-level visits continued right through the year 2013. In January, India's Defence Minister A.K. Anthony led a defence delegation to Myanmar. This was followed by the visit of a parliamentary delegation, headed by Meira Kumar, speaker of the Lok Sabha. The minister for commerce, industry and textiles, Anand Sharma, attended the World Economic Forum on East Asia at Naypyitaw in June 2013. Ranjan Mathai, the foreign secretary, led a delegation to participate in the 13th round of Foreign Office Consultations in July 2013.

The flood of Indian VIPs in Myanmar was matched by a series of high-level visitors from the Myanmar side throughout the period

2011–13. Some of the important visits were those by Thura Shwe Mann, speaker of the lower house of the Parliament (December 2011), Foreign Minister U Wunna Maung Lwin (January 2012), Vice Senior General Min Aung Hlaing, Commander-in-Chief, Defence Services of Myanmar (August 2012), Finance Minister U Win Shein (May 2013) and Myanmar Chief of Naval Staff (July 2013). Two visits that helped to wrap up the year 2013 were by U Khin Aung Myint, speaker of the upper house of the Parliament and by Vice-Senior General Soe Win, the army chief and deputy commander-in-chief of the *Tatmadaw*.

Prime Minister Manmohan Singh paid a second visit to Myanmar in March 2014, primarily to participate in the 3rd BIMSTEC Summit. That it took the seven-member states[86] over two years to agree on the dates of the summit was quite disappointing. However, the meeting demonstrated the continuing relevance of the grouping, especially as around this time China had begun pushing its own concept of cooperation in the subregion through Bangladesh, China, India and Myanmar (BCIM) initiative.

The visit was also an occasion for the leaders of Myanmar and India to update themselves on bilateral relations, and for the Indian prime minister to bid his goodbye as he completed the last foreign tour of his ten-year long tenure.

Recent visits

In the early months of 2014, India was preoccupied with parliamentary elections and the formation of a new government. A decisive mandate and a clear majority given to the Narendra Modi–led Bharatiya Janata Party (BJP) and National Democratic Alliance (NDA) was welcomed in Myanmar as a sign of India's stability and growing political strength. Experts expressed the hope that development of North East might now receive priority.[87] Advocates of closer India–Myanmar relations, however, expressed disappointment that only SAARC leaders and the prime minister of Mauritius were invited to the swearing-in ceremony of Prime Minister Modi and his government on 26 May. Inclusion of the president of Myanmar in this exclusive list of neighbours would have, they felt, gone a long way to place Myanmar on the list of India's priorities.[88]

The new government arranged the 14th round of Foreign Office Consultations between India and Myanmar quickly. Held in Delhi on 23 July 2014, they were led by Sujatha Singh, foreign secretary of India and U Thant Kyaw, deputy minister of foreign affairs of Myanmar. Both sides 'reviewed the entire gamut of bilateral relations' and expressed 'satisfaction at the friendly relations between the two countries'.[89]

External Affairs Minister Sushma Swaraj paid a four-day official visit to Myanmar from 8 August 2014. While her main goal was to participate in India–ASEAN, ARF and EAS Ministerial Meetings, it is worth noting that a separate bilateral dimension was added to the visit by ensuring that she held discussions with Myanmar's leaders on various aspects of India–Myanmar relations.

In the discussions with Myanmar leaders, 'I raised', said Minister Swaraj, 'the issue of insurgent groups and told them that though the political leadership is again and again saying that their territory will not be used for terrorist activities, but on the ground, the situation is different'.[90] When journalists asked her about delay in projects being implemented by India in neighbouring countries, she observed: 'Old projects will be expedited and new projects will be started with time line.' She also discussed matters relating to Persons of Indian Origin (PIOs), visa issues and connectivity projects. She suggested that a direct flight linking Delhi, Bodh Gaya and Yangon should be started. The minister observed that India enjoyed 'very good relations' with Myanmar and termed her visit as 'very successful'.[91]

Prime Minister Narendra Modi's visit to Myanmar in November 2014 was primarily to participate in the India–ASEAN Summit and East Asia Summit, but a meaningful bilateral dimension was added through his meeting with President Thein Sein soon after his arrival in Naypyitaw. Meeting for the first time, the two leaders undertook a tour d'horizon of relations, assuring each other of the shared desire to deepen bilateral cooperation. Modi expressed full support for Myanmar's transition to democracy and economic reforms. Thein Sein observed that he considered India 'a brother'[92] and extended an invitation to the Indian prime minister to pay a full-scale visit later in order to experience the close cultural ties that linked the two countries.[93] Modi also met Aung San Suu Kyi, thereby demonstrating India's easy access to political forces outside the ruling combine. It was evident, however, that she was passing through a difficult phase as her bid to get the Constitution reformed for clearing the way for her presidential candidacy was losing steam. The prime minister made it a point to interact with representatives of the Indian Diaspora, despite his busy schedule.

Modi's visit was imbued with considerable significance for regional politics. At the India–ASEAN Summit, he highlighted India's shift from 'Look East' to 'Act East' policy, thereby stressing his interest in action on and implementation of previous agreements as well as enhanced

150 During reform period

focus on digital and institutional connectivity and people-to-people exchanges. At the East Asia Summit (EAS) the prime minister projected some 'urgency for the conclusion of a code of conduct between ASEAN nations and China thereby extending valuable support to the former in their current travails'.[94] New Delhi projected EAS as an important pillar of its Act East Policy. Clear signals were sent indicating that, under Modi's watch, India's relations with ASEAN and other key players in East Asia were set to grow rapidly.

The year 2015 opened with a five-day long official visit to India by Dr Sai Mauk Kham, Myanmar's first vice president. The visit from 19 to 23 January was at the invitation of Vice President Hamid Ansari. The visiting dignitary held discussions with India's top leaders. His visit was 'the latest in a series of high-level contacts' between the two countries and would 'further strengthen the close and friendly relations . . . .'[95] The dignitary called on Prime Minister Narendra Modi who stressed the significance of cultural and civilisational links between India and Myanmar. The Prime Minister's Office indicated that the two leaders discussed ways to enhance the bilateral partnership in view of India's 'Act East Policy', especially with regard to connectivity, infrastructure, trade, education and culture.

People-to-people exchanges

The relations between the two nations, if confined only to governments and business communities, remain 'transactional' in nature. Real vitality gets imparted to them when they encompass other sections of the society. This dimension was quite weak during the military era, but it gained salience during 2011–14. The quantum of exchanges involving parliamentarians, journalists, students and members of civil society increased significantly, a sure sign that peoples of the two countries were warming up to each other. But there was still a long way to go to realise the full potential.

A significant facet of people-to-people interaction was a gradually blossoming dialogue between the strategic communities. The reform period witnessed several visits by Myanmar experts to India to study its model of democracy and development and to discuss foreign policy issues with their counterparts in India. Institutions like Jamia Millia Islamia, Institute for Defence Studies and Analyses (IDSA) and Institute of Social Sciences hosted useful Track-II meetings in Delhi. Similar meetings were held in other cities.[96] A delegation of experts and business leaders representing Gateway House visited Myanmar in October 2012 to evaluate the impact of reform and emerging changes in Myanmar.[97] Research and Information System (RIS) sent a high-profile delegation to Myanmar in November 2013 to study and explore connectivity options. In this regard, one visit deserves a detailed mention here.

ICWA delegation's visit

This author was privileged to lead the Indian Council of World Affairs (ICWA) delegation on its important and highly fruitful visit to Myanmar in March 2013. It represented a coordinated endeavour to implement two of the 13 MoUs signed during the Indian prime minister's historic visit to that country in May 2012. The two MoUs were between the Myanmar Institute of Strategic and International Studies (MISIS) and the ICWA, and between the former and the Institute for Defence Studies and Analyses (IDSA). The delegation's visit enabled a major, structured dialogue between academic and strategic communities of the two countries.

The programme was developed in close consultation with MISIS. Apart from a one-day dialogue with a team of experts fielded by MISIS, the delegation had the opportunity to meet ministers, parliamentarians, academics, business leaders, media representatives and members of the Indian Diaspora in three cities, namely Yangon, Naypyitaw and Mandalay. The most important meeting was with the chairperson of NLD.

The ICWA–MISIS seminar on 'Change in Myanmar: Impact on India–Myanmar Relations' was held at the old Foreign Office complex in Yangon on 6 March. The delegation of MISIS, the recently restructured think tank, was led by its chairman, Ambassador Nyunt Maung Shein, a former director general of political affairs in the Ministry of Foreign Affairs. Other members were serving professors from various universities as well as a few retired diplomats, including a former Myanmar ambassador to India. The composition of the Indian delegation, which included two former ambassadors to Myanmar, viz. Shyam Saran and this author, helped greatly in establishing rapport with the host side and obtaining considerable political and media attention.

After the opening session, the seminar concentrated on four themes, with a separate session devoted to each of them, namely 'Reform Process: Achievements and the Way Forward', 'Bilateral Political Relations', Defence and Security Cooperation' and 'Bilateral Economic Engagements and Technical Cooperation'. The lead speaker from the Myanmar side spelt out key challenges facing the nation,

152 During reform period

two years after the reform process began. National reconciliation, involving ethnic groups on the one hand and political parties on the other needed to move forward. The process needed to be inclusive. Besides, socio-economic development remained the fundamental goal for which foreign investment, he emphasised, was crucial. 'Doubts existed', he said, about how inclusive the reform process would be in the future. There was consensus on his conclusion that developments between now and the next elections due in 2015 would determine the country's future, and that optimism was justified about its prospects of progress towards democratisation. It was also felt that the Myanmar Army, still a driving force, would continue to be influenced and guided by the Indonesian model of transition from an authoritarian rule to democracy. 'Gradualism is better' in overall political terms was another notable conclusion.

On bilateral relations, useful and interesting presentations were made by both sides, with Ambassador Shyam Saran articulating India's worldview, its Look East Policy, the changing power alignments in East Asia, 'the China factor' and the future evolution of India–Myanmar relations in the regional context. The Myanmar side accepted a number of suggestions put forward by the Indian experts, such as raising relations to the level of 'a strategic partnership', annual meetings at the head of government level, establishment of a ministerial-level joint commission, sustained and regular interaction involving economic ministers and encouraging exchanges between chief ministers of border states of the two countries. On defence and security issues, a view was expressed that governments needed to be more transparent and communicative about the actual situation pertaining to insurgency. The Myanmar side emphasised that military measures alone would not be adequate to resolve the problem, which needed both political dialogue and economic development. Discussions on economic facets of the relationship devoted considerable time to the proposed establishment of development corridors, connectivity issues, impediments to trade expansion and need for pro-active promotion of inflow of Indian investments.

Suu Kyi received the Indian delegation at her residence in Naypyitaw on 7 March. She was exceptionally warm, friendly and communicative and she spent nearly an hour with the delegation. A variety of issues including the NLD party congress (which opened the next day), the ethnic issue, constitutional reform and the impact of sanctions were discussed. On the ethnic issue, she observed that she was awaiting 'an invitation' from the government in order to contribute to the current dialogue process. Regarding constitutional reform, she drew some satisfaction from President Thein Sein's remark, made during his trip to Europe, that 'if people want reform', it could be considered. She noted with veiled glee that the government was 'a little nervous' because of her. Her message for Indian businessmen was that they should come in as 'responsible' investors and should be respectful of the Burmese sense of dignity. Foreigners should offer their technology and products in accordance with the needs and requests of the Burmese side. She greatly appreciated that the ICWA delegation had attempted to study Myanmar's problems and strengthen people-to-people relations, something she considered very important.[98]

Conclusion

Myanmar's reform period thus witnessed an unprecedented range of high-level political interaction between India and Myanmar. The link between reform and increased interaction was evident. The driving motivation for India was to assist a vital neighbour in its quest for development and democracy through increased cooperation across the board. The Myanmar government, set to reduce its excessive dependence on China, was willing to profit from enhanced attention and offers of assistance from all quarters, especially a strategic and powerful neighbour – India.

Another important gain was the Indian government's full public engagement with Myanmar's democracy camp. Aung San Suu Kyi's visit to India represented the completion of reconciliation between the NLD and the Indian political establishment, a process that began with Foreign Secretary Nirupama Rao's meeting with her in Yangon.

Two constraints, however, also became sharply visible towards the end of the said period. First, there were unspoken worries as to what might happen to the positive trends in bilateral relations if the reform train in Myanmar stalled. From about mid-2013, the equation between the Thein Sein government and Aung San Suu Kyi started to suffer as she began mobilising people's support for constitutional reform and reduced role for the military. Thein Sein was already facing criticism, both domestically and internationally, on account of deteriorating relations between the Muslim and Buddhist sections of the population. Observers in India agonised if political divisions within Myanmar might constrain the Indian policy once again. Second, it was also obvious that while political relations between India and Myanmar had warmed up considerably, economic cooperation would take more time to be strengthened. In this regard, India's ability to complete ongoing development projects would play a critical role.

During reform period

While welcoming a Myanmar dignitary, President Pranab Mukherjee said: 'India–Myanmar bilateral relations have seen accelerated growth and expansion over the last two years. India stands ready to build on this, particularly at a time when Myanmar is engaged in far-reaching political and economic reforms.'[99] Managers and well-wishers of India–Myanmar relations hoped that the saplings planted to strengthen cooperation in various fields would transform into fruit-laden trees in the fullness of time.

Notes

1 From the author's personal notes of the remarks made by Aung San Suu Kyi, after she had delivered the formal Jawaharlal Nehru Memorial Lecture on 14 November 2012, New Delhi.
2 www.livemint.com/Politics/nULJZTyRg5PmzjMrll4SiO/SM-Krishna-to-visit-Myanmar-on-Monday.html (accessed on 21 October 2013).
3 'Joint Statement on the occasion on the occasion of the State Visit of the President of the Republic of the Union of Myanmar to India.' http://www.mea.gov.in/bilateral-documents.htm?dtl/5326/Joint_Statement_on_the_occasion_of_the_State_Visit_of_the_President_of_the_Republic_of_the_Union_of_Myanmar_to_India (accessed on 20 October 2013).
4 *The New Light of Myanmar*, 17 October 2011, http://www.burmalibrary.org/docs12/NLM2011-10-17.pdf (accessed on 20 October 2013).
5 'Joint Statement on the occasion on the occasion of the State Visit of the President of the Republic of the Union of Myanmar to India.' http://www.mea.gov.in/bilateral-documents.htm?dtl/5326/Joint_Statement_on_the_occasion_of_the_State_Visit_of_the_President_of_the_Republic_of_the_Union_of_Myanmar_to_India (accessed on 20 October 2013).
6 Website of Smt. Pratibha Devisingh Patil, former president of India, http://pratibhapatil.nic.in/bqsp141011.html (accessed on 20 October 2013).
7 Thein Sein observed: 'Myanmar places a special emphasis on the policy of maintaining good and friendly relations with India and we highly appreciate India's "Look East" policy.' Website of the Embassy of the Republic of the Union of Myanmar, New Delhi, Archives, October 2011, 'President of the Republic of India hosts dinner to President U Thein Sein and wife Daw Khin Khin Win', http://myanmedelhi.com/president-of-republic-of-india-hosts-dinner-to-president-u-thein-sein-and-wife-daw-khin-khin-win/ (accessed on 20 October 2013).
8 The five prime ministers of India who visited Burma/Myanmar are: Jawaharlal Nehru, Lal Bahadur Shastri, Indira Gandhi, Rajiv Gandhi and Manmohan Singh.
9 *AsiaNews.it*, 30 September 2011. In a letter to the Parliament on 30 September 2001, Thein Sein said 'Our government is elected by the people so we must pay attention to the will of the people. . . . Thus the Myitsone Dam project will be suspended during the term of our government.' http://www.asianews.it/news-en/Burmese-President-stops-construction-of-Myitsone-dam-22780.html (accessed on 20 October 2013).

During reform period 155

10 Baladas Ghoshal in 'India Lacks Strategic Vision in Myanmar', *Imphal Free Press*, 27 April 2012.
11 'Building Bridges with Myanmar', *Business Economics*, 14 May 2012.
12 'Opening remarks by Foreign Secretary on Dr Singh's Forthcoming State visit to Myanmar', 25 May 2012, http://www.mea.gov.in/media-briefings.htm?dtl/19714/Transcript_of_the_Media_Briefing_by_Foreign_Secretary_in_Nay_Pyi_Taw_on_Prime_Ministers_ongoing_Myanmar_Visit (accessed on 20 October 2013).
13 Ibid. Statement by Dr Singh prior to his departure for Myanmar.
14 Transcript of Dr Singh's on-board press interaction en route from Yangon to New Delhi, 29 May 2012, http://www.mea.gov.in/media-briefings.htm?dtl/19675/Transcript_of_Prime_Ministers_onboard_Press_Interaction_en_route_from_Yangonto_New_Delhi (accessed on 2 June 2012)
15 'Myanmar's Capital, the Royal City, Is Not a Teeming Metropolis', *The Hindu*, 29 May 2012. See also 'The Making of a Capital in Myanmar', *The Indian Express*, 29 May 2012.
16 Manmohan Singh's Speech at the State Banquet hosted by the President of Myanmar, 28 May 2012, http://www.mea.gov.in/Speeches-Statements.htm?dtl/19746/Prime_Ministers_Speech_at_the_State_Banquet_hosted_by_the_President_of_Myanmar (accessed on 30 May 2012).
17 Ibid.
18 Banquet Speech by President Thein Sein on 28 May 2012. *India Digest Special Edition*, 2012, published by the Indian Embassy in Yangon.
19 Prime Minister Dr Singh's address to think tanks and business community, 29 May 2012, http://www.mea.gov.in/Speeches-Statements.htm?dtl/19749/PMs_address_to_thinktanks_and_business_community_at_an_event_organized_by_Myanmar_Federation_of_Chambers_of_Commerce_and_Industry_and_the_Myanmar_Deve (accessed on 1 June 2012).
20 Ibid.
21 Ibid.
22 Statements to media by the prime minster of India and Daw Aung San Suu Kyi, Media Centre, MEA, 29 May 2012, http://www.mea.gov.in/Speeches-Statements.htm?dtl/19747/Statements_to_Media_by_Prime_Minister_of_India_and_Daw_Aung_San_Suu_Kyi (accessed on 1 June 2012).
23 Ibid.
24 Transcript of Dr Singh's on-board press interaction en route from Yangon to New Delhi.
25 'PM to Meet Suu Kyi, Venue Not Fixed Yet', *The Indian Express*, 24 May 2012.
26 Dhiraj Nayyar, 'Out of the General's Shadow', *India Today*, 11 June 2012.
27 Informal enquiries with MEA revealed that gifts for Suu Kyi by the prime minister and his wife included a pashmina stole, choicest mangoes and framed photographs of the Burmese leader's college days in Delhi, an imaginative reminder of her old connection with India.
28 'Shwedagon – A Symbol of Strength and Serenity', http://shwedagon.8m.com/chap1.htm (accessed on 21 October 2013).
29 Text of Dr Singh's remarks, obtained from an official of MEA, New Delhi: 'I am deeply honoured at this opportunity to pay my respects at this holy

156 During reform period

site. The Shwedagon Pagoda has stood for more than two and a half millennia as a symbol of Lord Buddha's teachings of love and compassion. This hallowed place is a testament to the immortal values of peace and tolerance and an eternal symbol of the ancient and deep-rooted ties between India and Myanmar. It is a privilege for me to have been able to visit here in celebration of 2600 years of the Shwedagon Pagoda.'

30 Text of Dr Singh's remarks, obtained from an official of MEA: 'It is an honour for me to pay my respects at the last resting place of Bahadur Shah Zafar, the last Mughal Emperor, a poet and a great son of India. It is a great irony of the history of India and Myanmar that the mortal remains of the last King of one of India's greatest empires are located on the soil of Myanmar, while those of Myanmar's last King Thibaw are in Ratnagiri in India. The destinies of India and Myanmar are truly intertwined and the respect accorded to the Emperor's Mazar by the people of Myanmar symbolizes the strong bonds between our two nations and peoples. I am glad to see that the Mazar is being preserved and maintained carefully. The Government of India will continue to play a role in this important task.'

31 Text of the Joint Statement is at MEA website, http://www.mea.gov.in/bilateral-documents.htm?dtl/19893/Joint_Statement_by_India_and_Myanmar_on_the_State_visit_of_Prime_Minister_of_India_to_Myanmar (accessed on 5 June 2012).

32 Jubilant Energy secured an oil block located between Yangon and Naypyitaw. The three companies working since before Dr Singh's visit were Oil and Natural Gas Corporation Videsh Ltd. (OVL), Gas Authority of India Ltd. (GAIL) and ESSAR Oil. (The last-mentioned, however, withdrew later.)

33 Banquet Speech by President Thein Sein on 28 May 2012. *India Digest Special Edition*, 2012, published by the Indian Embassy in Yangon.

34 Dr Khin Zaw Win, 'Now Is the Time for India to Play a Role in Myanmar', *South Asia Monitor*, 13 May 2012, http://southasiamonitor.org/detail.php?type=n&nid=2388 (accessed on 25 April 2015).

35 'Namaste', *The New Light of Myanmar*, 30 May 2012, http://www.burmalibrary.org/docs13/NLM2012-05-30.pdf (accessed on 22 October 2013). Considering the long-term value of this editorial, which reflected the Establishment thinking, its full text has been added as Appendix II.

36 Transcript of the media briefing by Foreign Secretary in Naypyitaw on Dr Singh's ongoing Myanmar visit, 28 May 2012, http://www.mea.gov.in/media-briefings.htm?dtl/19714/Transcript_of_the_Media_Briefing_by_Foreign_Secretary_in_Nay_Pyi_Taw_on_Prime_Ministers_ongoing_Myanmar_Visit (accessed on 30 May 2012).

37 'On Burma Road', *The Hindu*, 1 June 2012.

38 C. Raja Mohan, 'Road to Naypyidaw', *The Indian Express*, 28 May 2012.

39 Ranjit Gupta, 'Not Just a Neighbourly Visit', *The Indian Express*, 1 June 2012.

40 Pramit Pal Chaudhuri, 'Singh Makes Up to Myanmar', *The Hindustan Times*, 29 May 2012.

41 'Myanmar Beckons', *The Times of India*, 29 May 2012.

42 Rajiv Bhatia, 'Striking the Right Note', *The Times of India*, 31 May 2012.

43 Cited by Zaw Win Than, in 'Indian PM Outlines Cooperation Vision', *Myanmar Times*, Vol. 32, No. 629 (4–10 June 2012), http://www.scribd.com/doc/117333970/201232629#scribd (accessed on 26 April 2015).

44 M.K. Bhadrakumar. 'Challenges in Myanmar'. *The Deccan Herald*, 2 June 2012, http://www.deccanherald.com/content/253391/challenges-myanmar.html (accessed on 5 June 2012).
45 William Boot. 'India's Discovery of Burma Still Waiting for the Train to Leave the Station'. *The Irrawaddy*, 5 June 2012.
46 Press release issued in New Delhi, *Foreign Affairs Record*, 8 May 1995. Inter alia it read as follows: 'Daw Aung San Suu Kyi has been chosen for the 1993 Jawaharlal Nehru Award for International Understanding for her brave, nonviolent and unyielding struggle for freedom, democracy and human dignity – the ideals that promote international understanding and goodwill and the ideals cherished by Pandit Jawaharlal Nehru for which the award was instituted.' http://www.mealib.nic.in/?999841 (accessed on 24 October 2013).
47 'Jawaharlal Nehru Memorial Lecture, 2012 "Discovery of Nehru" by Aung San Suu Kyi', 14 November 2012, http://www.mea.gov.in/Speeches-Statements.htm?dtl/20812/Jawaharlal_Nehru_Memorial_Lecture_2012_quotDiscovery_of_Nehruquot_by_Aung_San_Suu_Kyi (accessed on 16 November 2012).
48 From the author's personal notes.
49 This is based on the author's personal notes of the event.
50 Karan Thapar, 'The Lady in Delhi', *Hindustan Times*, 18 November 2012.
51 'I feel I am partly an Indian citizen: Myanmar's Aung San Su Kyi', PTI, 16 November 2012.
52 Shaswati Das. 'Suu Kyi Relives Memories at LSR, Her Alma Mater', *Hindustan Times*, 17 November 2012.
53 'Mahatma Gandhi Would Have Stood by Us: Suu Kyi', http://ibnlive.com/news/mahatma-gandhi-would-have-stood-by-us-aung-san-suu-kyi/305833-2.html (accessed on 17 November 2012).
54 'Let's Not Be Over-Optimistic about Burma', *The Hindu*, 13 November 2012.
55 'Mahatma Gandhi Would Have Stood by Us: Suu Kyi', http://ibnlive.com/news/mahatma-gandhi-would-have-stood-by-us-aung-san-suu-kyi/305833-2.html (accessed on 17 November 2012).
56 'Let's Not Be Over-Optimistic about Burma', *The Hindu*, 13 November 2012.
57 Ibid.
58 'Our People Won't Be Hostage to the Past,' *Outlook*, 26 November 2012.
59 'Let's Not Be Over-Optimistic about Burma', *The Hindu*, 13 November 2012.
60 Ibid.
61 'Mahatma Gandhi Would Have Stood by Us: Suu Kyi', http://ibnlive.com/news/mahatma-gandhi-would-have-stood-by-us-aung-san-suu-kyi/305833-2.html (accessed on 17 November 2012).
62 In an interview to Nirupama Subramanian, 'Let's Not Be Over-Optimistic about Burma', *The Hindu*, 13 November 2012.
63 Interview to NDTV, 15 November 2012, http://www.ndtv.com/article/india/full-transcript-my-farewell-message-for-my-husband-was-too-late-says-aung-san-suu-kyi-to-ndtv-292831 (accessed on 16 November 2012).
64 Ibid.

158 During reform period

65 Ibid.
66 'Mahatma Gandhi Would Have Stood by Us: Suu Kyi', http://ibnlive
.com/news/mahatma-gandhi-would-have-stood-by-us-aung-san-suu-
kyi/305833-2.html (accessed on 17 November 2012).
67 Indrani Bagchi. 'India Suu Kyi Bury the Past', *Times of India*, 15 November 2011.
68 *The Asian Age*, 16 November 2012.
69 'Engaging Myanmar', *Times of India*, 16 November 2012.
70 *Hindustan Times*, 12 November 2012.
71 'Suu Kyi's Message', *The Indian Express*, 15 November 2012.
72 Baladas Ghoshal, 'Pragmatic Road to Reconciliation', *The Hindu*, 17 November 2012.
73 Rajiv Bhatia, 'Significant Journey Underway', *The Times of India*, 21 November 2012.
74 MEA website, http://www.mea.gov.in/
75 Minister Khurshid, the author of a famous play named *Sons of Babur*, wrote the following line in the visitors' book of the Mazar, 'On visiting this place of pilgrimage, both spiritual and political, I feel a sense of fulfilment and inspiration. . . .' *NDTV*, 15 December 2012, http://www.ndtv.com/india-news/salman-khurshid-visits-bahadur-shah-zafars-mausoleum-in-myanmar-507599 (accessed on 26 April 2015).
76 A PTI news report in DNA (15 December 2012) termed Khurshid's activities relating to installation of the Buddha statue and the inauguration of the conference as 'a day of religious diplomacy'. www.dnaindia.com/india/report_khurshid.adopts-religious-diplomacy-to-woo-myanmar-people-1777933 (accessed on 3 January 2013).
77 This is based on a 'Brief Report' on the conference, prepared by the Indian Embassy in Yangon.
78 MEA website: http://www.mea.gov.in/
79 Notably Minister Khurshid concluded his speech with an extract from *The Light of Asia* by Edwin Arnold, which remains highly relevant today: '. . . such is the Law which moves to righteousness, which none at last can turn aside or stay; the heart of it is Love, the end of it, Is Peace and Consummation sweet. Obey!' MEA website, http://www.mea.gov.in/
80 IANS report, *Maktoob News*, 24 December 2012, https://en-maktoob.news.yahoo.com/myanmar-reaffirms-pledge-boost-asean-india-ties-063221123.html (accessed on 26 April 2015).
81 Zarni Mann, 'Thein Sein Visits Delhi for Summit amid Protests', *The Irrawaddy*, 20 December 2012 http://m.irrawaddy.org/burma/thein-sein-visits-delhi-for-summit-amid-protests.html (accessed on 28 April 2015).
82 *IANS* report, 'Myanmar Invites India to Invest in Infrastructure, Power', 22 December 2012, http://burmanationalnews.org/burma/index.php?option=com_content&view=article&id=3198:news-a-articles-on-burma-22-december-2012&catid=39:-news-a-articles-on-burma (accessed on 26 April 2015).
83 Thibaw was dethroned on 28 November 1885. Along with the queen and family, he lived in exile in Ratnagiri from 10 April 1886 until his death on 15 December 1916. He was 57. After the king's death, the queen and daughters requested the British government several times to send back

During reform period 159

the remains of the king to Mandalay Palace, but the request was not granted.

84 'President U Thein Sein Visits the last king's tomb in India', 23 December 2012, http://www.myanmarpresidentoffice.info/en/?q=briefing-room/news/2012/12/23/id-1292 (accessed on 26 April 2015).

85 *Bangkok Post*, 22 December 2012. www.bangkokpost.com/news/asia/327511/thein-sein-visits-kings-tomb (accessed on 5 January 2013).

86 These are: India, Sri Lanka, Nepal, Bhutan, Bangladesh, Thailand and Myanmar.

87 Sonu Trivedi, 'The Importance of Myanmar to Modi', *Asia Times Online*, 13 June 2014: 'Guided by realism and national interest, the new government in India may try to make the northeast region a center point and pivot for its connectivity to the rest of Asia by bridging missing trade links via Myanmar.' http://www.atimes.com/atimes/South_Asia/SOU-02-130614.html (accessed on 18 August 2014).

88 Rahul Mishra, 'Myanmar: Priority for the New Indian Government', Article No. #4545, 4 July 2014, *IPCS*, www.ipcs.org/article/india-the-world/myanmar-priority-for-the-new-indian-government-4545.html (accessed on 11 October 2014). The scholar opined: 'One may argue that like Mauritius, Myanmar could have also been invited as both the countries are, in geographical terms, part of Southern Asia.'

89 'Foreign Office Consultations between India and Myanmar', Ministry of External Affairs (23 July 2014), http://www.mea.gov.in/press-releases.htm?dtl/23716/Foreign+Office+Consultations+between+India+and+Myanmar (accessed on 18 August 2014).

90 'Myanmar Visit Was Successful, says Sushma Swaraj', PTI, 11 August 2014, http://www.firstpost.com/politics/myanmar-visit-successful-says-sushma-swaraj-1659747.html (accessed on 18 August 2014).

91 Ibid.

92 Portrayal of India as a 'brother' reminded old-timers of the use of the same word to depict India by General Aung San in 1946, as mentioned in Chapter 3.

93 An Indian official, briefing the media in Naypyitaw, stated: 'I think it is a unique relationship in that it has never been a troubled relationship. It has always been a relationship of cordiality and warmth.' Media Centre, Transcript of Media Briefing, 11 November 2014, http://mea.gov.in/media-briefings.htm?dtl/24227/Transcript+of+Media+Briefing+by+Official+Spokesperson+in+Nay+Pyi+Taw+on+Prime+Ministers+ongoing+visit+to+Myanmar (accessed on 15 November 2014).

94 Rajiv Bhatia, 'Eastward ho!' *Frontline*, 26 December 2014.

95 'MEA Press Release', http://www.mea.gov.in/press-releases.htm?dtl/24699/Official_visit_of_the_Vice_President_of_the_Republic_of_the_Union_of_Myanmar_to_India (accessed on 19 January 2015).

96 Some of the main ones were: Jamia Millia Islamia (December 5 2012); Aspen Institute Roundtable on Myanmar (4 May 2012); CENRS, Kolkata (17 September 2012); and Asia Centre Bangalore (9 June 2012).

97 'India–Myanmar: A New Impetus', Gateway House Report No. 10, February 2014, p. 12, *Gateway House*. Reporting on the visit, this think tank concluded: 'Clearly, Myanmar has begun its journey to become a

typical emerging market – a journey that India must participate in if we are serious about our place in Asia.'

98 The section on the visit of ICWA delegation to Myanmar is based on the author's personal notes.

99 'Chief of the Myanmar Army calls on the President', Rashtrapati Bhavan, New Delhi, 12 December 2013, http://www.presidentofindia.nic.in/press-release-detail.htm?164 (accessed on 26 April 2015).

Chapter 6

Bilateral relationship
Present state-of-play

> In fact, India needs Myanmar, and Myanmar also needs India, and that is the common ground. . . . So we say 'Namaste!' to our neighbours.
>
> – *The New Light of Myanmar*[1]

History reveals difficulties in putting an accurate label to the complex relations between India and Burma/Myanmar. Geographical contiguity, ethnic and cultural heritage, shared Asian values and the legacy of religions – Hinduism, Buddhism and Islam – have been permanent factors moulding these ties. The relationship, however, has fluctuated, from time to time.[2] The two countries have related to each other as neighbours, strangers and adversaries occasionally, but mostly as friends and partners. Neither country has treated the other as irrelevant to its national interests.

As the twenty-first century dawned, a new phase in their mutual discovery began, bringing them closer to each other. This trend gathered momentum from early 2011 as Myanmar embarked on a new journey of reform and renewal. Four years later, at the beginning of 2015, the state of bilateral relations was marked by progress and promise, but also constraints.

Key determinants

India–Myanmar ties are anchored in history, broader foreign policy perspectives and each country's assessment of the other's motivations and inclinations in the subregional and regional context.

Myanmar perceives itself 'sandwiched' between two Asian giants – China and India – that are also among the fast-growing economies in the world today. Naturally, it seeks cooperative relations with both,

162 Present state-of-play

keen to leverage its strategic location for deriving maximum benefits, while safeguarding its national independence. It is adept at projecting its membership and chair of ASEAN as well as the new openings towards the West as a means to enhance its strategic attractiveness to India.

From India's viewpoint, Myanmar is an immediate neighbour of vital importance for defence and internal security needs, stability and development in the North Eastern Region (NER) and expansion of its influence in the Bay of Bengal region and Southeast Asia. Myanmar is not where only China and India 'meet', it is also the intersection between South Asia and Southeast Asia. Thus, both Myanmar and India have a fundamental convergence in treating the former as the 'gateway' between India and ASEAN and beyond, through expansion of connectivity and cooperative links.

The North East angle

India's NER is bordered by Bangladesh, Nepal, Bhutan, China and Myanmar. Although landlocked, it is in close proximity to the Bay of Bengal. It is of immense importance for India from the perspective of strategy and maritime dimension, national defence and internal security, social and economic development. The pattern of India's relations with neighbours has a direct bearing on the security and development of NER. Hence the right kind of connectivity needs encouragement and the wrong kind of exchanges such as drug trafficking, smuggling, illegal trade and insurgent activity need to be curbed effectively.

Geography and ethnic bonds are the oldest links between India and Myanmar. A shared border and familial/tribal ties ensure a certain uniqueness to India–Myanmar relations if special attention is paid to NER. The people of the region view it as India's link to Southeast Asia.

India's Look East/Act East Policy is a vital subset of the foreign policy, but it is still not fully understood within the country. This author's visits to eastern India, especially the North East, and conversations held there indicated that not only the man on the street but even sections of informed public opinion and the elite seemed to think that this policy had something to do with looking east of Delhi and taking measures to accelerate economic development of eastern India consisting of NER, West Bengal and Orissa. One experienced the burden of this expectation and resulting perception of discontent on numerous occasions, while speaking to interlocutors in Bhubaneswar,

Kolkata, Shillong, Tezpur, Guwahati and Manipur, besides Delhi. It is, therefore, pertinent to analyse the situation in the NER in order to comprehend its potential both to help and harm the relationship with Myanmar.

Using a broader definition, one may point out that NER comprises 'seven sisters' and 'a brother'. These sisters are Arunachal Pradesh, Nagaland, Manipur, Mizoram, Tripura, Meghalaya and Assam, with Sikkim being the brother. Even a cursory look at the map shows the region's geostrategic significance. Without NER being at peace with itself and enjoying the fruits of stability, security and inclusive development, India as a whole can never develop fully. Therefore, NER must enjoy a place of priority in India's foreign policy, particularly its South Asia policy, China policy, Look/Act East policy and Myanmar policy.

For long, much of NER witnessed serious disturbances marked by insurgency, communal strife and violence.[3] Bodo–Muslim clashes in Assam in 2012 brought this facet to the fore again. Without delving into the past, it may be noted that parts of Assam, Nagaland and Manipur still remain affected periodically by popular disaffection, intertribal tensions and a general sense of instability and uncertainty. Analysts believe that unlawful elements – the Indian Insurgent Groups (IIGs) – have perfected the art of extortion, 'the compulsory tax' that they collect, under duress, from the populace including even government officials, particularly in Manipur.[4] With funds so raised, they maintain themselves and their illegal activities such as purchase of arms, smuggling, kidnapping, drug trafficking and general harassment of the people and security forces. They use local topography characterised by hills, forests and difficult terrain to go in and out of Myanmar, leveraging their tribal links in Myanmar's region bordering on Nagaland and Manipur. When these elements are under pressure from counter-insurgency action by Indian authorities, the former flee to Myanmar for the purpose of taking shelter and obtaining supplies and arms. Burmese insurgent groups (and victims of oppression from Burmese authorities) have sought shelter in India, following a well-established tradition of mutual assistance. Consequently, security forces of the two countries, although committed to cooperation, are unable to stamp out insurgency. This, of course, represents a benign view of the motivations of Myanmar military. Experts suggest that the Myanmar military speaks with two voices, assuring New Delhi of its good intentions and best possible efforts, while simultaneously advising and helping Indian militant groups as a lever of pressure on India.

Disturbed security conditions mean that private sector investment fails to come to the region in ample measure, resulting in minimum industrialisation, job creation and development. Huge injections of funding are given by the central government, but a considerable portion of it gets siphoned off, according to popular perception, by a well-functioning industry of corruption composed of multiple stakeholders, including political leaders, civil servants and business community – both in Delhi and various parts of the region. There are other reasons for poverty and privation, resulting in unemployment, a key factor responsible for insurgency. Facilities for education, training and skill development used to be limited, forcing youth to migrate to other parts of India. In recent years, much improvement in educational infrastructure has taken place, but in the absence of sufficient job opportunities, 'brain drain' still represents a major concern. Another important factor is the plethora and diversity of rules and regulations, taxes and non-tariff barriers emanating from as many as eight governments at the state level and a much larger number of municipal institutions. Economic experts have suggested that a free trade and investment area needs to be established within NER with the aim to securing its all-round development.[5] This, however, runs counter to regional and subregional aspirations and diversities. That is why coordination was thought to be a better route, utilising the instrumentality of North Eastern Council (NEC). It has proved, at best, a partial success as the plan set out in NER's 2020 vision has remained largely unimplemented.[6]

In the complex security-development paradigm, security experts tend to argue that insurgency cannot be eliminated through military means alone; therefore, the political class must sustain dialogue and find lasting solutions. Those advocating the cause of development point out that the results achieved so far represent 'only a half-glass-full' situation. To do better, India needs to change its mindset, understand the reasons why a person from the North East feels alienated, and find a way to respect and accept him as an equal citizen. Wisdom of this suggestion came into bold relief in August 2012 when, a massive stream of SMSs, threatening the security of thousands of workers from the North East in Bengaluru and other places in South India, triggered their mass exodus.[7] Fortunately the conspiracy, apparently hatched through a Pakistani connection, was exposed quickly and the government took timely steps to reassure the affected people, facilitating their return.[8] The short point is that Indians belonging to other parts of the country must

Present state-of-play 165

do more to accept the North East people as an integral part of the large Indian family.

Border region and ethnicity

Conditions in the India–Myanmar border region have been deeply influenced by the factor of ethnicity that defines populations on both sides of the border. The arbitrariness of the political boundary drawn by the colonial authority played a significant role in creating insurgencies following independence. 'The artificial delineation of the border was one of the major factors that led to the newly independent states of India and Burma reaping a harvest of insurgencies since 1947–48.'[9] These insurgencies remain a fact of life over six decades later, although they are of reduced intensity today than in the past.

Existing literature sheds ample light on the issues and contestations involved in the complex pattern of ethnic linkages between four border states and their adjacent regions in Myanmar.[10] Both sides clamour for freer movement, easier border trade and more exchanges at the people's level. Myanmar residents want easy access to medical and educational facilities available in the NER. On the Indian side, demands vary. Much support exists in Arunachal Pradesh for establishing a link to the Stilwell Road. The other three states also want closer connectivity to the heartland of Myanmar and, through it, to Southeast Asia and China in such a manner that, instead of being a gateway, the North East becomes an integral part of a vast thriving development corridor. In contrast to huge expectations, present-day links through underdeveloped roads remains a source of disappointment.

To Indian authorities, the success of insurgent groups in securing shelter and assistance in Myanmar continues to be a serious concern. Of late, the two governments have been engaged in mild contestation about border-fencing, fixing and repairs of border pillars and other aspects of border management. In the reform era, a new trend relates to the frequency of exchange of visits by chief ministers and other officials of the border regions. This is expected to strengthen understanding and cooperation.

Border regions have a sense of disconnect with the central authority, marked by a perception that their well-being and development have been neglected by governments located in far-off regional towns or national capitals, and that an approach of self-help and consolidation of traditional ethnic ties between communities on the two sides of the border should be continued. On the other hand, from the national

166 Present state-of-play

angle, border regions have generally been perceived as a land where nefarious activities abound: smuggling, drug trafficking, gun-running and defiance of central authority, especially attacks against Indian security forces. The last-mentioned feature has been a distinguishing characteristic of the Indo–Myanmar border region. Here insurgents have essentially operated against India, whereas the Kachins and Wa in the China–Myanmar border areas and the Karens located along the Thai–Myanmar border waged long-drawn wars against the Myanmar military. Thus, three of Myanmar's immediate neighbours – China, India and Thailand – have been the key stakeholders in the country's ethnic politics. As was noted in Chapter 2, ethnic groups play a vital role in the Myanmar polity. 'On the ethnic issue, it is in the country's best interest to address the question of autonomy of the ethnic minority.'[11]

The impact of ethnicity should always, therefore, be kept in view, while evaluating India–Myanmar relations. One could hardly overemphasise that, without ameliorating the socio-cultural and economic situation in the border region that links the two countries, it may not be possible to add new substance to their cooperation.

Connectivity

A major consideration, while considering the challenges in NER, is its geographic location. Its optimal potential for development can never be realised unless it is connected with the region on its west, north and east. That is how 'connectivity' has come to assume a vital role in NER's development, in the development of Myanmar (and Bangladesh) and in the potential expansion of India's relations with Myanmar (and Bangladesh). While many ambitious projects have been drawn up and a few have even been implemented, the Indian government has received much criticism for delays in the execution of two of its flagship projects – the Trilateral Highway project that would link India, Myanmar and Thailand, and the Kaladan Multi-modal Transport project that would link Kolkata via Sittwe with Mizoram (Map 2). When they are completed in the future, NER may have very useful and productive openings towards Southeast Asia.[12]

At a brainstorming session hosted by the Research and Information System (RIS) for Developing Countries, New Delhi, in April 2012, where this author was present, participants agreed that Myanmar represented 'a significant opportunity for India to position itself as a key economic partner of Myanmar. . .' Further, they emphasised the need to keep 'the larger regional perspective in mind' by considering India's

Present state-of-play 167

participation in 'both the Kyaukpyu deep water port project on the Rakhine coast and the Dawei port project on the Tanintharyi coast'.[13]

Connectivity through stronger infrastructural links is only a means to the end of promoting more travel, tourism, trade and other friendly activity between India and Myanmar. Such links may also be extended to China, but security experts tend to articulate their reservations on this aspect, given their perception of the Chinese threat. On this score, they disagree and clash with economic experts who believe that an effective way to reduce or dilute the sense of threat from China is to encourage commercial and people-to-people links. On the question of India working to connect its road system to the Stilwell Road in Myanmar, the Indian establishment is divided: even as public opinion and development experts in Arunachal Pradesh and NER in general favour the idea, security people remain firmly opposed to it. In contrast, there is no divergence – only unanimity – over the question of forging all-round connectivity with Myanmar in the central and southern sectors. It is also maintained that, going beyond infrastructure, other kinds of connectivity, viz. through development corridors, assistance for education, health and human resource development, civil society linkages and people-to-people contacts, would help the two countries realise the huge potential of their relationship.

Mani Shankar Aiyar, former diplomat and cabinet minister who has been a strong proponent of the development of NER and forging its close connections with Myanmar, stated:

> In many ways, I would suggest Burma matters much more than Pakistan; whereas the west part of India can live with suspended economic activity with Pakistan, north east India can never break off from its trap of backwardness without active cooperation of Burma or Myanmar.[14]

In this context, the two governments, which articulated a promising vision on many occasions, should lend full support to the implementation of their shared vision. The yawning gap between words and action, commitments and delivery needs to be bridged in order to enhance credibility and reduce scepticism prevalent in the public domain.

India has a good NER policy in the 2020 vision document, but it too needs to be implemented. A good Myanmar policy already exists. Its value and impact could be enhanced by forging multi-dimensional connectivity between NER and Myanmar. In doing so, full care should be taken that our North East does not become merely a transit station for passage of goods from India to Southeast Asia and vice versa. Value addition and sharing the fruits of investment and development must also be enjoyed by the people of NER and of the border regions of Myanmar. Only then they will have stakes in supporting connectivity projects.

An effective way to 'sell' India's Eastern policy and the need for closer relations with Myanmar would be to take the people of eastern India into confidence and take care of their economic interests.[15] They need to be sensitised much more about the rationale of the policy and how it is designed to help in their development. It was, therefore, heartening to note that, while addressing a special session of the Arunachal Pradesh Assembly on 29 November 2013, President Pranab Mukherjee stressed that the development of border areas was 'vital' and must receive 'our attention'. He stated:

> The north east of India provides a natural bridge between us and South East Asia. The essential philosophy of our Look East Policy is that India must find its destiny by linking itself more and more with its Asian partners and the rest of the world.[16]

China factor

Finally, a holistic look at the India–Myanmar–China triangle is the key to obtaining an accurate read on India–Myanmar relations. Is it a zero-sum game in which China's gains are seen as India's losses and vice versa? It need not be so, but generally it is perceived as such because the pattern of India–China ties is stamped by competition and rivalry.

After two decades of mounting dependence on China, Myanmar, of late, has been giving clear signs of seeking greater room for manoeuvre in its external relations. This comes in the backdrop of the country heading towards more inclusive governance and transition to democracy. Further, under the leadership of President Xi Jinping, China has been pushing proposals like Bangladesh–China–India–Myanmar (BCIM) Economic Corridor and the proposed Maritime Silk Road (MSR) that aims to connect China, Southeast Asia and South Asia.

These developments have the potential to reduce the negative impact of 'the China factor' and provide new opportunities to concerned countries, especially India in view of its age-old links with the 'Golden Land'. This important aspect will be examined in detail in the next chapter.

The focus here is on analysing the state of India–Myanmar relations and cooperation as it existed at the beginning of 2015.

A multifaceted relationship

It is normal to depict India–Myanmar ties as 'a multi-faceted relationship'. This depiction has two vital connotations. Firstly, at all four levels of interaction, that is, multilateral, regional, subregional and bilateral, the two countries are linked closely and they interact on a regular basis. Secondly, in all the main sectors of bilateral exchanges, cooperation is becoming fairly substantial. In this context, seven major pillars of the relationship need to be viewed closely and critically.[17]

I Political cooperation

Recent years spanning from 2000 to 2014 witnessed a regular dialogue at the highest levels of the government. This demonstrates a shared commitment to the growing importance of the relationship and the common desire to add more content to it and diversify it. Deriving inspiration from the Five Principles of Peaceful Co-existence, the leaders repeatedly affirmed that a further expansion of engagement would help the two countries politically and for securing their goal of economic progress. A combination of important values and hard interests has driven the relationship forward.

Shared perceptions and plans for further cooperation took shape in the statements issued after recent high-level bilateral visits, listed in Table 6.1.

Table 6.1 Recent high-level visits

No.	VVIP	Year(s)
1.	Vice Chairman SPDC Maung Aye	2000 and 2008
2.	Vice President Bhairon Singh Shekhawat	2003
3.	SPDC Chairman Than Shwe	2004 and 2010
4.	President A.P.J. Abdul Kalam	2006
5.	Vice President M. Hamid Ansari	2009
6.	PM/President Thein Sein	2008, 2011 and 2012
7.	Prime Minister Manmohan Singh	2012 and 2013
8.	Prime Minister Narendra Modi	2014
9.	Vice President Dr Sai Mauk Kham	2015

170   Present state-of-play

The unique visit of NLD Chairperson Aung San Suu Kyi to India (2012) also contributed to the process of relationship building.

A key highlight of the recent period is the continuous exchange of visits at the level of top office-bearers of the parliaments, ministers, service chiefs and senior officials handling subjects pertaining to the main facets of bilateral cooperation. Another significant feature is the conclusion of a large number of Agreements and MoUs that govern almost every aspect of interaction between India and Myanmar.[18]

The two governments have also been on the same page about forging regional and subregional cooperation. Myanmar has been consistently appreciative of India's deepening engagement with ASEAN, particularly its assistance to CLMV countries. Further, convergence in the developmental domain has motivated the two countries to strengthen subregional cooperation through BIMSTEC, Mekong–Ganga Cooperation (MGC) and BCIM channels. Myanmar's entry in SAARC as an Observer in 2008 is also relevant as it helped in deepening Indians' consciousness of the country as a part of South Asia.

Various institutional mechanisms have been developed to forge and nurture bilateral cooperation in a variety of sectors. These include the following: Foreign Office Consultations (FOC) for an annual review of all bilateral issues at the level of foreign secretary/deputy minister level; National Level Meeting (NLM), Sectoral Level Meetings (SLM) as well as Army Border Liaison Committee (ABLC) and Regional Border Committee (RBC) meetings to review security cooperation matters; Joint Working Groups on Railways and Shipping to discuss connectivity issues; Joint Working Group on Agriculture and allied sectors; Joint Trade Committee; Border Trade Committee; and Joint Working Group on Science and Technology.

India and Myanmar share a 1,643-kilometre-long boundary.[19] Management of border-related issues forms part of regular interaction between officials of the two governments. Joint survey, maintenance, repair and reconstruction of the Boundary Pillars (BP) are undertaken by the two Survey Departments on a regular basis. The heads of the Survey Departments meet annually to discuss boundary management issues.

In a break from the past, the boundary issue drew considerable media attention in mid-2013 as the Myanmar side alleged the presence of Indian constructions within the agreed '10-metre no-construction zone' along the international boundary line.[20] The constructions were identified in the sectors between BP 145–146 (Nagaland), BP 79–81 (Manipur) and BP 155 (Nagaland).[21] A few media reports spoke unconvincingly of intrusions by the Myanmar Army.[22] Authorities on both sides strove to address the problem pragmatically in order to resolve it to their mutual satisfaction.[23]

Cooperation in institutions

Myanmar's membership of ASEAN, BIMSTEC and MGC has introduced important regional and subregional dimensions to bilateral relations and imparted additional significance to them in the context of India's LEP. As the only ASEAN country sharing the land border with India, Myanmar is also a bridge between South and South East Asia and a pivotal and visible link between India and ASEAN. India has been enthusiastic about and supportive of Myanmar's chairmanship of ASEAN. It has extended visa on arrival facility to seven ASEAN countries, including Myanmar.

On numerous multilateral issues, the two countries maintain a common position, based on shared perceptions. They favour a strong United Nations as a key factor in tackling global challenges and advocate UN reform, including expansion of the Security Council in order to make it more representative, credible and effective. India greatly appreciates Myanmar's consistent support for the former's quest for permanent membership of the Security Council and its generally friendly policy towards India in the context of South Asian affairs.

In recent years, both sides cooperated closely at the UN and other regional and international fora. Myanmar supported India's candidature for the non-permanent membership of the UN Security Council for the term 2011–12. Myanmar acquired the status of 'Observer' in SAARC with India's support.

2 Defence/security cooperation

Given the geostrategic factors as well as defence inter-linkage between India's NER and Myanmar's north-western region, it is natural that defence cooperation should be an important component of bilateral relations. This has witnessed significant strengthening through a series of regular visits at high levels, provision of training facilities, visits by naval ships, supply of equipment and, above all, a continuing dialogue on professional matters and strategic issues. Comparing it to what the

172 Present state-of-play

cooperation is between China and Myanmar is not the only way to measure it; an alternative is to compare the present-day defence cooperation to what had existed a decade back. A valid point though is that defence cooperation has considerable potential for further expansion and diversification.

For long, much of the India–Myanmar border region has been the theatre of negative activities. In particular, operations by certain IIGs against Indian authorities, the ability of IIGs to use north-western Myanmar as a base or shelter, and the nexus between them and sources of arms supplies from third countries through Myanmar, have caused serious problems. To counter these negatives, the two governments have set up several dialogue mechanisms, signed legal instruments and agreements, and have made arrangements for intelligence exchange and security cooperation.

Nevertheless, as problems in the border region have a long history and continue to fester, hard questions are raised in India from time to time.[24] Broadly, India's perception is that although Myanmar authorities extend cooperation, it is episodic and inadequate. As mentioned in the previous chapter, the Indian government seems to have become rather candid in its public pronouncements on the subject.[25] The Myanmar view, on the other hand, is that greater infrastructure development in the region would facilitate more security cooperation. In this context, the two governments' agreement in 2011 on ensuring effective cooperation and coordination between security forces in tackling the menace of insurgency and terrorism assumed significance. Recognising the importance of this issue, the two sides strengthened, in May 2012, their resolve to fight the scourge of terrorism and insurgency 'in all its forms and manifestations'.[26]

Border security management promised to remain a critical challenge in the future. An MoU on Border Area Development was signed during the visit of the prime minister in May 2012. Projects for the year 2012–13 under the MoU (US$5 million per annum for five years) were approved. Further, an MoU on Border Cooperation with Myanmar was signed in May 2014.[27]

With the ushering in of the Thein Sein government, defence cooperation registered a marked upswing in tune with the overall development of bilateral ties. This was best reflected in a non-stop stream of VIP visits in the defence sector. Moreover, assistance in training formed an important aspect of defence cooperation. This included training under the ITEC programme and in different sectors covering diverse areas ranging from counter-insurgency to teaching of the English language. Besides, Myanmar Navy participates in the biennial naval exercises at Port Blair. Navy and Coast Guard ships regularly call at Yangon port. Indian Navy ship *Sandhayak* made a port call in January 2012. A Myanmar naval ship visited Visakhapatnam in March 2013.[28] Two battleships and a coast guard frigate from the Indian Navy conducted joint exercises with the Myanmar Navy in April 2014.[29] Experts believe that, given the strategic significance of the Bay of Bengal, the potential of naval and maritime cooperation involving India, Myanmar and Bangladesh should be explored optimally, and expansion in areas of mutual benefit should be arranged in the future.

Sports exchanges are held every year on a reciprocal basis between the two Defence Forces. Indian golf and football teams visited Myanmar to participate in the Chief of Defence Forces Friendly Golf Tournament and the five-nation Armed Forces Invitational Tournament respectively in July 2013. India accepted the old Myanmar argument that good roads helped in curbing insurgents' activities. Hence, road construction equipment and spare parts are gifted to the Myanmar side from time to time. This supply witnessed some increase in value and frequency in recent years, according to knowledgeable sources. At Myanmar's request, supply of seven sets of bailey bridges for use in areas with difficult terrain was also arranged in July 2013.

3 Economic cooperation

Economic cooperation covers a vast area, including trade, border trade, investment, technical cooperation, energy, infrastructure and other joint projects. There is need to assess the present position concerning all these sectors.[30]

Trade

At the time of writing, India was the fourth largest trade partner of Myanmar, as shown in Table 6.2.

India–Myanmar trade has been rising steadily. In 2011, both sides agreed to double the bilateral trade to US$3 billion by 2015. Trade grew from US$1.497 million in 2009–10 to US$2,180 million in 2013–14. Trade balance has been consistently unfavourable to India. Table 6.3 indicates the trends.

Table 6.2 Myanmar's trade with ASEAN and neighbouring countries (US$ millions)

Country	2011–12			2012–13			2013–14		
	Exp	Imp	Total	Exp	Imp	Total	Exp	Imp	Total
China	2055.77	2796.55	5052.32	2238.07	2719.47	4957.54	2910.75	4105.49	7016.24
Thailand	3823.83	691.15	4514.98	4000.57	696.81	4697.38	4306.28	1376.99	5683.27
Singapore	542.75	2516.13	3058.88	291.35	2535.43	2826.78	694.03	2910.22	3604.25
India	1037.12	333.9	1371.02	1018.62	301.7	1320.32	1143.59	493.51	1637.1
Malaysia	152.04	303.41	455.45	97.92	360.90	458.82	108.87	839.69	948.86
Indonesia	40.94	431.82	436.76	31.54	195.23	226.77	60.04	438.82	498.86
Vietnam	81.09	62.29	143.38	81.24	74.22	155.96	112.39	170.23	282.62
Bangladesh	70.59	14.22	84.81	–	–	–	48.26	8.94	57.2
Philippines	34.32	14.64	48.96	18.22	–	–	12.8	21.11	33.91

Source: Embassy of India, Yangon

Table 6.3 India–Myanmar trade (US$ millions)

Year	2009–10	2010–11	2011–12	2012–13	2013–14
India's exports	207.97 (6.17%)	320.62 (54.17%)	545.38 (70.1%)	544.66 (-0.13%)	785.46 (44.21%)
India's imports	1,289.80 (38.84%)	1,017.67 (-21.1%)	1,381.15 (35.72%)	1,412.69 (2.28%)	1394.82 (-1.27%)
Total trade	1,497.77 (30.17%)	1,338.29 (-10.65%)	1,870.20 (39.75%)	1,957.35 (1.6%)	2180.28 (11.39)

Source: DGFT, Department of Commerce, India

Figures in brackets indicate variation from previous year(s)

India's imports from Myanmar are dominated by agricultural and forest-based products. Myanmar is the second largest supplier of beans and pulses to India and contributes to nearly one-fifth of India's imports of timber. Trends are indicated in Table 6.4.

India's exports are dominated by iron and steel products and pharmaceuticals as indicated by Table 6.5.

Discrepancies in the above-cited figures are due to their different sources, that is, official agencies in India and Myanmar.

Table 6.4 India's major imports from Myanmar (US$ millions)

	Commodity	2008–09	2009–10	2010–11	2011–12	2012–13	2013–14
1	Pulses and beans	611.78	851.53	570.82	628.57	552.12	468.68
2	Wood and articles of wood	311.01	404.95	419.16	388.71	402.28	605.54
3	Products of animal origin	2.93	6.22	12.32	0.56	1.07	–
4	Others	2.34	7.19	7.88	14.65	25.72	30.23
5	Raw hides and skin	–	2.05	4.55	3.41	0.84	
6	Coffee, tea, mate and spices	0.91	3.07	2.94	1.22	–	
7	Rice	–	–	–	–	–	18.17
8	Medical equipment			–	–	–	40.44

Source: Central Statistical Organization (CSO), Myanmar

Table 6.5 India's major exports to Myanmar (US$ millions)

Sl. No.	Commodity	2008–09	2009–10	2010–11	2011–12	2012–13	2013–14
1	Others	94.17	79.85	111.4	110.12	129.86	147.48
2	Meat and edible meat offal	–	1.91	71.59	13.31	0.29	–
3	Pharmaceuticals	49.92	55.98	61.29	76.09	94.55	74.17
4	Iron and steel	63.93	43.66	40.21	26.29	59.60	168.91
5	Sugar and sugar confectionery	–	0.07	21.27	–	0.09	–
6	Electrical machinery and equipment	13.62	16.69	16.39	26.81	26.03	58.34
7	Chemicals and allied products	–	9.81	12.27	5.4	7.20	–
8	Oil well and mining equipment	–	–	–	75.88	0.85	–

Source: Central Statistical Organization (CSO), Myanmar

Border trade

Although trade in traditional goods on head load basis has been the customary practice since long, the Border Trade Agreement signed in January 1994 gave it a legal framework. The Moreh–Tamu border trade point in the Manipur sector was operationalised in April 1995. The second border trade point was opened in January 2004 at Zokhawthar-Rhi, near Champhai. A third border trade point has been proposed. India and Myanmar agreed to upgrade the status of Border Trade to normal trade and to expand the list of tradable items from 18 to 62 since November 2012. Both sides also agreed to set up border *haats* along the India–Myanmar border to encourage local border trade. The first border *haat* has been proposed at Pangsau Pass, Arunachal Pradesh.[31] Table 6.6 shows the trends in the development of border trade in recent years.

It should be noted that 'informal trade', the euphemism for smuggling or illegal trade, is estimated to be far, far bigger than legal border trade.

Investment

India Inc. has been lagging behind in investing in Myanmar. Sectors like pharmaceuticals, fertilisers, cement, manufacturing, agro-processing and small industry offer attractive potential for green field investments and joint ventures. During Chairman Than Shwe's 2010 visit, Minister for Science and Technology U Thaung observed frankly that the Indian business community was taking 'too long to come, unlike China and ASEAN countries'.[32]

Table 6.6 India–Myanmar border trade ($ millions)

Year	Myanmar exports	Myanmar imports	Total trade	Balance of trade
2005–2006	11.28	4.13	15.41	7.14
2006–2007	11.02	4.75	15.77	6.27
2007–2008	10.91	3.92	14.83	6.99
2008–2009	5.49	4.43	9.82	1.05
2009–2010	7.79	5.95	13.73	1.84
2010–2011	8.30	4.50	12.80	3.80
2011–2012	8.87	6.54	15.41	2.33
2012–2013	26.96	11.67	38.63	15.20
2013–2014	30.92	17.71	**48.63**	13.21

Source: Department of Border Trade, Ministry of Commerce, Myanmar

178 Present state-of-play

Recent years witnessed much discussion and frank examination of what held India Inc. back and what kind of business and investment promotion should be undertaken jointly in future. On his visit to Myanmar, Prime Minister Singh was accompanied by a high-powered business delegation, which interacted not only with the Myanmar business community but also with President Thein Sein. Before a largely business audience in Yangon, the Indian prime minister spelt out his vision of India–Myanmar relations as a partnership for progress and regional development.

In 2013, India was the tenth largest investor in Myanmar. So far, both private and public sector companies from India are understood to have invested to the tune of $273 million, of which $257 million have been in oil and gas sector and $16 million in the manufacturing sector. Further details appeared in a useful report in the *Economic Times* in October 2013.[33]

The two countries signed several bilateral agreements to facilitate trade and investment. These included the Bilateral Investment Promotion Agreement (BIPA) and Double Taxation Avoidance Agreement (DTAA).

In 2008, the United Bank of India signed three banking agreements with the banks of Myanmar, namely Myanma Foreign Trade Bank (MFTB), Myanma Investment Commercial Bank (MICB) and Myanma Economic Bank (MEB) in order to facilitate bilateral trade. The Union Bank of India opened its representative office in Yangon in December 2012.

4 Energy cooperation

Before reforms

From British times, the rich potential of hydrocarbons in the general area of Assam, western Myanmar and the offshore waters was recognised. But, the involvement of Indian companies in oil and gas exploration in independent Myanmar is only a decade and half old. Indian public sector companies, Oil and Natural Gas Corporation Videsh Ltd. (OVL) and Gas Authority of India Ltd. (GAIL) secured stakes in two offshore blocks: A-1 (in April 2002) and A-3 (in March 2006) in the Shwe development and production area.[34] OVL holds 20 per cent and GAIL 10 per cent equity, whereas the Korean companies, Daewoo International Corporation and Korean Gas Corporation (KOGAS), have a total of 70 per cent equity, that is, 60 and 10 per cent, respectively.[35]

During the author's tenure (2002–05), more blocks were offered by Myanmar, but Indian companies were unable to avail themselves of the opportunity. Further, a serious endeavour was made by the authorities in India, Myanmar and Bangladesh to transport natural gas from the two blocks mentioned above to India through an on-land pipeline passing via Bangladesh. A trilateral meeting of the energy ministers was held in Yangon. However, the proposal did not register progress due to the lack of cooperation by Bangladesh. Other options such as the shallow-water pipeline and direct shipping were also considered, but they were not found to be commercially feasible. It was in this backdrop that two years later, in mid-2007, the Myanmar government chose to devise arrangements with the Indian companies and the Chinese side to sell gas to China, triggering an ugly public spat between India's Ministry of External Affairs and Ministry of Petroleum and Natural Gas as to 'who lost Myanmar?' or, to be more precise, Myanmar gas. In a separate development and due to the Indian Embassy's energetic diplomacy, an Indian private company, ESSAR, succeeded in winning exploration rights for A-2 and L blocks, but later it had to withdraw due to technical difficulties.

An MoU on cooperation in the petroleum sector was signed between the governments of India and Myanmar during the Indian president's visit in March 2006. During the visit of Murli Deora, minister of petroleum and natural gas, to Myanmar in September 2007, new production sharing contracts were signed for three deep water exploration blocks (i.e. AD-2, AD-3 and AD-9) between OVL and the Myanma Oil and Gas Enterprise (MOGE). India also offered a Line of Credit of $20 million for revamping of the Thanlyin refinery in Myanmar, with the project assigned to M/s Novatech for execution. While the Indian minister welcomed 'the happy development',[36] his visit was mired in controversy as pro-democracy activists criticised it severely, especially as it coincided with the 'Saffron Revolution'. In a statement, the protesters in Delhi said:

> It is a shame for the world's largest democracy to send its cabinet minister to Burma for reasons of exploiting more natural gas from the country at the time people and monks are protesting against the fuel shortages and economic hardships in Burma.[37]

On the question of energy cooperation between India and Myanmar in the context of China's successes in this field, Marie Lall conducted extensive studies. In her 2008 paper, she concluded that 'although

180 Present state-of-play

today Indo–Myanmar relations have improved, India has, in essence, been too slow to develop this important relationship and is now loosing [sic] out to China'.[38] Nevertheless, it is worth noting that by 2010 OVL and GAIL had reportedly invested approximately $1.33 billion in exploration and upstream activity. A portion of this would also go towards shareholding in a company laying a 110-kilometre-long offshore pipeline to bring the gas to landfall point on the Ramree Island.

Thus, pressures from the democracy camp and competition with China continued to serve as 'pull and push' factors on India's energy cooperation policy towards Myanmar.

After reforms

According to an expert view, Myanmar resources are 'estimated to be 50 million bbl of oil and 283.3 billion cum of natural gas, and the country has seen very limited exploration'.[39] Immediately after launching economic reforms, the Myanmar government accorded high priority to accelerating oil and gas production. Ministry of Energy offered 18 onshore blocks in the first licensing round in 2011–12.[40] Eight blocks were awarded, one of which was won by the Indian company, Jubilant Energy.

Subsequently, other licensing rounds were arranged in 2013 for 18 onshore and 30 offshore blocks. While old-timers OVL and GAIL drew blank, two other Indian companies scored success. Reliance Industries Ltd. (RIL) won two shallow-water blocks (i.e. M-17 and M-18) in Moattama Basin. Further, the public sector company Oil India Ltd. (and its partners – Mercator Petroleum and Oilmax Energy) secured two blocks (i.e. M-4 and YEB).[41]

Success of Indian companies in winning new energy projects during the reform era is highly encouraging. This has not been accompanied by controversy in India now, given the ongoing transition to democracy in Myanmar. Yet in comparison, China's energy footprint remains far bigger than that of India. The construction and operationalisation of twin gas and oil pipelines linking the south western shores of Myanmar to China's Yunnan province fulfils two essential purposes: carry gas from Shwe development area, and also transport gas and oil imported by China from other sources (such as the Middle East and Africa), once the deep sea port at Kyaukphyu becomes ready. This will help China to skip the longer route through the Strait of Malacca, providing enormous strategic advantage to the Asian giant. The gas pipeline became operational in 2013 and the oil pipeline was ready and waiting to be made operational in January 2015.[42]

5 Development cooperation

The Indian government extended a number of general and project-specific credit lines to Myanmar in the last decade. In 2012, New Delhi placed the total value of past development cooperation assistance at $1.2 billion.[43] A new concessional Line of Credit of $500 million was made available subsequently. Projects executed by Indian companies in recent years covered a variety of sectors such as roads, railways, telecommunication, automotive, energy and remote sensing. RITES, a public sector company, assisted Myanmar in improving its railway transport system. Indian Space Research Organisation (ISRO) set up and subsequently upgraded a data processing centre for remote sensing applications. Tata Motors set up a turbo-truck assembly plant with assistance from a Line of Credit by the Indian government. Earlier, a project for high-speed link in 32 Myanmar cities was completed by the telecommunication company, Telecommunications Consultants India Ltd. (TCIL).

Judging by the joint statement of May 2012, it was evident that the two governments reviewed candidly the status of big-ticket projects. Hydroelectric power projects at Tamanthi and Shwezaye in the Chindwin river valley, which were under discussion, study and investigation for over two decades, were apparently abandoned. Focus in recent years has been on two flagship projects. The first is the Kaladan Multi-modal Transport project for which construction commenced in December 2010. It aims to link Kolkata and other East Indian ports through coastal shipping to Sittwe on the Arakan coast in Myanmar and provide further connection through the Kaladan river route and road to Mizoram on the Indian side. It was expected that the port and river-related components of this project would be completed in 2014, but the road link to the Indian side might take another two or three years. The second is the Trilateral Highway project, which aims to link Moreh in Manipur to Mae Sot in Thailand through Myanmar. It has been under execution for many years, and its completion is now expected in 2017.

Other important projects include Rhi-Tiddim road project, which relates to the development of 80-km long road in Myanmar connecting Rhi to Tiddim. The upgradation of 160-km long Tamu-Kalewa-Kalay (TKK) road was continuing. The ground-breaking ceremony for construction of the Myanmar Institute of Information Technology (MIIT) complex in Mandalay took place in June 2014. The Indian 'mentor' for this institution is the Indian Institute of Information Technology (IIIT), Bangalore. The government of Myanmar completed

182 Present state-of-play

construction of the Advanced Centre for Agricultural Research and Education (ACARE) in Yezin and it was expected to be operationalised in early 2015. Rice Bio Park, also in Yezin, would serve as a training and demonstration centre for conversion of rice biomass into 'market driven products'. Besides, the upgradation of Yangon Children Hospital and Sittwe General Hospital proceeded in accordance with agreed plans. Assistance was also provided to establish language laboratories and e-resource centres at the ministry of foreign affairs in Naypyitaw and at its branch office in Yangon.[44]

Reviewing recent interactions, three key points need to be made here. First, India's Lines of Credit became substantial in quantum in view of Myanmar's needs and its growing importance for India. Second, in earlier years, emphasis was laid on expanding connectivity, mainly through port and road construction as well as upgradation. Third, while choosing new projects, special attention was accorded to capacity building and skill development in IT, agriculture and health care areas.

6 HRD cooperation

Human resource development (HRD) and capacity building emerged as a point of principal focus in recent years. There has been substantial support by the Indian government for strengthening Myanmar's human resource capacity. Through concerted efforts and guided by a long-term vision, the two governments collaborated successfully to establish and operate India–Myanmar Centres relating to enhancement of IT skills, entrepreneurship development, English language training and industrial training. They showed their worth through their popularity in Myanmar and their ability to train hundreds of young people every year. This innovative approach demonstrated the huge potential for further cooperation in this domain. The current stress on increasing cooperation in the select sectors by building new institutions and upgrading the existing ones was particularly helpful to Myanmar.

In this context, initiatives covered training for government officials, assistance under the ITEC programme as well as the TCS and ICCR scholarship schemes. In 2011–12, Myanmar was given 185 ITEC slots, 75 TCS slots, 10 ICCR GCSS slots, 10 MGCSS slots and 15 AYUSH slots. During the prime minister's visit, it was announced that, in keeping with India's commitment to developing human resource capacity in Myanmar, the number of training slots under the ITEC programme would be doubled from the current 250 to 500. Besides, India also offered 24 police training courses for Myanmar police personnel annually. India instituted ten research fellowships for Myanmar researchers for joint research in Indian universities under the cooperation programme in the science and technology sector. The first fellowship was awarded for research at IIT, Indore.[45] Moreover, training programmes in parliamentary procedures and practices have been conducted by the Bureau of Parliamentary Studies and Training for members and officials of Myanmar's parliament since July 2012.

7 Other areas of cooperation

Cooperation in other areas is also an important pillar, notable for its diversity and capability in terms of influencing people's lives. Education, culture, tourism and other means of strengthening people-to-people relations have been employed with imagination and vigour in order to deepen Myanmar–India friendship. Media exchanges and civil society contacts too have been promoted.

Tourism promotion and expansion of transport links received added attention. An Air Services Agreement was signed in May 2012 to enhance direct air connectivity between India and Myanmar. India's ministry of civil aviation gave the green light to SpiceJet to operate a daily flight on the Delhi–Dhaka–Yangon sector. Air India already flies twice a week on the Kolkata–Yangon–Kolkata sector. In October 2014, the Shipping Corporation of India commenced a direct container shipping service between India and Myanmar.[46]

The role and contribution of the Indian Diaspora in Myanmar should also be factored in. Over the years, Persons of Indian Origin (PIOs) did not receive fair treatment by the Myanmar government. Through sustained dialogue and cooperation at the government level, efforts should be continued to address their grievances. Government and business level relations have a chance to get real momentum only when people-to-people links are revitalised. In the reform era, both sides have an unprecedented opportunity to carry this cooperation forward in a decisive manner.

In May 2012, top leaders of the two countries emphasised 'the centrality of culture' through increased cooperation for education, capacity building and people-to-people relations. India and Myanmar share close cultural ties. There is a deep sense of kinship, particularly amongst the Buddhist community, given India's association with the

184 Present state-of-play

Buddha's life. Cultural performances by Indian troupes in Myanmar have been organised on a regular basis. Myanmar troupes have regularly participated in South Asian and ASEAN cultural events in India. A host of events were organised in Yangon and Mandalay to commemorate the 150th birth anniversary of Rabindranath Tagore.[47] The Cultural Exchange Programme for 2012–15 was signed during the prime minister's visit. India has been assisting Myanmar in the restoration and conservation of the famous Ananda Temple in Bagan.[48] An international conference on Buddhist cultural heritage was jointly organised in Yangon in December 2012. The conference was inaugurated by the vice president of Myanmar and the minister of external affairs of India. In an earlier chapter, reference was made to the development of people-to-people exchanges, especially the structured efforts that began, in 2013, to facilitate regular discussions between the strategic communities.

Indian authorities responded promptly to assist Myanmar in humanitarian relief operations, following natural calamities like Cyclone Nargis in 2008 and the earthquake in Shan state in 2010. Relief materials, medical assistance, supplies for rehabilitation work, biomass gasifiers, solar torches and lanterns were arranged. Sixteen damaged transformers were replaced and a special grant was made available to repair the Shwedagon Pagoda complex in Yangon. Assistance for relief and reconstruction work in the quake-affected zone was provided to finance reconstruction of schools.

In August 2012, a grant was extended to the Myanmar government as India's assistance towards the relief and rehabilitation of victims of the violence in the Rakhine state. The external affairs minister also gave assistance for community centres and schools in the Rakhine state, during his visit to Myanmar in December 2012.

Final picture

Projects of various kinds represent a vital dimension of bilateral cooperation. Table 6.7 shows the relevant details.

The preceding account makes it amply clear that India–Myanmar relations have been marked by considerable substance, much diversity and growing momentum. It was also apparent at the beginning of 2015 that while government-to-government ties registered significant progress, business-to-business exchanges were moving forward rather slowly, and people-to-people interaction also needed a bigger boost through imaginative and sustained action.

Table 6.7 Recent government of India-assisted developmental projects in Myanmar

S. No.	Project	Approx. value in Rs Crore (round off)	Approx. value in US$ million (1US$=INR 60) (round off)	Under implementation (UI) or completed (C)
1	Kaladan Multi-modal Transit Transport Project (KIVITTP)	1,842	307	UI
2	Tamu-Kalewa-Kalay Road (TKK) upgradation + 71 bridges	65 crore for TKK road. Feasibility report under preparation by consultants for 71 bridges	11 million. Feasibility report under preparation by consultants for 71 bridges	UI
3	Trilateral Highway Project (Kalewa–Yagyi road segment)	Feasibility report under preparation by consultants	Feasibility report under preparation by consultants	UI
4	Rhi-Tiddim Road Project	298	50	UI
5	Myanmar Institute of Information Technology (MITT), Mandalay	186	31	UI
6	Advanced Centre for Agricultural Research and Education (ACARE), Yezin	48	8	UI
7	Rice Bio Park, Yezin	9	2	UI
8	Upgradation of Yangon Children Hospital and Sittwe General Hospital	41	7	UI
9	Upgradation of Monywa General Hospital, Sagaing	12	2	UI
10	Industrial Training Centre, Pakokku and Industrial Training Centre, Myingyan	34	6	C

(Continued)

Table 6.7 (Continued)

S. No.	Project	Approx. value in Rs Crore (round off)	Approx. value in US$ million (1US$=INR 60) (round off)	Under implementation (UI) or completed (C)
11	Border Areas Development Project (Chin State and Naga Self-Administered Zone in Myanmar)	150 crore (Rs 30 crore every year for five years at 1US$ = Rs 60)	25 million ($5 million every year for five years)	UI
12	Language Laboratories and E-Resource Centre, Ministry of Foreign Affairs	2	0.3	UI
13	India-Myanmar Center for Enhancement of Information Technology Skills (IMCEITS)	2	0.3	C
14	Cardamom Plantation Project	0.06	0.1	UI
15	Reconstruction and Reconciliation assistance in Rakhine State	6	1	C
16	Restoration of Ananda Temple, Bagan	20	3	UI
17	Supply of tractors and agricultural machinery to Myanmar	50	10	C
18	Supply of 20 Bio mass gasifiers	0.5		C
19	Construction of ten food storage silos	10.0	2.0	C

Notes

1. Outlay/costs for Kalewa-Yagyi project, upgradation of bridges TKK project depend on Feasibility reports/DPR/EPC.
2. Myanmar India Entrepreneurship Development Centre ($0.3 million) and Myanmar India Center English Language Training ($ 0.1 million in 2009) were undertaken under initiative for ASEAN integration.
3. Costs are based on MoU/DPRs/commitments declared/agreements signed.

Source: Ministry of External Affairs, New Delhi

Notes

1 *The New Light of Myanmar*, 30 May 2012, http://www.burmalibrary.org/docs13/NLM2012-05-30.pdf (accessed on 25 October 2013).

2 Renaud Egreteau, 'India's Unquenched Ambitions in Burma', in *Burma or Myanmar? – The Struggle for National Unity*, L. Dittmer, (ed.), Singapore: World Scientific, 2010, pp. 296–7. 'India has always had a peculiar relationship with its Burmese neighbor. . . . The Burmese frequently have been bitterly suspicious of India and the Indians. . . . On the other hand, Indians have generally had a rather positive image of Burma, which has traditionally been perceived as a part of India's wider sphere of influence.'

3 Sreeradha Datta, 'What Ails the Northeast: An Enquiry into The Economic Factors', Strategic Analysis, IDSA, April 2001, Vol. XXV, No. 1, pp.73–87, and 'Security of India's Northeast: External Linkages' Strategic Analysis, IDSA, November 2000, Vol. XXIV, No. 8, pp. 1495–516. For a detailed diagnosis of challenges facing the people of North East, please refer to these two excellent articles.

4 Sanjoy Hazarika, 'Ethnic Conflict and Civil Society in the Northeast', *The Little Magazine*, 25 June 2012. The author stated: 'The entire network of cadres, recruits, informers and political leaders is based on extortion and extraction: extortion from business houses and petty traders, from professionals, contractors and politicians. Few are spared.' http://www.littlemag.com/bloodsport/sanjoyhazarika.html (accessed on 5 October 2014).

5 For further details on the economy of the North East Region, please see 'India's North-East: Diversifying Growth Opportunities', Report by Indian Chamber of Commerce, https://www.pwc.in/en_IN/in/assets/pdfs/publications/2013/north-east_summit-2013.pdf (accessed on 7 October 2014).

6 Gorky Chakraborty, 'North East Vision 2020: A Reality Check', Institute of Development Studies Kolkata (IDSK). In this detailed assessment, the author observed: 'Mere lip service regarding border trade and showcasing North East as the arrowhead of the much hyped Look East Policy will mean "little" to the people in the region if their growing realisation suggests that under the present scenario securing the pathway for trade (with only few commodities from the region) is prime for the Indian state, while ameliorating their condition happens to be the secondary agenda.' www.idsk.edu.in/common/file/oc-33.pdf (accessed on 31 August 2014).

7 *The Hindu*, 16 August 2012.

8 'Bulk SMSes: Pakistan denies role in hatemongering: 74 websites blocked for objectionable content'. *The Economic Times*, 20 August 2012, http://articles.economictimes.indiatimes.com/2012-08-20/news/33287779_1_home-ministry-assam-chief-minister-tarun-gogoi (accessed on 26 April 2015).

9 Sushil K. Pillai, 'The Invisible Country Ethnicity & Conflict Management in Myanmar', South Asia Terrorism Portal (SATP), http://www.satp.org/satporgtp/publication/faultlines/volume7/Fault7-GenPillaiF.htm (accessed on 24 September 2014).

10 The chapter 'Myanmar Situation and India's Northeast' in Rakhee Bhattacharya's book, on *Northeastern India and its Neighbours: Negotiating Security and Development*, New Delhi: Routledge, 2015, presents an excellent and updated analysis.

188 Present state-of-play

11 Medha Chaturvedi, 'Myanmar's Ethnic Divide: The Parallel Struggle', Institute of Peace and Conflict Studies, June 2012. The author added: 'There is a need for inclusion and participation of all ethnic groups in the country's affairs and giving them the status of stakeholders.' http://www.ipcs.org/pdf_file/issue/SR131-SEARP-Medha.pdf (accessed on 24 September 2014).

12 For details on this point, interested readers may refer to 'India's Moment with Myanmar: The Promise and Challenges of a New Relationship', A Report by Aspen Institute of India, http://www.anantaaspencentre.in/pdf/India_moment_myanmar.pdf (accessed on 26 April 2015).

13 Shyam Saran, 'Key Recommendations of the Brainstorming Meeting on Myanmar organised by Research and Information System for Developing Countries', *RIS*, 13 April 2012.

14 Mani Shankar Aiyar, 'India Would Be More Comfortable with a Democratic Regime', India-Burma Relations: Trends and Developments (1990–2011), New Delhi: Burma Centre Delhi, 2011, p. 19.

15 Subir Bhaumik, 'Look East through Northeast: Challenges and Prospects for India', ORF Occasional Paper #51 (June 2014), Observer Research Foundation, p. 30. The author stated: 'India needs to pursue its Look East policy through Northeast to boost the region's economy by allowing it to leverage the neighbourhood markets.'

16 Speech by the President of India Pranab Mukherjee to the Members of Arunachal Pradesh Legislative Assembly, 29 November 2013, http://presidentofindia.gov.in/sp291113-1.html (accessed on 30 November 2013).

17 Concerning the following section, I have drawn material from a special briefing given to us by officials of the Ministry of External Affairs (MEA) on the occasion of ICWA delegation's visit to Myanmar in March 2013.

18 List of Agreements is provided in Appendix 1.

19 (i) Briefs on Foreign Relations, Myanmar, MEA official website, http://www.mea.gov.in/#&panel1-1 (accessed on 9 October 2014).
(ii) According to *CIA the World Factbook*, the total length of land boundaries of Myanmar is 6,522 km. The breakup is: Thailand – 2,416 km; China – 2,129 km; India – 1,468 km; Laos – 238 km; and Bangladesh – 271 km. https://www.cia.gov/library/publications/the-world-factbook/geos/bm.html (accessed on 5 October 2014).
(iii) Other sources such as *Border Darshan* and *The Indian Page* maintain that the length of India–Myanmar boundary is 1,643 km. Its breakup is: Arunachal Pradesh – 520 km, Manipur – 398 km, Mizoram-510 km and Nagaland 215 km. http://archive.is/6KkUu (accessed on 15 May 2012).

20 See 'After China, Myanmar Intrudes into Indian Territory, Attempts Fencing along Manipur Border', *The Indian Express*, 28 August 2013, and 'Are India and Burma Likely to Resolve the Border Issues Soon?' in *The Asian Age*, 4 September 2013.

21 For further details, please refer to the website of India's Ministry of Home Affairs, http://mha.nic.in/northeast_new?&fontsize=small (accessed on 27 October 2013).

22 'Myanmar Army Intrudes into Manipur Border Village, Tries to Set Up Base Camp' *India Today*, 28 August 2013.

23 Iboyaima Laithangbram, 'Manipur Committee on Myanmar Border Issues to Submit Report on Monday', *The Hindu*, 8 September 2013.

24 This subject has figured in official bilateral discussions from the times of U Nu and Ne Win as demonstrated by MEA's annual reports pertaining to the 1950s and 1960s.

25 See the comments by External Affairs Minister Sushma Swaraj in the previous chapter.

26 Joint Statement, http://www.mea.gov.in/bilateral-documents.htm?dtl/19893/Joint_Statement_by_India_and_Myanmar_on_the_State_visit_of_Prime_Minister_of_India_to_Myanmar (accessed on 5 June 2012).

27 'India and Myanmar Sign Memorandum of Understanding on Border Cooperation', Ministry of External Affairs (May 10, 2014), http://www.mea.gov.in/press-releases.htm?dtl/23315/India+and+Myanmar+sign+Memorandum+of+Understanding+on+Border+Cooperation (accessed on 31 August 2014).

28 'India–Myanmar Naval Diplomacy', *The Indian Express*, 11 March 2013.

29 Press Release, Embassy of India, Yangon, http://www.indiaembassyyangon.net/index.php?option=com_content&view=article&id=146:press-release-goodwill-visit-of-three-indian-navy-ships&catid=28&Itemid=132&lang=en (accessed on 26 April 2015).

30 Lavina Lee, 'Myanmar's Transition to Democracy: New Opportunities or Obstacles for India?' *Contemporary Southeast Asia*, Vol. 36, No. 2 (2014), p. 304: 'Overall, India's economic engagement has been impressive in terms of aspiration and vision, but poor on implementation.'

31 V.S. Seshadri, 'Transforming Connectivity Corridors between India and Myanmar into Development Corridors', Research and Information System for Developing Countries (RIS), New Delhi: RIS, 2014. For further details, see pp. 37–56.

32 From my personal notes.

33 Subir Bhaumik, 'Look East policy: India Underperforming Its Role in Myanmar', *The Economic Times*, 2 October 2013. The article reported, 'Total foreign investment (FDI) in Myanmar crossed $43 billion in August 2013, according to the Myanmar Investment Commission.' It further stated: 'India's investment in Myanmar is now around $273.5 million. It is expected to soar to $2.6 billion over the next few years.' http://articles.economictimes.indiatimes.com/2013-10-02/news/42617389_1_foreign-investment-total-trade-volume-china (accessed on 30 November 2013).

34 For details, please see the official website of ONGC Videsh Ltd., http://www.ongcvidesh.com/assets/cis-far-east/ (accessed on 26 April 2015).

35 Ibid.

36 Press Release, Press Information Bureau, 24 September 2007, http://pib.nic.in/release/rel_print_page.asp?relid=31405 (accessed on 28 September 2014).

37 'Myanmar Activists Protest Murli Deora's Visit', Reuters, 24 September 2007, http://in.reuters.com/article/2007/09/24/idINIndia-29693820070924 (accessed on 28 September 2014).

38 Marie Lall, 'India–Myanmar Relations – Geopolitics and Energy in Light of the New Balance of Power in Asia' ISAS Working Paper No. 29, 2 January 2008, http://www.burmalibrary.org/docs09/Geopolitics&Energy-Lall-red.pdf (accessed on 30 November 2013).

39 'Myanmar Awards Exploration Blocks', *Oil & Gas Journal*, 26 March 2014, http://www.ogj.com/articles/2014/03/myanmar-awards-exploration-blocks.html (accessed on 28 September 2014).

40 'Exploring Opportunities: New Oil and Gas Blocks Continue to Attract International Companies', The Report: Myanmar 2014, Energy, Oxford Business Group, http://www.oxfordbusinessgroup.com/news/exploring-opportunities-new-oil-and-gas-blocks-continue-attract-international-companies (accessed on 28 September 2014).

41 'Myanmar Awards Exploration Blocks', *Oil & Gas Journal*, 26 March 2014, http://www.ogj.com/articles/2014/03/myanmar-awards-exploration-blocks.html (accessed on 28 September 2014).

42 Hereward Holland, 'In Myanmar, China's Scramble for Energy Threatens Livelihoods of Villagers', *National Geographic*, 5 September 2014, http://news.nationalgeographic.com/news/energy/2014/09/140905-myanmar-china-burma-drilling-oil-energy-asia-petroleum/ (accessed on 28 September 2014).

43 Refer to para 21 of the joint statement at MEA website, http://www.mea.gov.in/bilateral-documents.htm?dtl/19893/Joint_Statement_by_India_and_Myanmar_on_the_State_visit_of_Prime_Minister_of_India_to_Myanmar (accessed on 5 June 2012).

44 *Source*: The useful website of the Indian Embassy in Yangon.

45 This information has been compiled from official documents.

46 *The Economic Times*, 4 October 2014.

47 'Spotting Signs of a Political Thaw', *The Myanmar Times*, 12–18 September 2011. This event, hosted by the Indian Embassy in Yangon, was attended by Aung San Suu Kyi as the reform period began in Myanmar.

48 'India to Renovate Temple in Myanmar', *IANS*, 21 June 2011, http://archaeologynewsnetwork.blogspot.in/2011/06/india-to-renovate-temple-in-myanmar.html#.VTzUx5PCZKo (accessed on 26 April 2015).

Chapter 7

India–Myanmar–China triangle

> To the surprise of Beijing the Myanmar government carried out major political reforms which China did not anticipate. . . . However, Myanmar still has to attach importance to its big neighbour because of its traditional ties of friendship dating back many centuries. . . . India is now gaining momentum in its relations with Myanmar mainly also to counter the influence of China and loosen the grip which it has on Myanmar.
>
> – U Nyunt Maung Shein[1]

The year was 2002. Within a few weeks of the presentation of credentials to Senior General Than Shwe, chairman SPDC, the author received an invitation for lunch with Foreign Minister Win Aung. We learnt that only four persons would attend it: the foreign minister and his wife, the Indian ambassador and his wife. The venue was the guest house of the ministry of foreign affairs, located adjacent to our residence, 'India House', in Yangon.

My wife and I arrived a few minutes before the scheduled time, picking up the Burmese habit of showing respect to the host. Win Aung and Daw San Yone stood at the entrance to welcome us, with a smile and unfailing courtesy. We ascended a flight of stairs and took our places in a small cosy room. The host and hostess were gracious; the hospitality was warm and generous; and the atmosphere was very friendly and relaxed. This was Burmese diplomacy at its best, designed to sensitise a newcomer to the military-ruled Myanmar and its myriad mysteries. The government's keen interest to strengthen relations with India and Win Aung's wish to play a personal, pro-active role in the process came through clearly.

But what the foreign minister stated right at the outset was perhaps the most important of all the messages he conveyed on that day. 'This', he said, referring to the exclusive lunch with the foreign minister and his wife, 'is reserved for ambassadors of only two countries – China and India, our two most important neighbours'.

Clearly the triangle involving India, Myanmar and China is a key to understanding the substance of Myanmar's foreign policy as well as India–Myanmar relations.

The notion of a triangle composed of the three countries may not be as pertinent in Beijing, but it has always mattered to Delhi.[2] It certainly weighs heavily with the Burmese at all levels. Prime Minister U Nu famously depicted Burma as a country 'hemmed in like a tender gourd among the cacti'.[3] The celebrated author, Thant Myint-U, chose to devote his recent book to this concept, calling it *Where China Meets India: Burma and the New Crossroads of Asia*.[4]

Through the ages, the perception in Myanmar has been that their country, surrounded by two giant neighbours in the west and the north, should watch out carefully for the preservation of its security, territorial integrity and other interests. If not handled properly, these neighbours could pose serious threats, but if tackled wisely, they could be a source of valuable support and assistance. Traditionally the fundamental approach of authorities in Myanmar has been to engage in a balancing exercise between relations with China and with India.[5] They may not have always succeeded in their endeavours, but that is the goal policymakers strive for. They are aware that the operation of the said triangle depends not only on them but also on the development of India–China relations as well as developments in the larger region surrounding the three countries. Hence both a focussed and broad perspective are essential to comprehend the changing dynamics of this triangle.

Myanmar–China relations: evolution

It is noteworthy that the triangle is not static; it has been susceptible to fluctuations. Evidently its evolution through history is remembered much more in Myanmar than in the other two countries.[6] The impact of Indian and Chinese cultures on Burma through history has been a subject of immense interest.[7] Its faith, Buddhism, came from India, whereas cultural influences came from both India and China. Burma suffered many invasions from the north, and its kings carried out several attacks in the west.[8] Hence the tendency to fear the northern neighbour and to consider friendship with the western neighbour as an easier possibility has always been a part of the nation's mindset.[9]

This blend of fear of China and kindly sentiments towards India came into a sharp focus immediately after Burma's independence when the newly installed government of Prime Minister U Nu confronted a near mortal threat from rebels comprising various ethnic groups, Communist factions and some units of the army. Rangoon turned towards New Delhi for urgent help. Jawaharlal Nehru's bold decision to supply much-needed arms saved the first democratic government of Burma, denying an early victory to Communist forces that received inspiration, if not assistance, from the north.

In the years after independence, Burma showed activism in nurturing cordial ties with China. With India's acquiescence, it became the first non-communist country in the world to grant recognition to the People's Republic of China. Subsequently the two countries, Burma and China, were engaged in a peculiar tango that saw them resolving their border disputes in an exemplary fashion, a sphere in which India and China failed. On the other hand, the Communist Party of Burma (CPB) continued to be used by China as a tool to destabilise Burma. Rangoon took clear-cut and firm diplomatic measures to oppose the presence of remnants of Nationalist China's troops on its territory which enjoyed US backing, fearing that their activities would invite an invasion by Communist China.

Throughout Ne Win's years in power, he took care to cultivate China, a country he visited 12 times during his 26-year rule. In contrast, under him Burma's relations with India were cordial but they lacked substance, despite his warm ties with Indira Gandhi. It is notable that Ne Win took numerous harsh measures that led to the expulsion of a huge number of Indians from Burma. He closed Burma's doors to the world, but he just stopped short of shutting them totally on its immediate neighbours. In other words, he strove to maintain limited interaction with Delhi and Beijing, which was conducted through him and his government only, not through the party or the people.

Burma had to devise its own clever ways to deal with the CPB, which caused immeasurable trouble to the government with full support and connivance of Beijing. Ne Win was denounced by Radio Peking as a 'contra-revolutionary, fascist and reactionary', as mentioned by Bertil Lintner.[10] China, driven by fervour of the Cultural Revolution, felt no hesitation in pressing the CPB to stir trouble by staging demonstrations and fuelling insurgency in Burma. The nadir was reached in June 1967 when reaction came in the form of attacks by Burmese on Chinese community members and their properties. Attempted attacks and demonstrations in front of the Chinese Embassy in Rangoon were

194 India–Myanmar–China triangle

followed by similar but larger demonstrations against the Burmese Embassy in Peking. In 1968, a large force composed of Burmese communists that enjoyed Chinese armed support captured a part of Burmese territory in the northeast. 'It was nothing less than an invasion from China.'[11] Ne Win steadily curbed CPB without attracting China's wrath. Eventually the CPB ceased to be a potent political factor only when it was disbanded in 1989.[12]

Hence, while the 1950s were largely a happy time for China–Burma relations, the next decade and half recorded marked deterioration, marked by ill-will, bitterness and disappointment that spilled over to the people's level. From the late 1970s, as radicalism in China subsided, China–Burma relations began returning to an even keel, displaying mutual pragmatism. Deng Xiaoping's visit in 1978 did much to restore cordiality and warmth as he withdrew considerable support to the CPB, thus paving the way for what eventually became a relationship between *Pauk-Phaw* (cousins or kinsfolk).[13] Taking an overall view of the pre-military rule period, Josef Silverstein observed: 'Burma has demonstrated that it can live alongside a powerful neighbour and pursue an independent policy in the face of pressures from across the border.'[14] Throughout the 1980s, the Ne Win government seemed to work harder on relations with China than with India. This trend gathered momentum once the military rule replaced his government.

Following Ne Win's departure from the political scene and with the commencement of direct military rule, first under SLORC and then under SPDC, an entirely new and unprecedented situation was created. The military's ruthless crackdown on the pro-democracy movement in 1988–89 and the rejection of the electoral verdict in 1990 heralded a new era in Burma's relations with the international community.[15] Western governments and civil society responded with unbridled criticism, stern measures and sanctions against the military regime for suppressing the people's democratic urges and violation of human rights. The West was not alone but was largely joined by others, including India, Japan, Australia and other neighbours. Burma's isolation was now complete. This complex situation coincided with a similar phenomenon in China where the government launched its own repressive policy against the people with the crackdown at Tiananmen Square in June 1989. In effect, therefore, as the 1980s ended and the next decade began, both governments found themselves under severe international censure. Finding themselves in the same uncomfortable corner, they simply moved closer to each other in order to face together a hostile world.

Thus began the period of the most enticing opportunities during which China strove to develop and expand its relationship with Myanmar. The period from 1988 to 2010 was the time when bilateral relations blossomed rapidly, deepening Yangon's dependence on China. Nevertheless, it is worth underlining that the country did not completely abandon its policy of balancing China and India even during this phase. It explains why India's Myanmar policy, after its review and revision in 1992–93, received an increasingly positive response, resulting in slow but steady growth of understanding and cooperation between Myanmar and India. However, during the 1990s India–Myanmar relations did suffer from their own quota of ups and downs because India's revised policy was subjected to many contradictory, internal pulls and pressures. This situation improved considerably from the year 2000 onwards, resulting in stronger growth of India–Myanmar cooperation.

Undertaking a detailed comparison of the policies of China and India towards Myanmar, Le Chenyang argued that Myanmar had the 'same importance' for the two countries 'in both the geopolitical and geo-economic sense'.[16] He identified access to the Indian Ocean, stability in border areas, energy security, economic cooperation and maintaining friendly relations with other developing countries as China's objectives.[17] He explained that strengthening relations with Southeast Asian countries, containing China's influence, solving the ethnic minority issue in the North-Eastern states and obtaining access to gas and oil were India's objectives in Myanmar. Evaluating the success of China and India in achieving their objectives, the scholar drew the conclusion that China's policy showed 'a high degree of consistency', while India's policy went through three phases: 'criticism and opposition from 1988 to 1992, normalizing relations form 1993 to 2000, and comprehensive cooperation since 2002'.[18]

Against the above backdrop, President Thein Sein's broad approach on foreign policy, neighbourhood relations and particularly ties with India and China should be examined critically. Many determinants of the policy remain unchanged, but new factors entered the calculus. Geography has ordained that Myanmar shares a much longer border with China than India. Ethnicity is a common but complex bond. Kachins, living in the border region adjacent to China, have been engaged in armed insurgency against the Myanmar government, whereas the tribes in India–Myanmar border region, ranging from Kachins, Nagas, Kukis and Mizos, have had more grievances against authorities in India than those in Myanmar. The result, as viewed from Myanmar, is the prevalence of a mixture of nefarious activities causing concern rather than outright insurgency in tribal areas in the west. Clearly during recent years, Myanmar's north was much more disturbed than the west. Hence, while the Myanmar Army fought against armed Kachin groups, the refrain of the two governments, India and Myanmar, has been to expand trade and connectivity at the people's level in their border region. But, it should also be noted that China secured much greater success in expanding border trade and connectivity with Myanmar than what India achieved.

According to Myanmar's thinking, both neighbours and indeed other foreign powers are perceived to be craving for the country's natural resources – oil, gas, minerals, jade and precious stones, teak, rice and agricultural produce, and even land (in case of the Chinese). Hence the tendency to be wary and cautious may be considered as another determinant. Further, Myanmar's innate impulse for striking a balance remains relevant.[19] Most importantly, leaders and policymakers seemed engaged in reviewing and internalising geopolitical and geostrategic implications of the change in Southeast and East Asia that began from about 2009. This related to the steady rise of China, its impressive economic growth and massive increase in military expenditure, its aggressive behaviour towards several of its neighbours, especially on the South China and East China issues, as well as the adverse reactions within the region, and the robust response by the US in the shape of its 'pivot' and later 'rebalancing' towards Asia. Naypyitaw demonstrated, through its calibrated policy on China, that it had proceeded with a blend of caution and resilience in dealing with its northern neighbour, while ensuring continuous support and assistance for its newly launched reform process from the western world and others. Recent years have, therefore, contributed to situating the India–Myanmar–China triangle within the larger geostrategic matrix of the Asia-Pacific Region or, to use the latest phrase, the Indo-Pacific Region.

Key facets

In the past quarter of a century (1988–2014), Myanmar–China relations have registered progress but also a few setbacks.[20] Ties with China represent Myanmar's most comprehensive and multidimensional relationship with a foreign country. Our intention here is not to detail facts and figures but to pinpoint key facets of the relationship as it has emerged today.

Firstly, as many scholars have pointed out, strategic and development considerations drive China's long-term vision of its relationship with Myanmar. Accelerated development of central and western China, especially the Yunnan province, is seen as contingent on breaking through the subregion's landlocked situation by securing a permanent access to the Indian Ocean through Myanmar's territory.[21] That this would give to China immense strategic and security advantages vis-à-vis India and other major rivals has been quite evident. Whether development or security is the principal motivation may be debatable, but what is beyond doubt is that both goals would be served through China's success in building and maintaining an extensive network of road, rail, gas and oil pipelines connecting its southern border to Myanmar's south-western coast through a multipurpose north–south corridor running through Myanmar. Li Chenyang stressed that 'Myanmar is China's best shortcut to the Indian Ocean'.[22] S.D. Muni too placed importance on this factor, calling it 'access and strategic depth'.[23] With the gas pipeline already operational[24] and the oil pipeline expected to be operational in January 2015, China is clearly set to take major strides in promoting its triple interests: energy security, economic development and strategic advantage.[25] The economic impact of pipelines will be far reaching, considering their area coverage.[26]

Second, proximity in the political and diplomatic domain is the basis of the relationship. In the military era, both sides depicted it as a relationship between 'cousins'. Mention of this phrase is made less frequently at present. High-level visits including at the level of heads of state and government were regular and frequent then. This is markedly less so now, especially from the Chinese side. In his tenure so far, Thein Sein visited China four times, but the Chinese have not reciprocated these visits.[27] After Thein Sein's first visit to China as president in May 2011, the two governments stressed that the relationship had been elevated to the level of 'a comprehensive strategic cooperative partnership'. Thein Sein described the ties with China as 'the closest and most important diplomatic relationship'.[28] At other levels, political and diplomatic interaction continued unabated.

Third, defence cooperation is the area where ties warmed up in the earlier part of the military rule, though gradually salience has shifted to economic cooperation. Myanmar's large military needed arms and equipment, training and exposure to concepts of modern warfare and counter-insurgency. Much of this type of assistance came from China. Analysts estimated that the value of arms aid received from China in the post–Ne Win period was between US$2 and 3 billion. In fact, it could be more. Smaller supplies came from other sources, including India. Gradually it dawned on the Myanmar side, according to defence analysts, that Chinese equipment was generally substandard. Language posed problems in the imparting of training. Nevertheless, on the basis of a meticulous comparative study, Muni drew the conclusion: 'On the whole, therefore, we find that the nature and extent of military cooperation between Myanmar and China is much closer than with the rest of Indo-China region.'[29]

An important motivation behind Myanmar's opening towards the West seemed to be the desire to obtain cooperation with the UK and US military. The decision by the US to permit Myanmar's participation in annual 'Cobra' exercises in Thailand; visit by India's Defence Minister A. K. Antony in January 2013, preceded by the visits of all three Service Chiefs (Army, Air and Navy) earlier; and visit of the UK Chief of Defence Staff Gen Sir David Richards to Myanmar in June 2013 were straws in the wind that indicated limitations on Myanmar's defence cooperation with China as well as the former's imperative need to diversify its military links.

Fourth, economic relations continued to flourish, despite changing political attitudes. According to Myanmar's Directorate of Investment and Company Administration, China was Myanmar's largest trade partner. China's cumulative investment in Myanmar reached the level of US$14.45 billion by 31 August 2014.[30]

At the time of writing, approximately 71 Chinese projects were being executed in Myanmar. While other foreign companies including those from India encountered difficulties in doing business and finding suitable local partners, the notable fact was that Chinese companies seemed to have cracked the formula. They had established numerous partnerships involving Myanmar's Chinese community as well as the mainstream business community, and they faced a much easier time in dealing with the political class and bureaucracy. This success stemmed probably from the two sides having worked closely during the military rule. Even now senior army officers and top politicians are said to enjoy close relations with China's business community. The nexus between the military's business enterprises and Chinese companies had been well known, although it was perhaps on the decline, with the Myanmar market having been opened for wide international competition.

Fifth, infrastructure is a very significant field where China has scored spectacular and substantive success in Myanmar. Its assistance in building roads, bridges, dams and ports as well as a large part of the new capital testified to it. This success would help China forget, to a large extent, the massive reverse and humiliation it had to suffer when President Thein Sein decided to 'suspend' the construction of Myitsone Dam project in September 2011. Later, even the project to connect China's southern border with south-western Myanmar through a railway line was quietly abandoned due to the lack of interest on part of the Myanmar government.

Sixth, cooperation in other areas – diplomatic coordination at UN and other international fora, culture, education, tourism, training, human resource development and people-to-people relations – is talked about much less, but it is of considerable significance as well. Myanmar, it seems, has always been willing to profit from China's generosity, but at the same time segments of the Myanmar elite are never tired of telling their foreign interlocutors about their unhappiness over China's growing footprint in Myanmar. In short, Myanmar is adept at playing the 'China card' in its interaction with the world, and its 'world card' (or 'US card', 'India card' etc.) in its interaction with China.

In his excellent book, Maung Aung Myoe argued that, while Myanmar–China relationship is 'an asymmetric one, tilted in favour in Beijing', Myanmar has displayed skill in playing the 'China card' and it 'still enjoys considerable space in her conduct of foreign relations'. This scholar views Myanmar's China policy as 'located somewhere between balancing and bandwagoning. . . .' According to him, the juxtaposition of accommodating China's regional strategic interests and resisting Chinese influence and interference in Myanmar's internal affairs represent 'a hallmark of Myanmar's China policy', which is likely to remain unchanged.[31]

Finally, as regards the Chinese community and immigration of Chinese citizens into Myanmar, it should be treated as an important factor for bilateral relations. Although much of the Burmese population is of Mongoloid antecedents, Chinese and Indian communities were both minorities in the country; however, the former was seen as closer to local Burmese people. During the Ne Win era, both communities suffered – Indians because their properties and businesses were nationalised and Chinese because they were seen as the fifth column for CPB and Communist China. The subsequent period of military rule was marked by two notable developments: (i) huge immigration, legal or otherwise, of Chinese people from border areas of China into Myanmar's northern and central parts and (ii) growing integration of Myanmar's border regions with the economic infrastructure of China. For example, it was estimated that Mandalay had become 20 per cent

200　India–Myanmar–China triangle

Chinese, and Lashio, the northern city, was 50 per cent Chinese as regards the composition of their population.[32] Based on interviews in Yangon conducted in May 2001, Muni observed: 'In terms of communications, cultural structure, consumer items and currency transactions, the northern border areas are more closely integrated with Yunnan than with Yangon.'[33] This trend gained much momentum in the following decade. Increasingly the Chinese presence was seen by the local population as an economic and even cultural threat.

During a visit to Yangon, this author had an interesting conversation with a senior official. Besides expressing concern on the growing Chinese influence, he seemed particularly anxious about another issue, namely reported incidents on a large scale of Chinese groups luring, forcing or kidnapping Burmese women and arranging their migration to China for the purpose of serving as wives to one or more Chinese men. This, he underlined, was seen as a very serious and adverse phenomenon by the Myanmar people.

Important implications

At this stage, a number of implications arising from the pattern of China–Myanmar relations need to be spelt out.

China has enjoyed a rather imbalanced equation with Myanmar in the sense that throughout SLORC/SPDC era, it focused attention exclusively on the government, essentially ignoring the opposition forces clamouring for democracy. The result was that its links with the NLD and other political parties were tenuous and limited. At periodic luncheon meetings in Yangon, the Chinese ambassador and this author used to exchange notes on Myanmar's internal and external developments. Our discussions often centred on what NLD was doing and whether it had any chance of prevailing in the long term. His questions revealed not only normal diplomatic curiosity but also China's respect for India's diplomatic resilience. This flexibility allowed India to support, encourage and keep in touch with the pro-democracy movement, while continuing to strengthen its relations with the military government.

After Thein Sein's presidential tenure began, the Chinese government felt handicapped by the unidimensional approach towards political players within Myanmar, even though Aung San Suu Kyi always made it a point to say a few nice things about China and its role in her country.[34] At the beginning of the reform process some observers thought that the Chinese government would lose no time in inviting her to visit China just as invitations from all parts of the world were pouring in.

In 2011, as a former ambassador, this author suitably advised the Indian officials to invite the NLD leader to India before the Chinese invitation came through. But the invitation from Beijing did not come, and fortunately she came to India in November 2012. Later, when this author visited Beijing and Shanghai in late 2012, my interlocutors in the strategic community conveyed that, while they were aware of the rising importance of the NLD leader in Myanmar politics, there were few takers in the Chinese government for her visit, given (a) the intricate power transition that was underway in China at the time and (b) the political value system she represented. Suu Kyi's visit to China had not taken place till the time of this writing. Evidently, Beijing had left it largely to its ambassador in Yangon to nurture ties with her and her party. It can, therefore, be argued plausibly that New Delhi scored over Beijing when it came to managing relations with the complex polity that Myanmar is today.

Fresh insights were obtained about changing attitudes in Myanmar during the visit of the ICWA delegation to Myanmar in March 2013. Conventional narrative had not changed, which stressed that Myanmar was a country surrounded by two giant neighbours and Yangon was keen on maintaining friendly relations with both. Our Myanmar interlocutors, however, showed more freedom and self-confidence by pointing out that 'they felt anxiety about Myanmar's relations with China but not over its relations with India'. Besides, they maintained that 'there was a new recognition that the country had other options, other suitors'.[35]

Another implication concerns President Thein Sein's attitude towards China. During my tenure, the highest decision-making body, the SPDC, seemed dominated by generals who favoured close relations with China. At the very apex of the power pyramid, however, the trio of generals appeared to display divergent attitudes. Prime Minister Khin Nyunt, the No. 3, was viewed as pro-China. Vice-Senior General Maung Aye, enjoying the No. 2 spot, supported the initiative to deepen ties with India. But, the Chairman of SPDC, Senior General Than Shwe and the No. 1 in the hierarchy as well as the most powerful leader of the country, favoured maintaining a balance that involved (i) keeping up special ties with China and (ii) persevering with the initiative of opening towards India. It was the latter approach that led to Than Shwe's historic first visit to India in 2004.

At that time Thein Sein was much lower on the power ladder and his attitude towards the two most important neighbours was hardly known. However, after he became the president in 2011, his words and, more importantly, his actions showed where he stood. With

India, he followed the Maung Aye-Than Shwe line of consolidation and expansion of relations in all fields of mutual interest.[36] As far as China was concerned, he no doubt dealt them a major setback by his adverse decision on the Myitsone Dam project, but beyond that, he has been very careful in not causing any annoyance. On the US$1 billion copper mining project at Letpadaung (in Sagaing division in the north-western region) in which interests of a Chinese company were involved, he set up an investigation committee, with Suu Kyi as the chair, to inquire into local protests and the crackdown by security authorities. In due course, the committee expressed its support for the project, to the relief of both Beijing and Naypyitaw. To secure a cease-fire agreement with Kachin Independence Army (KIA), his government showed little hesitation in accepting mediation by China. This was eventually signed in May 2013. Finally, while executing his 'pivot' to the West, Thein Sein repeatedly stated that improving relations with the US and other Western countries was not targeted against any country, least of all China. He sincerely believed that maintaining close and cooperative relations with the northern neighbour was a goal of the highest importance for anyone who was entrusted with the responsibility of the country's foreign policy.[37]

The next point concerns a new factor that has a bearing on the triangle under discussion. It relates to Japan, a country that has impacted on Burma's modern history in multiple ways.[38] During the reform era, the Japanese government showed exceptional activism, imagination and generosity towards Myanmar, especially during the visit of Prime Minister Shinzo Abe in May 2013, which was preceded by a number of high-level visits. One of Japan's obvious motivations has been to help Myanmar reduce its dependency on China's financial resources and political support. Japan's policy towards Myanmar has been briefly evaluated in Chapter 2. It is suffice to note here, that given strained political relations between China and Japan and growing strategic partnership between India and Japan in recent years, Japan's Myanmar policy and its position on the India–Myanmar–China triangle may be viewed by many as a studied attempt to weigh in against the People's Republic of China. In Myanmar, China did not fear competition from India in the past, but the rising footprint of India, Japan and the West could be a new powerful phenomenon that Beijing can hardly ignore. But this assessment should be tempered by the apt perception that New Delhi views its relations with China and its ties with Southeast Asia in inclusive, not Cold War, terms.[39]

A critical question that needs to be answered is why the military-ruled Myanmar chose to become so deeply dependent on China, whereas during Thein Sein's rule the country found an effective way to exercise its freedom and limit its relationship with China up to a degree. Min Zin provided a convincing answer to the first part of the question by stressing: 'Burma's dependency on China is more of an unintended consequence of the junta's survival struggle than its intentions, given its marked nationalism and Sinophobia.'[40] The answer to the latter part of the query lies in the new Myanmar's capability to find other balancers such as the US, driven by its view that India alone could not balance China in Myanmar. However, writing at the time when the Kokang episode[41] was unfolding, Min Zin went on to predict that 'China will more actively promote the goal of national reconciliation in Burma but it will not likely take the lead in pressing Burma to make it happen'.[42] In fact, judging by developments in recent years, there has been very little evidence to back this prediction.[43] It is a given that China places a high degree of importance on stability in its southern neighbour. However, a considered view is that stability in Myanmar will stem only from constructive and inclusive actions by the country's government and ethnic groups rather than those of Beijing. The latter can cause instability but can hardly ensure stability in Myanmar.

During the visit of the Indian Council of World Affairs (ICWA) delegation to China in September 2013, this author obtained views of the Chinese strategic community on reforms in Myanmar and the broadening of the country's foreign policy options. In answer to the issues one raised, experts of a prestigious think tank in Beijing conveyed the following:

1. In the beginning, i.e. when the reforms began, China suffered from 'much anxiety', but 'we are now more adapted to the change'. It was noted that China could not stop the change. Besides, it did not favour Myanmar's isolation.
2. However, China felt that the change was happening on 'too wide a scale'. New problems had come up now such as the question of religious strife.
3. NLD would win the next elections. Whether Suu Kyi became the president was not important to the party; it was important only to her.
4. Military's influence would be reduced further in future.
5. Referring broadly to Indo-China states, he said that China did not want them to go in the direction of 'democratic chaos', but that too was part of political development and history. Nevertheless, they (including Myanmar) 'cannot run away from their geography, from China'. Myanmar would still rely on China's loans and investments.

204 India–Myanmar–China triangle

6. Cancellation of Myitsone project was indeed a setback for China, but it sent out a negative signal concerning Myanmar – that foreign investments were not safe there. Many anti-China nongovernmental organisations (NGOs) were active there now. The entire experience would be good for Chinese companies. They would learn to acquire transparency and good corporate practices, drawing lessons for future.
7. China, he stressed, was 'not so worried' as before about 'political diversification' in Myanmar.

Addressing the same issues, a leading figure of another Chinese think tank, based in Shanghai, observed that China was now quite used to the reform process unfolding in Myanmar. It was never in a position to prevent it. But China still enjoyed good relations with the country. Asked as to why Suu Kyi had not visited China yet, he responded: 'Maybe she feels that she would lose votes if she undertakes the visit!' This was an indirect admission that China was not quite popular in Myanmar at present. He then added that it could also be a question of timing.[44] In November 2013 there was some speculation that Suu Kyi had received an invitation and was contemplating to undertake her visit to China. Her party NLD, however, strongly denied such reports.[45] This episode indicated that all was not well with China's relations with the party, but the two sides were working to improve them. A delegation representing NLD, which was led by Nyan Win, Suu Kyi's spokesman, visited China in December 2013.

From the Indian perspective, an unmistakable consensus has existed among former policymakers as well as analysts, which underlines the importance of China's role in Myanmar as a principal factor in shaping India's post-1992 policy. J. N. Dixit,[46] former foreign secretary and Rajiv Sikri,[47] former secretary in MEA, presented plausible explanations of India's motivations.

India–China relations

The trajectory of relations between India and China has had its peculiar, fluctuating impact on Myanmar and its ties with the two big neighbours. As noted earlier, Burma at its independence felt closer to India than China. The positive phase of India's engagement with China in the 1950s – the Panchsheel phase – encompassed U Nu's Burma in a creative manner. But once the New Delhi–Peking equation came under severe stress resulting in military conflict in October 1962, it posed a difficult situation for Burma. Ne Win lost no time in moving towards neutrality and showing preference for the militarily more powerful neighbour (China) with which it already had a series of problems. Between the early 1960s and the late 1980s, the China–India estrangement was almost absolute. After the thaw began with Prime Minister Rajiv Gandhi's visit to China in December 1988, Myanmar under the post–Ne Win military rule began to increase its dependence on China.

In this backdrop, the present state of China–India relations, as showcased during President Xi Jinping's state visit to India in September 2014, merits a brief mention. In Prime Minister Narendra Modi's foreign policy calculus, East Asia has received a high priority. His visit to Japan (before Xi's arrival in India) and the agreements reached between New Delhi and Tokyo demonstrated India's inclination to deepen its economic and strategic cooperation with a technology- and capital-rich country, which faced an exceedingly assertive China. The Chinese president's discussions in Ahmedabad and New Delhi were assessed to be productive. They led to new accords on economic cooperation (e.g. collaboration for industrial parts, smart cities, railways, nuclear cooperation, among others), but they were overshadowed by a tense stand-off between the troops of the two countries on the Line of Actual Control in the Chumar region in eastern Ladakh (and in Demchok where the stand-off involved civilians). The visit thus demonstrated a whole range of opportunities and limitations of the complex relationship between Asia's two giants.

Through their joint statement, the two governments decided 'to strengthen political communication, deepen strategic thrust as well as intensity of political dialogue and consultations at all levels'. Through the Strategic Economic Dialogue they planned 'to explore new areas of cooperation in crosscutting fields', and separately to focus on increasing cooperation in other fields such as culture, tourism and people-to-people exchanges. They recognised peace and tranquillity in the border areas as 'an important guarantor for the development and continued growth of bilateral relations'. The joint statement also reflected their belief that 'the 21st century should be marked by peace, security, development and cooperation'.[48]

Delivering a public address at the special event hosted by the ICWA, President Xi Jinping stated: 'China regards good relations with neighbours as a basis for a peaceful existence and development.'[49] This, however, appeared inadequate in cutting through the wall of scepticism that exists in India in view of its past experiences and present-day monitoring of China's actions in parts of South Asia and East Asia. Nalin Surie, former Indian ambassador to China, wrote: 'The India–China relationship . . . is destined in the foreseeable future to be marked by

The triangle: recent developments

As opposed to the narrative of India–China competition in Myanmar, the potential of cooperation scenario should also be considered. Important developments relating to this scenario took place recently.

At China's initiative, the 60th anniversary of the proclamation of Panchsheel or Five Principles of Peaceful Co-existence was celebrated, with more enthusiasm and fanfare in China rather than in India and Myanmar. The climax came as top leaders of the three countries – President Xi Jinping, President Thein Sein and Vice President M. Hamid Ansari – assembled for a special commemorative event in the Great Hall of the People in Beijing on 28 June 2014. Tracing the origin of Panchsheel philosophy to Buddhism, Buddhist traditions in India and Myanmar and the views of Confucius, Ansari observed: 'It is thus evident that Panchsheel emanated from the civilizational matrix of Asia and is Asia's contribution towards building a just and democratic international order.'[51] Arguing that Panchsheel had 'overcome the test of time', President Thein Sein expressed Myanmar's confidence that it would 'play even a greater role in inter-state relations in the future'.[52]

Speaking on this occasion, President Xi Jinping stressed that it was 'no coincidence that the five principles of peaceful coexistence were born in Asia, because they embody the Asian tradition of loving peace', adding that thanks to the contributions made by the three countries – China, India and Myanmar – 'those principles are accepted in other parts of Asia and the world'.[53]

C. Raja Mohan, a respected strategic analyst, interpreted Panchsheel celebrations as the tool for China to mobilise 'regional political support . . . for a new security framework' promoted by China.[54] Two big ideas for economic cooperation involving these three countries (and others) drew special attention. The first was Bangladesh, China, India and Myanmar (BCIM) Economic Corridor and the second was Maritime Silk Route (MSR), comprising construction and renovation of a string of ports and other facilities linking China's south-eastern shores to destinations in Southeast Asia, South Asia and beyond. The first proposal received a fillip during the visit of Chinese Premier Li

Keqiang in May 2013 when China and India agreed to set up a joint study group on strengthening connectivity in the BCIM region and for closer economic, trade and people-to-people linkages. This came up for further deliberation during President Xi Jinping's visit to India in September 2014. He also publicly suggested discussions on the MSR project. It was noted that, while Myanmar showed some interest in both proposals, India was receptive to the first one and indifferent to the second.[55]

Future prospects

What is likely to be the future shape and direction of the triangle under discussion? From his detailed study, Maung Aung Myoe concluded:

> . . . if Myanmar's engagement with China in the past decades offers any lesson for future reference, it is most likely that Myanmar will be very cautious in dealing with China, because Myanmar is thoroughly convinced that China, like all other countries, will determine its policies toward Myanmar according to the calculations of her own interests.[56]

The tone and state of India–China relations will continue to exercise influence on the triangle. The relationship between Asia's two giant nations has been marked by friendship and conflict in the past, and by dialogue, cooperation, competition and rivalry in the present. Assuming this mix will continue in the coming years, China and India will remain actively engaged in competing with each other in order to expand their areas of influence in Myanmar. Naypyitaw will be happy to encourage this competition as long as it does not degenerate into a conflict or harm Myanmar's interests. India's strategic concerns and security, both in relation to defence against external attack and insurgent groups as well as imperatives concerning the socio-economic development of the North East, will remain unchanged. This guarantees Myanmar a spot of high priority in India's worldview.

Future prospects may be determined by yet another factor. Ranjit Gupta, a former ambassador, aptly argued that 'an enormous gulf remains between the relative positions of China and India in Myanmar'. Noting with satisfaction that considerable progress was achieved in the development of India–Myanmar relations since 2011, he opined that there was 'no need for India to contest China's position in Myanmar or to compete with China in Myanmar' and advised India to continue with its 'pro-active engagement' with Myanmar.[57] This may be a wise line, but the inescapable fact is that public perception, both in India and abroad, of an ongoing competition or even contest between India and China remains deep and widespread.[58] This is continuously reinforced by media.[59] India is far behind in the race, but it possesses a few valuable assets, the principal being Myanmar's traditional inclination to maintain and promote some kind of equilibrium, not parity, between Myanmar–China relations and Myanmar–India relations.[60]

During the visit of the ICWA delegation to Myanmar in March 2013, 'the China factor' inevitably came up in discussions among strategic experts as the Myanmar side expressed apprehensions about possible rivalry between India and China in Myanmar. Ambassador Shyam Saran made it amply clear that India was not interested or engaged in such a rivalry for this would not suit its interests. India sought peace and cooperation with China, both bilaterally and regionally, and it favoured a multipolar world and a multipolar Asia. He, however, stressed that India would not accept 'the unilateral assertion of dominance' by China, suggesting that this would be unacceptable to ASEAN too. While articulating their current perceptions of China–Myanmar relations, our Myanmar interlocutors stressed that they felt 'no anxiety' over Myanmar–India relations, implying that the latter should be expanded and deepened further.[61]

In this context, Renaud Egreteau and Larry Jagan made an apt suggestion in a recent work:

> Burma needs to cultivate both neighbors, find a strategic equilibrium between the two (meaning during the 2010s reducing Chinese clout, and enhancing India's role in development and capacity-building), but will most certainly resist being utilized as a pivotal state.[62]

They argued against the view of 'an inevitable China–India rivalry-in-the-making'.[63] Disagreeing with them, one would maintain that the debate is not about whether or not there is a rivalry between China and India in Myanmar, it is, in fact, about the nature, key triggers, involvement of other stakeholders, future trajectory and outcome of the rivalry.

Elaborating Myanmar's attitude towards its large neighbours, Li Chenyang observed:

> Myanmar will maintain friendly relations with China and India but will not allow either of them to have a dominant influence. Myanmar is a country with strong nationalist sentiments. Its top

leaders do not trust China and have little confidence in India. Like other Southeast countries adopting a balance-of-power strategy, Myanmar will adhere to its traditional neutral position and continue to balance its relations with China, India, ASEAN, and the Western democracies.[64]

As Thant Myint-U noted, to many people in Burma, 'India is in some ways a much more familiar place than China, in large part because of the ancient bonds of religion.' This has created 'a natural or at least historical pull towards India that perhaps is not there with China'. However, he added that it was unclear 'whether this will be a major factor going forward'.[65]

The peculiar functioning of the India–Myanmar–China triangle is likely to be affected in new ways by Myanmar's 'pivot' towards the US, EU, Japan and its other partners in East Asia. These equations have the potential to curb further growth in Myanmar's dependence on its northern neighbour. Therefore, the triangle should be viewed and assessed not in isolation but in the wider context of Myanmar's worldview since independence, and the gradual transformation of its foreign policy in recent years.

Notes

1 U Nyunt Maung Shein, 'External Players and Their Impact on Domestic Politics', Myanmar Institute of Strategic and Studies and International Studies, 20 September 2013, http://www.myanmarisis.org/index.php/research-a-publication-of-misis#s5_scrolltotop (accessed on 29 November 2013).

2 The importance of Burma for India in the context of great power relationships was perceptively visualised by Sardar Patel, India's Deputy Prime Minister and Home Minister from 15 August 1947 to 15 December 1950. In the celebrated letter dated 7 November 1950, addressed to Prime Minister Nehru, Patel observed: 'It is possible that a consideration of these matters (i.e. those pertaining to India and China) may lead us into wider question of our relationship with China, Russia, America, Britain and Burma. This, however, would be of a general nature, though some might be basically very important, e.g., we might have to consider whether we should not enter into closer association with Burma in order to strengthen the latter in its dealings with China. I do not rule out the possibility that, before applying pressure on us, China might apply pressure on Burma. With Burma, the frontier is entirely undefined and the Chinese territorial claims are more substantial. In its present position, Burma might offer an easier problem to China, and therefore, might claim its first attention.' http://www.vigilonline.com/index.php?option=com_content&task=view&id=1142&Itemid=1 (accessed on 15 July 2013).

3 Min Zin, 'China–Burma Relations: China's Risk, Burma's Dilemma', in *Burma or Myanmar?* Lowell Dittmer (ed.), Singapore: World Scientific, 2010, p. 269.
4 This reminded me of a chapter titled 'Burma: Where India and China Meet' in *Burma* by John L. Christian, 1945.
5 Rajiv Bhatia, 'Crafting a Richer India–Myanmar Partnership', *The Hindu*, 11 October 2012. 'Now curiously enough, there is talk of Myanmar playing China against India and India against China. It does not require rocket science to realize that the best policy for Myanmar is to befriend both.'
6 D. G. E. Hall, *Burma*, London: Hutchinson's University Library, 1950, p. 7. 'The Indo-Chinese Peninsula became a battle-ground between the Indian and Chinese civilizations. There was some blending, but in the long run Indian culture triumphed everywhere save in Annam and Tongking.'
7 G. E. Harvey, *Outline of Burmese History*, London: Longmans, Green and Co., 1947, p. 4. 'The Burmese are a Mongolian race, yet none of their traditions hark back to China or to Mongolian things: all hark back to India.'
8 Josef Silverstein, *Burma: Military Rule and the Politics of Stagnation*, New York: Cornell University Press, 1977, p. 170. 'Until 1954, Sino-Burmese relations were colored by the past – China's invasion and destruction of Pagan in the thirteenth century and Burma's stout defense and resistance to four invasions by the Chinese in the eighteenth century.' The memory of Burma having served as a vassal state to China but experiencing continuous success in retaining its independence as a kingdom stayed with the people and rulers throughout pre-colonial times.
9 John Silverstein, (ed.), *The Political Legacy of Aung San*, New York: Southeast Asia Program, Cornell University, 1993, pp. 146–7. Before the advent of independence, Aung San spelt out Burma's worldview in the Presidential Address at the Supreme Council Session of AFPFL in August 1946. He suggested that Burma would strive for 'closer understanding, increasing cooperation and coordination and of mutual efforts for the solution of mutual problems with nationalist India and democratic South East Asia' as well as 'contact and understanding with the rest of Asia, particularly China in our case. . . .'
10 Bertil Lintner, *Burma in Revolt: Opium and Insurgency since 1948*, Bangkok: Silkworm Books, 1999, p. 242.
11 Thant Myint-U, *Where China Meets India*, London: Faber and Faber Limited, 2011, p. 52.
12 Robert Taylor, *The State in Myanmar*, London: Hurst Publishers Ltd., 2009, p. 469. 'China from 1988 made it clear that it would not directly involve itself in Myanmar's domestic affairs.'
13 Maung Aung Myoe, *In the Name of Pauk-Phaw*, Singapore: ISEAS, 2011, p. 8. 'Myanmar reserves this term exclusively to describe her relations with China. China also accepts it.'
14 Silverstein, *Burma: Military Rule and the Politics of Stagnation*, p. 180.
15 Myoe, *In the Name of Pauk-Phaw*, p. 7. 'Chi-shad Liang, a China-watcher with a special interest in Myanmar, argues that the Sino-Myanmar relationship since 1988 has been marked by a shift from "delicate friendship" to "genuine cooperation".'
16 Li Chenyang. 'The Politics of China and India toward Myanmar', in *Myanmar/Burma: Inside Challenges, Outside Interests*, Lex Rieffel (ed.),

Washington DC: Brookings Institution Press and the Konrad Adenauer Foundation, 2010, p. 113.

17 David I. Steinberg, *Burma/Myanmar, What Everyone Needs to Know*, New York: Oxford University Press, 2010, p. 120. 'Although we can only speculate on Chinese motivation for the close relationship with the Myanmar authorities, strategic and economic issues seem paramount.'

18 Li Chenyang, 'The Politics of China and India toward Myanmar', in *Myanmar/Burma*, Rieffel (ed.), p. 124.

19 Prem Mahadevan, 'The Changing Politics and Geopolitics of Burma', *Strategic Analysis*, Vol. 37, No. 5 (September–October 2013), p. 606. 'The Thein Sein government, with the backing of the Tatmadaw leadership, seems to be adroitly exploiting the desire of both China and India to gain influence in Burma. It is maintaining a balance between the two powers by partially cooperating with each.'

20 Myoe, *In the Name of Pauk-Phaw*, p. 1. 'Myanmar's relations with China have never been easy and have been subjected to numerous strains over the years.' For a brief review of literature on Sino-Myanmar relations, see pp. 7–8.

21 Zhao Hong, *China and India Courting Myanmar for Good Relations*. EAI Background Brief No. 360, 6 December, 2007, p. i. 'Myanmar is part and parcel of China's strategic design to develop its western region. Myanmar is the only passage for China to reach South Asia from Yunnan and an important access to the Indian Ocean.'

22 Chenyang, *Myanmar/Burma*, Rieffel (ed.), p. 114. On the same page he cited Voon Phin Keong, the director of the Centre of Malaysian Chinese Studies in Kuala Lumpur: 'An outlet on the Indian Ocean would add a new dimension to China's spatial relations with the world. It would enable China to overcome its "single-ocean strategy" and to realize what would constitute a highly significant plan for a 'two-ocean strategy.'

23 S.D. Muni, *China's Strategic Engagement with the New ASEAN*, New Delhi: Institute of Defence and Strategic Studies, 2002, IDSS Monograph no. 2, p. 80. He added: 'Comprehensive use of the proposed corridor will give China a tremendous advantage in projecting its power in the Indian Ocean as well as in the South China Sea.' p. 83.

24 Energy Global, 'CNPC Announces China–Myanmar Gas Pipeline Open', 30 July 2013, http://www.energyglobal.com/news/pipelines/articles/CNPC_announces_ChinaMyanmar_natural_gas_pipeline_open.aspx#.Umdoe_66YkI (accessed on 23 October 2013).

25 H. Shivananda, 'China's Pipelines in Myanmar', IDSA Comment, Institute of Defence and Studies Analyses, 10 January 2012. For more details, see this useful document, http://www.idsa.in/idsacomments/ChinasPipelinesinMyanmar_shivananda_100112 (accessed on 23 October 2013).

26 *Myanmar Investment & Industry Information Weekly News*, June 1–7, 2013, p. 85. The oil and natural gas pipelines run in parallel and start near Kyaukphyu, run through Mandalay, Lashio and Muse and in Burma before entering China at the border city of Ruili in Yunnan Province. The oil pipeline, which eventually terminates in Kunming, capital of Yunnan province, is 771 kilometres. The natural gas pipeline will extend further from Kunming to Guizhou and Guangxi in China in China, running a total of 2,806 kilometres, http://www.gunhongmyanmar.com/assets/files/issue19-jun-1-7.pdf (accessed on 28 October 2013).

27 President Thein Sein visited China in May 2011, September 2012, April 2013 and June 2014. The last visit from China at the head of state or government level was by Prime Minister Wen Jiabao in June 2010.

28 Wang Yan 'China, Myanmar Forge Partnership, Ink Deals on Myanmar President's Maiden Visit', *Xinhua*, 27 May 2011, http://news.xinhuanet.com/english2010/china/2011-05/27/c_13897797.htm (accessed on 12 October 2012).

29 Muni, *China's Strategic Engagement with the New ASEAN*, p. 80.

30 For more details, please see Directorate of Investment and Company Administration (DICA), under sub-heading 'Data and Statistics', http://dica.gov.mm.x-aas.net/ (accessed on 27 April 2015).

31 Myoe, *In the Name of Pauk-Phaw*, p. 9.

32 Silverstein, *Burma, Military Rule and the Politics of Stagnation*, p. 121.

33 Muni, *China's Strategic Engagement with the New ASEAN*, p. 51.

34 Rajiv Bhatia. 'The Extraordinary Icon Who Matters'. *The Hindu*, 22 July 2011.

35 Rajiv Bhatia, 'New Glitter on the Golden Pagodas'. *The Hindu*, 15 March 2013.

36 Rajiv Bhatia, 'Rebuilding Eastern Connections through Myanmar', *The Hindu*, 22 October 2011. 'Experts believe that Myanmar has been looking for options, a mindset that drives it to strengthen links with other neighbours and to seek openings with the West.'

37 Rajiv Bhatia, 'Myanmar on the Road Less Travelled', *The Hindu*, 14 December 2011. 'As to its equation with China, it will not remain static, evolving in the direction in which Myanmar enjoys greater policy space for balancing relations with key stakeholders.'

38 Rajiv Bhatia, *India–US Insight*, Vol. 2, Issue 1 (ICRIER-Wadhwani Chair in India–US Policy Studies), 2 January 2012. 'Japan has always felt a special emotional and historical bond with Myanmar, given the former's role in overthrowing British rule and assisting General Aung San and his comrades in their liberation struggle. While adhering to the broader western line on Myanmar in the past, Tokyo always found a way to be helpful to its constituency in that country. This trend is now gathering strength.'

39 Rajiv Bhatia, 'Striking the Right Note', *Times of India*, 31 May 2012. 'The neglected neighbour of past decades, Myanmar is now viewed as a critical partner in India's Look East policy and "an economic bridge between India and China and between South and Southeast Asia".'

40 Min Zin, 'China–Burma Relations: China's Risk, Burma's Dilemma', in *Burma or Myanmar?* Dittmer (ed.), p. 292.

41 In August 2009, serious fighting erupted between the Myanmar Army and the Kokang militant group based along the China–Myanmar border. This resulted in thousands of refugees, mostly Chinese, fleeing into China. Beijing's reaction was to provide shelter to them and to administer a reprimand to the Myanmar government.

42 Zin, 'China–Burma Relations', *Burma or Myanmar?* Dittmer (ed.), p. 263.

43 Nevertheless, it should be conceded that the Chinese government played a useful role by offering its good offices to facilitate a ceasefire agreement between the Myanmar military and Kachin Independence Army (KIA) in May 2013. However, the noteworthy point here is that the Chinese

authorities got into the act only when Myanmar shells began to fall on the Chinese side of the border.

44 This section is based on my personal notes. Names of institutions and experts have been withheld due to my adherence to the Chatham House Rule.

45 'NLD Denies Suu Kyi Planning to Visit China - delegation leaves Myanmar on November 17', *Democracy for Burma*, 8 November 2013. NLD spokesperson Win Myint said, 'The news is spreading that our chairperson Aung San Suu Kyi has been invited to visit China and she is going there. This is not true. There is no official invitation from China.' https://democracyforburma.wordpress.com/2013/11/08/nld-denies-suu-kyi-planning-to-visit-china-delegation-leaves-myanmar-on-november-17/ (accessed on 26 April 2015).

46 J.N. Dixit, *My South Block Years*, New Delhi: Pauls Press, 1966, p. 167. While explaining the 'considerations which influenced India's policies towards Myanmar from the end of 1991 onwards', the author stressed on two specific ones, namely 'Myanmar's geostrategic importance for India', and the imperative of ensuring that 'Myanmar does not become part of an exclusive area of influence of other great powers'.

47 Rajiv Sikri, *Challenge and Strategy*, New Delhi: Sage Publications, 2009, p. 66. Calling Myanmar 'a somewhat underrated neighbour', the author flatly observed: 'India's Myanmar policy is also driven by the China factor.' Expansion of China's influence in India's eastern neighbours, Bangladesh and Myanmar could be a cause of serious concern, he argued. 'A China-sponsored link-up between Myanmar and Bangladesh would bring China right on India's doorstep and complete China's encirclement of India from the east.'

48 'Joint Statement between the Republic of India and the People's Republic of China on Building a Closer Developmental Partnership', 19 September 2014, http://www.mea.gov.in/bilateral-documents.htm?dtl/24022/Joint+Statement+between+the+Republic+of+India+and+the+Peoples+Republic+of+China+on+Building+a+Closer+Developmental+Partnership (accessed on 6 October 2014).

49 'Address by H.E. Mr. Xi Jinping, President of the People's Republic of China', 18 September 2014, http://www.icwadelhi.info (accessed on 6 October 2014).

50 Nalin Surie, 'Cooperation, Competition and Peaceful Confrontation', *Indian Foreign Affairs Journal*, Vol. 9, No. 1 (January–March 2014), p. 16.

51 'Address by Hon'ble Shri M. Hamid Ansari, Vice President of India', 28 June 2014, http://vicepresidentofindia.nic.in/contents.asp?id=500 (accessed on 7 October 2014).

52 'Opening Speech of H.E. U Thein Sein, President of the Republic of the Union of Myanmar on commemorating the 60th Anniversary of the Announcement of the Five Principles of Peaceful Co-existence by China, India and Myanmar (28th June 2014, Beijing, P.R.China)', http://www.mofa.gov.mm/?p=3057 (accessed on 7 October 2014).

53 'Xi's speech at 'Five Principles of Peaceful Coexistence' anniversary', China.org.cn, July 7, 2014, http://www.china.org.cn/world/2014-07/07/content_32876905.htm (accessed on 7 October 2014).

214 India–Myanmar–China triangle

54 C. Raja Mohan, 'Panchsheel 2014', Observer Research Foundation, 4 July 2014. He added: 'The Panchsheel is at the very heart of Xi's conception of a new security order in Asia.' http://www.orfonline.org/cms/sites/orfonline/modules/analysis/AnalysisDetail.html?cmaid=68679&mmacmaid=68680 (accessed on 20 September 2014).

55 Joint Statement on the State Visit of Chinese Premier Li Keqiang to India, 20 May 2013, http://www.mea.gov.in/bilateral-documents.htm?dtl/24022/Joint+Statement+between+the+Republic+of+India+and+the+Peoples+Republic+of+China+on+Building+a+Closer+Developmental+Partnership (accessed on 20 September 2013).

56 The BCIM proposal figured in the joint statement issued after Xi Jinping's visit, but there was no mention of the second proposal in it, http://www.mea.gov.in/bilateral-documents.htm? (accessed on 20 September 2014).

57 Myoe, *In the Name of Pauk-Phaw*, p. 9.

58 Ranjit Gupta, 'China, Myanmar and India: A Strategic Perspective'. *Indian Foreign Affairs Journal*, Vol. 8, No. 1 (January–March 2013), pp. 80–92.

59 Asia Society Task Force (March 2010). Report on 'Current Realities and Future Possibilities in Burma/Myanmar: Options for US Policy', p. 16. 'As a result of its location between two of Asia's giants – China and India – Burma is now the focus of a geopolitical contest for influence between the region's biggest powers, which have economic and strategic interests in the country.' http://asiasociety.org/files/pdf/ASBurmaMyanmar_TaskForceReport.pdf (accessed on September 2012).

60 Myint-U, *Where China Meets India*, p. 221. 'Just before Than Shwe visited New Delhi (in 2010) and before he travelled to Beijing, *The Economist* ran the cover story "China and India: Contest of the Century", arguing that the relationship between the new powers was destined to shape world politics.'

61 Ibid., p. 74. The author quoted a former Burmese officer telling him: 'We know that India can't really balance China for us.'

62 From the author's personal notes.

63 Renaud Egreteau and Larry Jagan, *Soldiers and Diplomacy in Burma: Understanding the Foreign Relations of the Burmese Praetorian State*, Singapore: NUS Press, 2013, p. 338.

64 Ibid., p. 339.

65 Li Chenyang, *Myanmar/Burma*, Dittmer (ed.), p. 129.

66 Myint-U, *Where China Meets India*, p. 31.

Chapter 8

Bilateral relations
Future directions

> Myanmar is a critical partner in India's 'Look East' policy and is perfectly suited to play the role of an economic bridge between India and China and between South and South-East Asia.
>
> – Manmohan Singh[1]

The reader's journey through the previous chapters may have helped him or her to comprehend the complex pattern of the development of India–Myanmar relations in the context of changing times.[2] On the basis of this study, we are now in a position to reflect on what might happen in the future.

A scholar is, of course, not an astrologer. One is also fully conscious of how experts end up making forecasts that prove wrong, especially concerning Myanmar. Yet, it is necessary to spell out where the future trajectory of the relationship may and should lie. Only then a scholarly work can be truly helpful to the policymaker, the opinion maker and indeed the next generation of students of Myanmar affairs. It is in this spirit that this – the last – chapter will attempt to imagine the future, with the proposed exercise anchored in our in-depth examination of the past and the present.

Determinants of future

The future of the relationship will obviously be moulded by developments in the Indo-Pacific Region (IPR), ASEAN region and the sub-region in which Myanmar is located. The larger area stretching from India to Japan and Australia has been witnessing significant changes in US–China equations in recent years. The spectacular growth in China's economy, military power, political influence, activism and assertiveness abroad has compelled many nations to revisit their strategic

216 Future directions

calculations and policy assumptions. Each actor on the regional stage, including China and the US, claims to promote security and development for all, but at the same time each suffers from insecurity, experiencing concern regarding others' behaviour.

Analysts will continue to interpret and monitor the action–reaction cycle of nations, big and small, in order to determine if IPR would head towards an era of peace and prosperity, or tensions and cold war, or confrontation and conflict or a combination of it all.[3] Evolving India–China equations in Myanmar are also relevant here.[4] These scenarios, in turn, will impact on ASEAN, shaping not only its future strength and solidarity but also its ambitious project of community-building and promoting integration of its newer members – the CLMV countries. The regional perspective thus will continue to be highly relevant to whatever happens in Myanmar in the coming years. Its geopolitical and geo-economic importance is now clearly recognised by its immediate neighbours and all other players in the region.

What happens in India in the politico-economic sphere, its approach towards its North East Region (NER), neighbourhood policy, Look/Act East Policy and Myanmar policy too should be factored in. Parliamentary elections, held in mid-2014, brought in a new government that promised forward-looking governance under a strong prime minister, Narendra Modi. India's neighbourhood policy and Act East policy[5] are likely to receive a major thrust, with added emphasis on crafting a balance in India's relations with ASEAN, Japan, China and other regional powers. Regarding its Myanmar policy, adequate national consensus has been built by now. Therefore, it is realistic to assume that the policy will continue. But how vigorously it will be executed, whether it will be backed by optimal political will and ample financial muscle, and whether it will entail the fullest possible engagement of the North East are valid questions. Answers to them would be shaped by the leadership that the Modi government provides and the difference it makes in motivating the bureaucracy and India Inc. to engage Myanmar.

The most important determinant will undoubtedly be Myanmar itself, particularly the road that it takes in the next decade and, more precisely, in course of 2015–16. It is maintained that there is a link between peace and stability in Myanmar and further blossoming of India–Myanmar relations; it is a link that works both ways.

Whither Myanmar?

An objective evaluation indicates that the nation's performance in reforming its political system, economy, media and other sectors and in recalibrating its foreign policy during the period 2010–14 has been quite impressive. The Thein Sein government has achieved more than what was expected of it at the commencement of its innings. Many factors have been responsible for it: the people's strong yearning for change, the *Tatmadaw's* revised strategy, Thein Sein's zeal and prudence to craft and execute reform, the decision by Suu Kyi-led NLD to become a cooperative partner and notably a favourable external environment. The results have been there for all to see. Myanmar economy has been growing at a decent rate of 7.8 per cent.[6] Aid and investment have been flowing in, albeit slowly. The parliament has become far more independent and assertive than was expected in 2010. The president is well-liked, both within and outside Myanmar. Suu Kyi has been free and engaged in contributing to political life and influencing the reform process. In short, Myanmar is quite a different place from what it used to be just a few years back.

However, the reform period drew global limelight to the serious fault lines of the nation. Sectarian strife and violence have exposed the ugly side of Myanmar society. Ethnic reconciliation has been on top of the agenda, but even a serious dialogue between the government and ethnic groups has been unable to improve the atmosphere of scepticism and pessimism about the future prospects. The national reconciliation process remains incomplete. In his radio broadcast marking the beginning of the traditional New Year in April 2013, President Thein Sein observed:

> Our society not only achieved successes that had not [sic] hoped for but also encountered saddening and horrifying events that had not [sic] expected. During the long road to democracy, we have to maintain our already achieved successes, take lessons from the losses and be prepared to face and overcome the challenges ahead. In preparation for the challenges, we have to strive for the success with patience, tolerance and diligence.[7]

As the year 2013 neared its end, NLD progressively showed its commitment to seek constitutional reform before the 2015 elections. The party stepped up its campaign for amending the Constitution speedily in order particularly to remove discriminatory restrictions imposed on Suu Kyi's candidature. Section 59(f) stipulated that a presidential candidate's spouse, children or children's spouse may not hold foreign citizenship.[8] In this context, Suu Kyi made numerous statements favouring constitutional reform, both within the country and also during her visits to Europe and Australia. She also publicly called

218   Future directions

for a quadripartite dialogue involving the speaker, the president, the Tatmadaw commander-in-chief and the NLD with a view to crafting a consensus on the subject. The NLD scotched speculation about possible boycott of 2015 elections by stating categorically that it would participate in them even without the required amendments to the Constitution. As if responding to this position, USDP issued a statement supporting constitutional reform, including the removal of restrictions concerning Suu Kyi's candidature. But, its position was only partially satisfactory as it indicated its willingness to remove the foreign citizenship requirement of the spouse but not of the children of a presidential candidate. In the first televised address of 2014, President Thein Sein gave fillip to Suu Kyi's chances by expressing himself in favour of constitutional reform, including the restrictions on Suu Kyi.[9] Responding, Suu Kyi observed: 'We have to accept openly that the constitution is not fair, not in accordance with democratic standards and not a charter that is good for our country's future.'[10] Turning her attention to the military, she called on its leadership to come out in support of constitutional reform.

The army, however, continued to be cautious and opposed to the introduction of a full democracy in a hurry. It seemed to take inspiration from the Indonesian model of gradualism in change. Baladas Ghoshal, presenting a comparison between experiences of the two countries, concluded: 'Despite these minor differences, the pathology, the ideological outlook and the experiences of the two countries are so similar that Myanmar is likely to follow the same trajectory in its movement towards democracy. . .'[11]

The amendment of the 2008 Constitution thus became a top political issue, and the parliament remained seized with it. The amendment debate encompassed two other matters, namely the need to change Section 436 dealing with the constitutional amendment procedure, and the question of switching to proportional representation as a substitute for the present 'first-past-the post'. The latter could even be introduced without amending the Constitution. However, as the year unfolded, the likelihood of progress on constitutional reform was wrapped in uncertainty. The nation was running out of time, with the next parliamentary elections scheduled for the end of 2015.

Whether key constitutional reforms happen may determine the answer to the oft-raised question: who will be the president of Myanmar after 2015 elections? Of the four possible 'candidates' in mid-2014, one (Thein Sein) seemed reluctant but still interested; two others (Speaker Thura Shwe Mann and Suu Kyi) were declared candidates, although the latter remained disqualified under the present

Constitution; and the fourth was an undeclared candidate (*Tatmadaw* Commander-in-Chief Min Aung Hlaing). Besides, a dark horse could not be ruled out, especially if Suu Kyi were to follow 'the Sonia Gandhi model', as some advised her to do.[12] Without an amendment to the Constitution, Suu Kyi could at best hope to become the speaker of the lower house of the parliament if her party performed well in the forthcoming elections. Lex Rieffel wrote: 'The single best word to sum up the outlook is: uncertain.' He aptly explained that Myanmar's politico-economic prospects would depend on its ability to resolve the ethnic issue and the success or failure of its 'quasi-democratic system, which will face a crucial test in the 2015 national election'.[13]

As one looked ahead, reversion to a brutal, full-fledged military rule appeared an unlikely scenario. Transition to genuine multiparty democracy seemed set to be characterised by gradualism and caution. However, many well-wishers of Myanmar and supporters of Myanmar's democracy felt that the military has had its chance to govern the country from 1962 till date. Therefore, it was now time for the country's reins to be given to democratically elected, popular and charismatic leaders of the people.

As Aung San Suu Kyi headed the list of such leaders, she seemed to deserve a fair opportunity to contest the presidency, but she appeared unlikely to get it. At the end of 2014, Suu Kyi's advocates were losing hope about her becoming the next president in 2015 and veering round to the view that perhaps the year 2020 might see her succeed. 'My dream is about the kind of country I would like it to become – not sitting in a presidential suite or anything like that', she informed BBC in sharp contrast to what she had told the Indian media in 2012.[14] The politics in the coming years may witness many turns and twists.[15] Some Myanmar watchers continued to believe that, despite his retirement, Than Shwe, the last strongman, could still play a crucial role in influencing the political elite's choice of the next president.[16] After all, Myanmar is 'a country with a complicated present and murky future'.[17]

Bilateral relations: future possibilities

A fundamental convergence exists between India's recognition of Myanmar's geostrategic centrality and Myanmar's quest for an 'independent' foreign policy and a balance in its relations with neighbours and other major partners. Therefore, a whole set of factors that push the two countries towards a close and cooperative relationship will remain potent and unchanged, despite political changes that may occur in Myanmar in the foreseeable future. Those in power in New Delhi and Naypyitaw are obliged to respect the realities and move towards building on the strong foundations which have been laid in the past decade and half, especially since 2011.

Looking ahead from this perspective, we may critically analyse the prospects concerning three major pillars of the relationship, in the following discussion.

Politico-strategic cooperation

India is in a position to develop a close political relationship with Myanmar as long as the former recognises that (a) China, like India, has legitimate reasons to craft close cooperation with Myanmar, (b) Myanmar would not choose between China and India, desiring friendly relations with both and (c) China–Myanmar bilateral cooperation would continue to outweigh India–Myanmar bilateral cooperation in the coming years. But, even subject to these constraints, there is ample scope for further expansion and diversification of relations between India and Myanmar. A number of suggestions, given in the following, may be considered in this context.

First, the two nations should move forward to establish 'a strategic partnership'. Some may argue that a strategic partnership between Myanmar and India would offend China, but it is worth noting that President Then Sein employed this phrase for relations with both India and China. While speaking at a major Panchsheel event in Beijing, he remarked tellingly:

> Both our closest neighbours China and India have played a significant role in Myanmar's economic development and it is our firm belief that these two neighbours will continue to be our strategic partners in the years ahead.[18]

Contours and scope of strategic partnership should be developed through annual summits between the prime minister of India and the president of Myanmar. These summits would be a valuable tool to give boost to the relationship, helping the two governments to align views and positions on international, regional and bilateral issues.

Second, India would need to improve its image as 'a reluctant power' in Myanmar's eyes and consider taking bold steps to strengthen defence and security cooperation, especially with regard to its maritime dimension.[19] The views of military experts may be given due consideration.[20]

Third, India should continue to cultivate the *Tatmadaw* (which will remain a major power centre) and help it to assume an appropriate apolitical role in a democracy, should it be inclined in that direction. This requires astute coordination and close synergy among India's diplomats, intelligence officials, military brass, political experts and strategic analysts so that a harmonious approach is crafted and executed in this realm.

Fourth, the principal mechanism for bilateral interaction, Foreign Office Consultations, needs to be elevated to the political level, with the two foreign ministers serving as co-chairs. By meeting once a year, it will provide evidence of sustained political will to strengthen the relationship.

Fifth, recent initiatives to provide training and capacity-building assistance to the Myanmar parliament should be enlarged and sustained. They could be extended to regional assemblies of the border region opposite India's NER.

Sixth, given India's vast experience in addressing Centre–state relations, there exists potential for an in-depth dialogue and considerable practical cooperation among experts and stakeholders of the two countries. India's approach should be to share its experience and expertise in the field, while leaving it entirely to the Myanmar side as to what it would wish to accept, modify or reject. India should also recognise that the Myanmar government, parliamentarians etc. would continue to study and learn from other countries' experiences as well.

Seventh, India should continue to assist Myanmar in shouldering its responsibilities towards ASEAN, particularly the Initiative for ASEAN Integration (IAI) that aimed to bridge gaps between old and new members of the grouping. In doing so, New Delhi would not only strengthen bilateral relations but also advance its Act East agenda.

Finally, the two countries need to work out tangible and effective ways of increasing their cooperation in subregional institutions such as BIMSTEC, MGC and BCIM. It is time to convert commitments into action.

Economic cooperation

Economic cooperation has been a relatively weaker facet of bilateral ties, although a great deal has been written and talked about it. On trade and investment cooperation, progress has been slow as India Inc. has not been fully enthused about business attractiveness of Myanmar, due to a variety of reasons. The collective memory of past disruptions and forced migrations of Indians from Burma (during World War II, and in U Nu and Ne Win years) and sectarian violence during the reform period have been rather discouraging. But the opening up of Myanmar economy and the government's active efforts to seek foreign investment have not gone unnoticed. The more forward-looking section of India Inc. has joined the new international competition for a slice of Myanmar's market. A few top-ranking Indian companies have achieved initial success, but it should just be a beginning if India's competitive advantages could be leveraged fully. 'Our companies and industry associations,' wrote V. S. Seshadri, 'will however need to pack in a lot more punch to significantly improve our trade and investment ranking.'[21]

What should be done? A range of measures could be considered as relevant here. The governments should expand their dialogue on economic issues through a more diversified and sustained involvement of economic ministries and provincial authorities in both countries. The key is for the heads of the government and foreign ministers to motivate and persuade other actors to invest more in economic aspects of the relationship. Whether this can be achieved through a Ministerial-level Joint Commission or through an additional mechanism such as Strategic Economic Dialogue should be examined by relevant officials. Further, considering the near exhaustion of the recent Line of Credit (LOC) of US$500 million, New Delhi could strengthen its financial heft by announcing a new LOC of US$1 billion, to be used in next three years for the export of engineering goods, technology and projects from India.

Further, an expert stressed the need for the Indian business community to devise 'suitable commercial strategies' building on development programmes and for the government 'to try and make the cost of doing business with Myanmar more competitive'.[22] Another suggestion meriting attention is that, with Japanese, Thai and Korean companies securing early advantage and foothold in the Myanmar market in the wake of economic reforms, it is logical and desirable for Indian companies to explore actively the possibilities of trilateral cooperation. Projects based on a blend of capital and high technology from those countries; management expertise and medium technology of Indian companies; and human resources drawn from the local population could be an alternative and mutually advantageous strategy.

Besides these initiatives, measures to monitor and ensure completion of the Kaladan Multi-modal Transport project and the Trilateral Highway project by the announced dates should firmly be put in place as a top priority. This is suggested in the light of indications that executing agencies may be running behind schedule once again. Stakes are high. India's strategic credibility in Myanmar is now dependent on the timely completion of these two major projects that were conceived over a decade ago.

Reference to the two projects brings us to a discussion of other proposals aimed at increasing connectivity – infrastructural, industrial and institutional. That many more road, shipping and air (and even railway) links should be established has been the thrust and conclusion of various studies done and discussions held in recent years.[23] But, the problem is that very little emerges in the form of government decisions and actions from these intellectual exercises. Where a broad consensus, however, has emerged is that not just roads but 'development corridors' are required. Special economic zones should be set up, both on the Indian side and Myanmar side of the border, so that goods are produced, jobs are created and real development is secured, thus leading to connectivity of the kind that benefits peoples of both countries. Focus should be on creating new manufacturing facilities, not only in the border regions but also in India's North East and the hinterland of Myanmar. A comprehensive report published by the RIS contains a blueprint that deserves serious consideration. As Shyam Saran, chairman RIS, put it:

> Our aim must be to promote a truly substantive and dynamic economic partnership between India and Myanmar, which could then serve as a platform for promoting the India–ASEAN Strategic Partnership.[24]

Third pillar

Besides the government-to-government and business-to-business facets, the third pillar of bilateral relations, people-to-people contacts, needs to be strengthened in an appreciable manner. Mouthing slogans and platitudes is easy. What is difficult is to achieve meaningful progress within a short time in the absence of a suitable platform or institution for this purpose. Hence the proposal to set up an India–Myanmar Foundation makes eminent sense.

It is suggested that the two governments as well as a few interested companies and other institutions may join hands to provide substantial funding for establishing the proposed foundation. It would consist of experts who may work under the supervision of the Indian

224 Future directions

Ambassador in Yangon and the Myanmar Ambassador in New Delhi. Its mandate would essentially be to develop and implement a set of programmes for strengthening people-to-people relations by promoting Buddhist pilgrimage in India, regular tourism by Indians in Myanmar, expanding educational exchanges, nurturing dialogues among strategic communities and providing scholarships to youth, women and civil society activists for study, travel and interaction. It is only by involving the society at large that we may hope to bring the two nations closer together.

Conclusion

Writing in the *New Light of Myanmar*, Indian academic Sonu Trivedi opined that three 'critical gaps' in bilateral relations needed to be bridged 'through immediate intervention'. These are: 'security and stability at the borders', 'connectivity with the Northeast' and expansion of 'border trade'. She believed that addressing them might 'go a long way in strengthening partnership and boosting ties for the two countries'.[25]

During Prime Minister Manmohan Singh's first visit to Myanmar, the well-known business leader, Sunil Bharti Mittal, dismissed the criticism that India had 'missed the bus' in Myanmar, adding:

> There is so much to be done. Every piece of infrastructure [in Burma] needs to be rebuilt and the warm, historic relationship that we enjoy will come in handy for Indian businessmen when they are competing with the rest of the world. While the world only discovered Myanmar now, I think India has discovered this place for a long time, more than a century. It's up to us now, how fast we can move into this country.[26]

Myanmar–India relations are likely to thrive further on their own steam. But through a conscious and well-planned endeavour, they could be strengthened and deepened in a far more perceptible manner and in a relatively short period. It is hoped that the two nations – not just their governments but their societies too – will make the necessary investment in this vital relationship. There is no dearth of good ideas. What is needed is an increased public awareness of the potential of the relationship, the geopolitical stakes involved and the costs of suboptimal action. A new fountain of synergy should be created in the future, which will be fuelled by a clear mutuality of interests, common values, shared experiences and a determined leadership.

Notes

1 Prime Minister Manmohan Singh's address to think tanks and business community in Yangon on 29 May 2012, http://www.mea.gov.in/Speeches-Statements.htm?dtl/19749/PMs_address_to_thinktanks_and_business_community_at_an_event_organized_by_Myanmar_Federation_of_Ch (accessed on 1 June 2012).

2 Contribution of individual policymakers to the development of relations in the past deserves mention here. During the British Raj, governors general at the crucial stages – Dalhousie, Dufferin, Curzon and governors in Burma – Sir Harcourt Butler and Sir Charles Innes, played exceptionally important roles. After independence, Jawaharlal Nehru and Indira Gandhi as well as U Nu and Ne Win left their imprints. Other figures who mattered include Dr M. A. Rauf, India's first ambassador to Burma, Foreign Secretary J. N. Dixit, SPDC Vice Chairman General Maung Aye and Deputy Foreign Minister Khin Maung Win. This subject needs to be researched further.

3 Asha Mary Mathew, 'Myanmar: The New Strategic Pawn in Asia Pacific?' *Air Power, Journal of Air Power and Space Studies*, Vol. 8, No. 4 (Winter 2013, October–December), pp. 184–6. The author argued: 'As a part of this larger strategy, the US and China will continue to engage closely with Myanmar in order to gain their strategic influence in the country. Japan's engagement with Myanmar becomes crucial as part of this power play.' She added: 'Owing to its strategic position in the region, Myanmar is bound to be used as a playground by external players to serve their larger geopolitical interests.'

4 David I. Steinberg and Hongwei Han, *Modern China–Myanmar Relations: Dilemmas of Mutual Dependence*, Copenhagen: NIAS Press, 2012, p. 368. The authors asserted: 'The dilemma for India is how much they might be prepared to invest in Myanmar, and whether their perceived goal of balancing China, or at least moderating China's internal role in Myanmar, is sustainable.'

5 The Modi government showed preference to use a new term – 'Act East' policy – as mentioned in the India–US Joint Statement of 30 September 2014. This was subsequently reiterated by the prime minister at the East Asia Summit on 13 November 2014. He stated: 'Since entering office six months ago my government has moved with a great sense of priority and speed to turn our "Look East Policy" into "Act East Policy". The East Asia Summit is an important pillar of this policy.' http://www.mea.gov.in/Speeches-Statements.htm?dtl/24238/Prime_Ministers_remarks_at_the_9th_East_Asia_Summit_Nay_Pyi_Taw_Myanmar (accessed on 15 November 2014).

6 Asian Development Bank. 'Myanmar's economy is on track to grow by 7.8% in both Fiscal Year 2014 (ending 31 March 2015) and in FY2015. Growth is supported by rising investment propelled by improved business confidence, commodity exports, rising production of natural gas, buoyant tourism, and credit growth – all complemented by the government's ambitious structural reform program.' http://www.adb.org/countries/myanmar/economy (accessed on 5 October 2014).

7 'Translation of radio address delivered by President of the Republic of the Union of Myanmar U Thein Sein on the occasion of Thingyan New Year',

226 Future directions

The New Light of Myanmar, 16 April 2013, http://www.burmalibrary.
org/docs15/NLM-2013–04–17-red.pdf (accessed on 30 November 2013).
8 *Constitution of the Republic of the Union of Myanmar* (2008).
Section 59(f):

'59. Qualifications of the President and Vice-Presidents are as follows :
(f) shall he himself, one of the parents, the spouse, one of the legitimate
children or their spouses not owe allegiance to a foreign power, not be
subject of a foreign power or citizen of a foreign country. They shall not
be persons entitled to enjoy the rights and privileges of a subject of a
foreign government or citizen of a foreign country.' www.burmalibrary.
org/docs5/Myanmar_Constitution-2008-en.pdf (accessed on 13 November 2013).

9 'Healthy Constitution Must Be Amended from Time To Time to Address
National, Economic, Social Needs of Society', Embassy of the Republic of
the Union of Myanmar, New Delhi, *The New Light of Myanmar*, 2 January 2014. 'I would not want restrictions imposed on the right of any citizen
to become the leader of the country. At the same time, we will need to have
all necessary measures in place in order to defend our national interests
and sovereignty.' http://myanmedelhi.com/healthy-constitution-must-be-
amended-from-time-to-time-to-address-national-economic-social-
needs-of-society/ pdfv (accessed on 26 April 2015).
10 'Suu Kyi Urges Myanmar Army to Back Charter Reform', *Channel News-
Asia*, 4 January 2014, http://www.channelnewsasia.com/news/asiapacific/
suu-kyi-urges-myanmar/943006.html (accessed on 4 January 2014).
11 Baladas Ghoshal, 'In Myanmar's Transition, Shades of Indonesia', *The
Hindu*, 9 January 2013.
12 This model would involve NLD finding a dependable ally who may be
helped to become the next president on the understanding that he would
allow Suu Kyi to rule from behind the throne. This view was mentioned to
me in a personal discussion by a Myanmar scholar and an Indian business
leader in Yangon during my visit in March 2013.
13 Lex Rieffel, 'Myanmar on the Move: An Overview of Recent Developments', *Journal of Current Southeast Asian Affairs*, Vol. 31, No. 4 (2012),
pp. 46–7. Published by GIGA German Institute of Globaland Area Studies, Institute of Asian Studies and Hamburg University Press, http://
journals.sub.uni-hamburg.de/giga/jsaa/article/view/581 (accessed on 17
December 2013).
14 Linday Murdoch, 'Aung San Suu Kyi Concedes She Won't Become Myanmar's Next President', *The Sydney Morning Herald*, 9 January 2015, http://
www.smh.com.au/world/aung-san-suu-kyi-concedes-she-wont-become-
myanmars-next-president-20150109-12knaw.html (accessed on 26
April 2015).
15 Peter Chalk, 'On the Path of Change', Special Report, December 2013,
Australian Strategic Policy Institute. This report contains a perceptive
analysis of the challenges facing Myanmar.
16 From the author's conversations with important visitors from Myanmar.
17 *The Economist*, 27 September to 3 October 2014. The quotation is from
the editor's note on the article 'The haze blocks the view'. Simon Willis,
the author, concluded: 'There are many uncertainties ahead for Myanmar.'

18 'Opening Speech of H.E. U Thein Sein, President of the Republic of the Union of Myanmar on commemorating the 60th Anniversary of the Announcement of the Five Principles of Peaceful Co-existence by China, India and Myanmar (28th June 2014, Beijing, P.R.China)', Ministry of Foreign Affairs, Republic of the Union of Myanmar, 30 June 2014, http://www.mofa.gov.mm/?p=3057 (accessed on 7 October 2014).

19 The phrase 'reluctant power' was used by a visiting Myanmar scholar in the course of his presentation at a seminar hosted by Institute of Defence Studies and Analyses (IDSA), New Delhi on 1 November 2013.

20 General V.P. Malik, *India's Military Conflicts and Diplomacy: An Inside View of Decision Making*, Noida: HarperCollins Publishers India, 2013, p. 233. 'India and Myanmar should enhance cooperation in maritime security, particularly in combating piracy, terrorism and gun running and for the security of their respective island territories. This would require bilateral and multinational arrangements and training.'

21 V.S. Seshadri, 'An Invitation from a Neighbour', *The Hindu*, 20 April 2013.

22 Ibid. The author added: 'Finally, our businesses have also to learn how to do business in Myanmar.'

23 Prabir De and Jayanta Kumar Ray, 'India–Myanmar Connectivity: Current Status and Future Prospects', *IFPS/CPWAS Occasional Paper Series No. 4*, New Delhi: KW Publishers Pvt. Ltd., 2013, pp. 59–60. In this excellent Paper, the authors drew the conclusion: 'India–Myanmar connectivity could be realized through enhanced physical infrastructure development, effective institutional arrangements and empowered people.' They stressed that in order to ensure a positive outcome of such endeavours, 'Myanmar, India and ASEAN need to respond to the opportunities offered by its geographical and natural advantages and to the competitive advantages brought about by regional and global market change.'

24 V.S. Seshadri, 'Transforming Connectivity Corridors between India and Myanmar into Development Corridors', *Research and Information System for Developing Countries – RIS*, New Delhi: RIS, 2014, p. vi.

25 Sonu Trivedi, 'Bridging the Critical Gaps: India–Myanmar', *The New Light of Myanmar*, 23 September 2014.

26 William Boot, 'India's "Discovery" of Burma Still Waiting for the Train to Leave the Station', *The Irrawaddy*, 5 June 2012. Sunil Mittal is the founder Chairman and Group CEO of Bharti Enterprises.

Epilogue

The Preface contained a reference to Seattle, the city where our elder son Siddharth lives. The seed for this book was sown at his home. Therefore, it is appropriate that two-and-a-half years later I write this Epilogue at the same place.

While looking at the green hills of Washington State, my mind drifted to the hilly regions of Myanmar we traversed a decade ago, soaking much of this unique land and its unforgettable people.

To craft this book, I undertook many more 'journeys' to Myanmar, not on airplanes but in the company of a variety of thinkers, travellers, scholars, authors and leaders who studied, reflected and wrote about this country. I am grateful to them all.

What sustained my focus on this project was the sustenance I received from Buddha's teachings, which fascinated me since long. I remembered him every day, not by reading a holy book but by glancing at his beautiful stone-carving, installed in the park opposite our home in a Delhi suburb.

As I sign off, I am tempted to share with the reader a snippet about the farewell visit we had paid to Mandalay in August 2005. My personal diary reads as below:

> On our farewell visit to Mandalay, I decided to go up the Mandalay Hill one last time. Then, we walked down to Dut Taw Pagoda which housed the Peshawar Relics.[1] A beautiful, white pagoda with a golden spire, it was over 100 years old; its wall paintings were fading and it looked abandoned. The keeper's wife, a friendly and helpful woman, informed us that the relics were shifted to the Hermit's Museum, located at the foot of the hill. We drove to the museum, wondering if we would be lucky enough to see the famous relics. The chief *sayadaw* came out to meet us, but he explained that the monk who had the keys of the relics' chamber

230 Epilogue

was away on some errand. It was getting dark and we had to rush off to an official dinner. It was agreed that we would return to the museum at 9:30 pm.

We returned to the venue ten minutes late, anxious that we might have offended the chief monk. But he, two other monks and several other men, were present in the museum hall. In the centre was placed a small table with a red velvet top with two spotlights trained on them. On the table were placed two objects: a small crystal vessel containing three bones of the Buddha, encased in ruby-studded gold holder, and a gold casket with the inscription stating that the British authorities had presented it to the Burmese Buddhist Society.

For me, the extraordinary experience came when the chief monk decided to bless us – Kumkum, myself, and the two officials of our Consulate accompanying us – by placing the crystal vessel on my head. At that moment, sitting on the soil of Burma/Myanmar, I felt connected directly to the revered founder of Buddhism, to his message and teachings, and indeed to the history of India dating back to over 2,500 years.

Note

1 A portion of Buddha's original relics (i.e. three small fragments of bone), known as the Peshawar Relics, were discovered through excavation in 1908–09 at a historic stupa. The stupa was constructed by the Kushan king Kanishka during the second century CE at a site that is located in today's Shah-ji-dheri on the outskirts of Peshawar, Pakistan. The British administration transferred the relics to Calcutta for safe-keeping. Later Lord Minto presented them to the Burmese Buddhist Society. The authenticity of the relics, though questioned by a few due to the anti-colonial sentiment of the time, was widely recognised. Eventually, it is all a matter of faith.

Appendices

Appendix I
List of Agreements/MoUs signed between India and Myanmar

1951 Treaty of Friendship
1967 Land Boundary De-limitation Agreement
1970 India–Myanmar Trade Agreement
1979 Air Transport Agreement
1986 Agreement on De-limitation of Maritime Boundary in the Andaman Sea, in the Coco Channel and in the Bay of Bengal.
1993 Agreement for Mutual Cooperation for Reducing Demand and Preventing Illicit Trafficking in Narcotics Drugs and Psychotropic Substances and Related Matters (30 March 1993)
1993 Tripartite Agreement between India, Myanmar and Thailand on the Tri-junction Point in the Andaman Sea [ratified on 24 May 1999]
1994 (i) Agreement on Border Trade
     (ii) Agreement on Cooperation between Civilian Border Authorities (21 January 1994)
1995 India–Myanmar Civil Aviation Agreement
1997 MoU on Cooperation in the Development of Roads in Myanmar along the Myanmar–India Border
1998 (i) Credit Agreement
     (ii) MoU on Cooperation in Agriculture and Allied Sectors
1999 Agreement on Cooperation in the Fields of Science & Technology
2000 (i) MoU on Banking Arrangements between the United Bank of India (UBI) and the Myanma Economic Bank (MEB)
     (ii) Credit Agreement providing for extension of a credit line of US$15 million to Myanmar
2001 (i) Agreement on Cultural Cooperation
     (ii) MoU on maintenance of Tamu–Kalemyo road
2003 (i) Protocol on Consultations between the Ministry of External Affairs of the Republic of India and the Ministry of Foreign Affairs of the Union of Myanmar

232 Appendix I

(ii) MoU between Government of India, Ministry of External Affairs and Ed.CIL and Government of the Union of Myanmar for the Deputation of Faculty Members in Various Disciplines for Conducting Seminars/Lectures/Training at the University of Yangon

(iii) MoU on the Establishment of Joint Trade Committee between the Government of the Union of Myanmar and the Government of India

(iv) MoU between the Ministry of Communications and Information Technology, Government of the Republic of India and the Ministry of Communications, Posts and Telegraphs, Government of the Union of Myanmar on Cooperation in Communications, Information Technology and Services

(v) Credit Agreement for credit line of US$25 million

(vi) Agreement on Visa Exemption for Official and Diplomatic Passport Holders

(vii) MoU on Education Exchange Programme between the Ministry of Education, Government of the Union of Myanmar and the Ministry of Human Resource Development, Government of India

2004 (i) MoU between the Government of the Republic of India and the Government of the Union of Myanmar for setting up Entrepreneurship Development Centre at Yangon

(ii) Letter of Understanding between Myanma Posts and Telecommunication and Telecommunications Consultant India Ltd., on Co-operation in Telecom Sector

(iii) Exim Bank's Line of Credit of US$56.358 Million to Myanmar for the Yangon–Mandalay Trunkline Railway Project

(iv) MoU on Cooperation in the field of Railways between the Government of India and the Government of the Union of Myanmar

(v) Dollar Credit Line Agreement of US$7 Million between Myanmar Foreign Trade Bank, Myanmar & Export–Import Bank of India

(vi) MoU between the Government of the Republic of India & the Government of the Union of Myanmar on Cooperation in the field of Non-traditional Security Issues

(vii) MoU between Ministry of External Affairs (MEA), Government of India & Department of Hydroelectric

Power (DHP), Ministry of Electric Power, Government of the Union of Myanmar

(viii) The Cultural Exchange Programme between the Government of the Republic of India & the Government of the Union of Myanmar, 2004–2006

2005 MoU for cooperation in petroleum sector between the Ministry of Energy of the Government of the Union of Myanmar and the Ministry of Petroleum and Natural Gas of the Government of the Republic of India

2006 (i) Framework Agreement for mutual cooperation in the field of Remote Sensing

(ii) MoU on Cooperation in Buddhist Studies

(iii) MoU on Cooperation in Petroleum Sector

(iv) Dollar Credit Line Agreement of US$20 million between Exim Bank of India and MFTB for renovation of Thanlyin refinery

2007 (i) Dollar Credit Line Agreement of US$60 million between Exim Bank and MFTB for Development of Thathatay Chaung Hydropower project [As requested by the GoM, in May'10, GoI has approved the loan to be used for railway project to be implemented by M/s RITES]

(ii) MoU on establishment of Myanmar–India Centre for Enhancement of IT Skills at Yangon

2008 (i) Avoidance of Double Taxation Agreement

(ii) Framework Agreement for Construction and Operation of a Multi-Modal Transit Transport Facility on Kaladan River

(iii) MoU on Intelligence Exchange Cooperation

(iv) Investment Promotion and Protection Agreement

(v) Three agreements with United Bank of India (UBI), Kolkata and Myanma Investment & Commercial Bank (MICB), Myanma Economic Bank (MEB), Myanma Foreign Trade Bank (MFTB) for facilitating of normal trade from border trade

(vi) Dollar Credit Line Agreement for US$64.07 million between Exim Bank and MFTB for 3 transmission line in Myanmar

(vii) Dollar Credit Agreement for US$20 million between Exim Bank and MFTB for seting up of ACSR factory [This LoC was converted into setting up of assembly/manufacturing of Tata vehicles in Myanmar and amendatory agreement was signed in 2009]

234   Appendix I

2009   (i) Setting up of Myanmar–India Industrial Training Centre at Pokokku, Myanmar
       (ii) Setting up of Myanmar–India Centre for English Language Training Centre
       (iii) Exim Bank's Line of Credit of US$20 Million to Myanmar for the Thanbayakan refinery project

2010   Agreement signed during Senior General Than Shwe's visit to India (27 July 2010)
       (i) Treaty on Mutual Assistance in Criminal Matters
       (ii) MoU on Information Cooperation
       (iii) Agreement on Cooperation in the fields of Science and Technology
       (iv) MoU on conservation and restoration of Ananada Temple in Bagan
       (v) MoU regarding Indian Grant Assistance for Implementation of Small Development Projects

2011   Agreement signed during External Affairs Minister's visit to Myanmar
       (i) MoU between India and Myanmar on Setting up of Indo-Myanmar Industrial Training Centre at Myingyan, Myanmar. Two agreements signed during President U Thein Seint visit to India:
       (ii) MoU on Upgradation of the Yangon Children's Hospital and Sittwe General Hospital
       (iii) Programme of Cooperation in Sc. & Tech for the period of 2012–2015

2012   Agreement/Memorandum of Understandings signed during Prime Minister Manmohan Singh's visit to Myanmar
       (i) Memorandum of Understanding on India–Myanmar Border Area Development
       (ii) Air Services Agreement between India and Myanmar
       (iii) Memorandum of Understanding towards setting up of Myanmar Institute of Information Technology (MIIT)
       (iv) Memorandum of Understanding of the Establishment of the Advance Centre for Agriculture Research and Education (ACARE), Yezin Agriculture University, Naypyitaw, Myanmar
       (v) Memorandum of Understanding on the Establishment of a Rice Bio Park
       (vi) Memorandum of Understanding on Establishing Border Haats across the Border between India and Myanmar

Appendix I   235

(vii) Memorandum of Understanding on Establishment of Joint Trade and Investment Forum

(viii) Cultural Exchange Programme 2012–15

(ix) Agreement on Cooperation between Institute of Defence Studies and Analysis (IDSA) and Myanmar Institute of Strategic and International Studies (MISIS)

(x) Memorandum of Understanding regarding a USD 500 million Credit Line between Export–Import Bank of India and Myanmar Foreign Trade Bank

(xi) Memorandum of Understanding between Calcutta University, Kolkata, and Dagon University, Yangon

(xii) Memorandum of Understanding on cooperation between the Indian Council of World Affairs (ICWA) and Myanmar Institute of Strategic and International Studies (MISIS)

(xiii) Memorandum of Understanding on cooperation between the Institute of Defence Studies and Analyses (IDSA) and Myanmar Institute of Strategic and International Studies (MISIS)

Post-PM Visit

Memorandum of Understanding on cooperation on construction/upgradation of the Rhi-Tiddim Road on Myanmar along the India–Myanmar Border.

2013   Memorandum of Understanding between the Government of Republic of India and the Government of the Republic of the Union of Myanmar for strengthening of India–Myanmar Centre for Enhancement of IT Skills (IMCEITS) signed on 31 October 2013 at Nay Pyi Taw

2014   (i) Memorandum of Understanding between the Government of Republic of India and the Government of the Republic of the Union of Myanmar on Border Cooperation – signed on 8 May 2014 at Nay Pyi Taw

(ii) Memorandum of Understanding between the Government of Republic of India and the Government of the Republic of the Union of Myanmar for setting up of Language Laboratories and E-Resource Centre in Myanmar – signed on 8 May 2014 at Nay Pyi Taw

Compiled by the author

* * * * * * * * *

Appendix II
The New Light of Myanmar

Perspectives

Namaste!
Wednesday, 30 May 2012

Thanks to our advancing democratization process, global interest in our country is rising making us busy with endlessly hosting foreign guests coming to us on business trips, diplomatic missions or other purposes that serve mutual interest. We are also welcoming leaders and dignitaries of foreign countries visiting Myanmar with packages of initiatives for fostering business, trade, cultural, people-to-people, and government-to-government relations. Some countries see us as a resource rich country, while others want to do business with us for its ongoing reforms, abundant labor, nice people and geographical positions that is strategic in the view of many global nations. Recently, Indian Prime Minister Dr. Manmohan Singh leading a large delegation visited Myanmar on a goodwill mission for further deepening the thousand-year-old cordial relations and enhancing areas of cooperation. During a meeting, President U Thein Sein thanked Dr. Singh for the Indian infrastructural assistance in border areas development as peace and stability of these remote regions running between the two countries is important for both. As for Myanmar, India is a giant neighbour whose long experience in democracy will be so valuable for its democratization process that needs international cooperation for achieving further acceleration. Besides, India is one of the global emerging markets with its consumption power in multiple sectors growing bigger and bigger every year. Especially, it is an energy hungry giant.

Moreover, this giant can help us create more job opportunities, acquire technology and set up light and medium industries through investments in multiple sectors. In fact, India needs Myanmar, and

Myanmar also needs India, and that is the common ground. We believe the visit of Indian Prime Minister is a herald of greater cooperation between the two friendly neighbours that may even contribute to regional peace, stability and progress. So we say "Namaste!" to our neighbours.

Source: http://www.burmalibrary.org/docs13/NLM2012-05-30.pdf (accessed on 25 October 2013).

* * * * * * * * *

Bibliography

Books

Abbott, Gerry. *Back to Mandalay: An Inside View of Burma*. Bangkok: Orchid Press, 2004.

Adas, Michael. *The Burma Delta – Economic Development and Social Change on an Asian Rice Frontier, 1852–1941*. Wisconsin: The University of Wisconsin Press, 1974.

Alexander, Garth. *Silent Invasion*. London: Macdonald & Company Limited, 1973.

Appadorai, A. and M.S. Rajan. *India's Foreign Policy and Relations*. New Delhi: South Asian Publishers, 1985.

Baruah, Sanjib. *Postfrontier Blues: Toward a New Policy Framework for Northeast India*. Washington DC: East–West Center Washington, 2007.

Basham, A.L. *The Wonder That Was India*. London: Sidgwick & Jackson, 1967.

Bhattacharya, Rakhee. *Northeastern India and its Neighbours: Negotiating Security and Development*. New Delhi: Routledge, 2015.

Bhattacharya Swapna (Chakraborti). *India–Myanmar Relations: 1886–1948*. Kolkata: K P Bagchi & Company, 2007.

Blackburn, Terence R. *The British Humilation of Burma*. Bangkok: Orchid Press, 2000.

Bose, Sugata. *His Majesty's Opponent*. New Delhi: Penguin Books India, 2011.

Brandon John J. (ed.). *Burma/Myanmar – Towards the Twenty–First Century: Dynamic of Continuity and Change*. Bangkok: Open Society Institute, 1997.

Byar Bowh Si, Oliver. *Solidarity and Civil Society: An Answer to Dictatorship in Burma*. CreateSpace Independent Publishing Platform, 2011.

Cady, John F. *A History of Modern Burma*. New York: Cornell University Press, 1958.

Callahan, Mary P. *Making Enemies: War and State Building in Burma*. Singapore: Singapore University Press, 2004.

Carey, Peter (ed.). *Burma: The Challenge of Change in a Divided Society* (Foreword by Aung San Suu Kyi). New York: St. Martin's Press, 1997.

240 Bibliography

Chakravarti, Nalini Ranjan. *The Indian Minority in Burma*. London: Oxford University Press, 1971.

Chakravarti, Sundeep. *Highway 39 – Journeys through a Fractured Land*. New Delhi: HarperCollins Publishers, 2012.

Chandra, Satish and Baladas Ghoshal (eds). *India and South East Asia: Cultural, Economic and Strategic Linkages*. New Delhi: Gyan Publishing House, 2011.

Cheesman, Nick, Monique Skidmore and Trevor Wilson (eds). *Ruling Myanmar: From Cyclone Nargis to National Elections*. Singapore: ISEAS Publishing, 2011.

Chit, Khin Myo. *A Wonderland of Burmese Legends*. Bangkok: Orchid Press, 1984.

———. *Colourful Myanmar*. Yangon: U Ye Myint, 1995.

———. *Festivals and Flowers of the Twelve Burmese Seasons*. Bangkok: Orchid Press, 2002.

Christian, John L. *Burma*. London: Collins, 1945.

Chung, Tan, Zhang Minqiu and Ravni Thakur (eds). *Across the Himalayan Gap: A Chinese Quest For Understanding India*. New Delhi: Konark Publishers, 2013.

Clinton, Hillary Rodham. *Hard Choices*. London: Simon & Schuster, 2014.

Colquhoun, Archibald Ross. *Amongst the Shans*. London: Field & Tuer, 1885.

Das Gurudas (ed.). *Indo–Myanmar Border Trade: Staus, Problems and Potentials*. New Delhi: Akansha Publishing House, 2005.

Datta–Ray, Sunanda K. *Looking East to Look West: Lee Kuan Yew's Mission India*. Singapore: ISEAS, 2009.

De Silva, K. M., Pensri Duke, Ellen S. Goldberg and Nathan Katz (eds). *Ethnic Conflict in Buddhist Societies: Sri Lanka, Thailand and Burma*. London: Pinter Publishers, 1988.

Devare, Sudhir. *India & Southeast Asia: Towards Security Convergence*. Singapore: ISEAS, 2006.

Dittmer, Lowell (ed.). *Burma or Myanmar? The Struggle for National Identity*. Singapore: World Scientific Publishing Co. Pte. Ltd., 2010.

Dixit, J. N. *Across Borders: Fifty Years of India's Foreign Policy*. New Delhi: Picus Books, 1998.

———. *My South Block Years: Memoires of a Foreign Secretary*. New Delhi: Pauls Press, 1996.

Donnison, F. S. V. *Burma*. London: Ernest Benn Limited, 1970.

Dubey, Muchkund. *India's Foreign Policy: Coping with the Changing World*. Delhi: Pearson, 2013.

Dutta Krishna and Andrew Robinson (eds). *Rabindranath Tagore: An Anthology*. London: Picado, 1997.

Egreteau, Renaud. *Wooing the Generals: India's New Burma Policy*. Delhi: Authors Press, 2003.

Elliott, Patricia W. *The White Umbrella: A Woman's Struggle for Freedom in Burma*. Bangkok: Friends Books, 2006.

Bibliography 241

Egreteau, Renaud and Larry Jagan (eds). *Back to the Old Habits: Isolationism or the Self- Preservation of Burma's Military Regime*. Bangkok: Institute of Research on Contemporary South East Asia (IRASEC), 2008.

Egreteau Renaud and Larry Jagan. *Soldiers and Diplomacy in Burma: Understanding the Foreign Relations of the Burmese Praetorian State*. Singapore: NUS Press, 2013.

Felfamkima, V.L. *Mizoram Border Trade: Emerging Trend & Future Prospects*. New Delhi: Akansha Publishing House, 2011.

Fink, Christina. *Living Silence: Burma under Military Rule*. Bangkok: White Lotus Company Company Ltd., 2001.

Foucar, E. C. V. *I Lived In Burma*. London: Dennis Dobson, 1956.

Furnivall, J. S. *Colonial Policy and Practice*. London: Cambridge University Press, 1948.

Ganesan, N. and Kya Yin Hlaing (eds). *Myanmar: State, Society and Ethnicity*. Singapore: ISEAS, 2007.

Gait, Sir Edward. *A History of Assam*. Calcutta: Thacker, Spink & Co, 1926.

Gassah, L. H. and C. J. Thomas (eds). *Democracy and Development in India's North-East: Challenges and Opportunities*. Delhi: Bookwell, 2015.

Geok, Ang Chin. *Aung San Suu Kyi: Towards a New Freedom*. Sydney: Prentice Hall, 1998.

Ghosh, Amitav. *Dancing in Cambodia and Other Essays*. New Delhi: Penguin Books India, 2008.

———. *The Glass Palace*. New Delhi: HarperCollins Publishers, 2000.

Grare Frédéric and Amitabh Mattoo (eds). *India and ASEAN*. New Delhi: Manohar Publishers, 2001.

Gravers, Mikael (ed.). *Exploring Ethnic Diversity in Burma*. Copenhagen: NIAS Press, 2007.

Hainsworth, Geoffrey B. *Globalization and the Asian Economic Crisis: Indigenous Responses, Coping Strategies, and Governence Reform in Southeast Asia*. Vancouver: CSEAR, University of British Columbia, 2000.

Hall, D. G. E. *Burma*. London: Hutchinson's University Library, 1950.

Harvey, G.E. *Outline of Burmese History*. London: Longmans, Green & Co. Ltd, 1926.

Hauff, Michael von. *Economic and Social Development in Burma/Myanmar: The Relevance of Reforms*. Marburg: Metropolis-Verlag, 2009.

Hazarika, Sanjoy. *Strangers of the Mist: Tales of War and Peace in India's Northeast*. New Delhi: Viking, 1994.

Holliday, Ian. *Burma Redux*. New York: Coumbia University Press, 2011.

Jelsma, Martin (ed.). *Trouble in the Triangle: Opium and Conflict in Burma*. Chiang Mai: Silkworm Books, 2005.

Johnstone, William C. *Burma's Foreign Policy: A Study in Neutralism*. Cambridge: Harvard University Press, 1963.

Kanchan, R. K. *Hindu Kingdoms of South-East India*. New Delhi: Cosmo Publications, 1990.

Keenan, Paul. *By Force of Arms: Armed Ethnic Groups in Burma*. Delhi: Vij Books, 2012–2013.

242 Bibliography

Kha, Tekkatho Tin. *The State Visits: the Milestones in history*. Yangon: U Soe Win News and Periodicals Enterprise, 2003.

Khosla, G. D. *The Last Mughal*. New Delhi: Navrang, 1986.

Kingdon-Ward, Frank. *Return to the Irrawaddy*. London: Andrew Melrose Limited, 1956.

Kingsbury, Damien. *South-East Asia: A Political Profile*. Michigan: Oxford University Press, 2001.

Koichi Fujita, Fumiharu Mieno and Ikuku Okamoto (eds). *The Economic Transition in Myanmar after 1988: Market Economy verses State Control*. Singopore: NUS Press, 2009.

Kyaw Yin Hlaing, Robert H. Taylor and Tin Maung Maung Than (eds). *Myanmar: Beyond Politics to Societal Imperatives*. Singapore: ISEAS, 2005.

Kyi, Aung San Suu. *Letters from Burma*. London: Penguin Group, 1997.

———. *The Voice of Hope: Conversations with Alan Clements*. New York: Seven Stories Press, 1997.

———. *Freedom From Fear and Other Writings*. New Delhi: Penguin Books India, 1991.

———. *Burma and India: Some Aspects of Intellectual Life under Colonialism*. New Delhi: Allied Publishers, 1990.

Lehman F. K. (ed.). *Military Rule in Burma since 1962*. Singapore: ISEAS, 1981.

Lewis, Norman. *Golden Earth: Travels in Burma*. London: Jonathan Cape, 1952.

Li Chenyang and Wilhelm Hofmeister (eds). *Myanmar: Prospect for Change*. Singapore: Select Books, 2010.

Liang, Chi-shad. *Burma's Foreign Relations: Neutralism in Theory and Practice*. New York: Praeger Publishers, 1990.

Lintner, Bertil. *Aung San Suu Kyi and Burma's Stuggle for Democracy*. Chiang Mai: Silkworm Books, 2011.

———. *Burma in Revolt: Opium and Insurgency since 1948*. Chiang Mai: Silkworm Books, 2011.

Maclean, Rory. *Under the Dragon*. London: HarperCollins Publishers, 1998.

Mahajani, Usha. *The Role of Indian Minorities in Burma and Malaya*. Bombay: Vora & Co, 1960.

Malik, General V. P. *India's Military Conflicts and Diplomacy: An Inside View of Decision Making*. Noida: HarperCollins Publishers India, 2013.

Marshall, Andrew. *The Trouser People*. London: Penguin Books, 2003.

Masters, John. *The Road Past Mandalay*. London: Cassell Military Paperbacks, 1961.

Maugham, W. Somerset. *The Gentlemen in the Parlour*. New York: Doubleday, Doran & Company, 1930.

Maung Maung (compiled and edited). *Aung San of Burma*. The Hague: Yale University, Southeast Asian Studies, 1962.

Maung, Maung. *Burma and General Ne Win*. Rangoon: Religious Affairs dept. Press, 1969.

Maw, Ba. *Breakthrough in Burma*. London: Yale University Press, 1968.

Bibliography 243

Majumdar, R. C. *Hindu Colonies in the Far East*. Calcutta: General Printers & Publishers, 1944.

Metraux Daniel A., Khin Oo (eds). *Burma's Modern Tragedy*. Lewiston: The Edwin Mellen Press, 2004.

Mishra, Pankaj. *From the Ruins of Empire*. London: Penguin Books, 2012.

Mohan, C. Raja. *Samudra Manthan: Sino-Indian Rivalry in the Indo-Pacific*. Washington, DC: Carnegie Endowment For International Peace, 2012.

Mole, Robert. *The Temple Bells Are Calling: A Personal Record of the Last Years of British Rule in Burma*. Michigan: Pentland Books, 2001.

Moore, Christopher G. *Waiting for the Lady*. Bangkok: Heaven Lake Press, 2003.

Muni, S. D. *China's Strategic Engagement with ASEAN*. New Delhi: Institute of Defence and Strategic Studies, 2002.

Myaing, Wai Wai. *A Journey in Time, Family Memoirs: Burma 1914–1948*. New York: iUniverse, Inc., 2005.

Myint, Soe. *Burma File – A Question of Democracy*. New Delhi: India Research Press, 2003.

Myint U, Thant. *The Making of Modern Burma*. Cambridge: University Press, Cambridge, 2001.

———. *Where China Meets India*. London: Faber and Faber Limited, 2011.

Myoe, Maung Aung. *In the Name of Pauk-Phaw*. Singapore: Institute of Southeast Asian Studies, 2011.

Nakanishi, Yoshihiro. *Strong Soldiers, Failed Revolution: The State and Military in Burma, 1962–88*. Singapore: NUS Press, 2013.

Nanda, Prakash. *Rediscovering Asia: Evolution of India's Look-East Policy*. New Delhi: Lancer Publishers, 2008.

Naw, Angelene. *Aung San and the Stuggle for Burmese Independence*. Chiang Mai: Silkworm Books, 2001.

Nehru, Jawaharlal. *An Autobiography*. New Delhi: Viking, 2004.

———. *Selected Works of Jawaharlal Nehru: Second Series – Volume – 3*. New Delhi: Jawaharlal Nehru Memorial Fund, 1985.

———. *The Discovery of India*. Oxford, 1956.

Nu, U. *U Nu: Saturday's Son*. London: Yale University Press, 1975.

Orwell, George. *Burmese Days*. London: Penguin Books, 1944.

Pandita, Sayadaw U. *In This Very Life: The Liberation Teachings of the Buddha*. Boston: Wisdom Publications, 1992.

Panikkar, K. M. *Lectures on India's Contact with the World in the Pre–British Period*. Nagpur: Nagpur University, 1964.

———. *In Two Chinas: Memoirs of a Diplomat*. London: George Allen & Unwin, 1955.

———. *Asia and Western Dominance*. London: George Allen & Unwin, 1953.

———. *The Future of South–East Asia: An Indian View*. New York: The Macmillan Company, 1943.

Paul, Erik. *Obstacles to the Democratization in Southeast Asia*. Sydney: Palgrave Macmillan, 2010.

244 Bibliography

Pedersen, Morten B., Emily Rudland and Ronald J. May (eds). *Burma Myanmar: Strong Regime Weak State?* Adelaide: Crawford Publishing House, 2000.

Phan, Zoya. *Undaunted: My Struggle for Freedom and Survival in Burma.* New York: Free Press, 2009.

Pradhan, Swatanter K. *New Dimesions in Indo-Burmese Relations.* New Delhi: Rajat Publications, 2000.

Pye, Maung Maung. *Burma in the Crucible.* Rangoon: Khittaya Publishing House, 1951.

Rajshekhar. *Myanmar's Nationalist Movement (1906–1948) and India.* New Delhi: South Asian Publishers, 2006.

Ram, Amar Nath (ed.). *Two Decades of India's Look East Policy: Partnership for Peace, Progress and Prosperity.* New Delhi: ICWA-Manohar Publishers, 2012.

Reddy K. Raja (ed.). *India and ASEAN.* New Delhi: New Century Publications, 2005.

Rieffel, Lex (ed.). *Myanmar/Burma: Inside Challenges, Outside Interests.* Washington, DC: Brookings Institution Press and the Konrad Adenauer Foundation, 2010.

Roberts, Christopher. *ASEAN's Myanmar Crisis: Challenges to the Pursuit of a Security Community.* Singapore: ISEAS, 2010.

Rogers, Benedict. *Than Shwe: Unmasking Burma's Tyrant.* Chiang Mai: Silkworm Books, 2010.

Romein, Jan. *The Asian Century: A History of Modern Nationalism in Asia.* London: George Allen & Unwin Ltd., 1962.

Rotberg, Robert I. *Burma: Prospects for a Democratic Future.* Washington, DC: Brookings Institution Press, 1998.

Roy, Arpita Basu and Subhadeep Bhattacharya (eds). *India and South East Asia: States, Borders and Culture.* Delhi: Shipra Publications, 2015.

Sakhuja, Vijay. *The Strategic Dynamics of the Indian Ocean.* Lecture, Abu Dhabi: The Emirates Center for Strategic Studies and Research, 2012.

Sakhuja, Vijay (ed.). *Reinvigorating IOR–ARC.* New Delhi: Pentagon Press, 2012.

San, Aung. *Burma's Challenge.* Rangoon, 1946.

Sanda, Sao. *The Moon Princess: Memories of the Shan States.* Bangkok: River Books, 2008.

Sangermano, Father. *The Burmese Empire – A Hundred Years Ago.* London: Westminster, Archibald Constable and Company, 1893.

Sargent, Inge. *Twilight Over Burma: My Life as a Shan Princess.* Chiang Mai: Silkworm Books, 1994.

Seekins, Donald M. *Burma and Japan Since 1940: From 'Co–prosperity' to 'Quiet Dialogue'.* Copenhagen: NIAS Press, 2007.

Seng, Koh Kim. *Misunderstood Myanmar: An Introspective Study of A Southeast Asian State in Tansition.* Singapore: Humanities Press, 2011.

Shah, Sudha. *The King in Exile: The Fall of the Royal Family of Burma.* Noida: HarperCollins Publishers India, 2012.

Bibliography 245

Sharan, P. *Government and Politics of Burma*. New Delhi: Metropolitan, 1983.

Sikri, Rajiv. *Challenge and Strategy: Rethinking India's Foreign Policy*. New Delhi: Sage Publications, 2009.

Silverstein, Josef. *Burma: Military Rule and the Politics of Stagnation*. New York: Cornell University Press, 1977.

Silverstein, Josef (ed.). *Independent Burma at Forty Years: Six Assessments*. New York: SEAP, 1989.

———. *The Political Legacy of Aung San*. New York: Southeast Asia Program, Cornell University, 1972.

Singh, Balwant. *Independence and Democracy in Burma, 1945–1952: The Turbulent Years*. Ann Arbor: CSSEAS Publications, 1993.

Singh, K. Natwar. *Walking with Lions: Tales from a Diplomatic Past*. Noida: HarperCollins Publishers India, 2013.

Singh, Kumar Badri Narain. *Freedom Struggle in Burma*. New Delhi: Commonwealth Publishers, 1989.

Singh, Langpoklakpam Suraj. *Movement for Democracy in Myanmar*. New Delhi: Akansha Publishing House, 2006.

Singh, Uma Shankar. *Burma and India: 1948–1962*. New Delhi: Oxford & IBH Publishing, 1979.

Skidmore, Monique. *Karaoke Fascism: Burma and the Politics of Fear*. Philadelphia: University of Pennsylvania Press, 2004.

Skidmore, Monique (ed.). *Burma at the Turn of the Twenty-First Century*. Honolulu: University of Hawaii Press, 2005.

Skidmore, Monique and Trevor Wilson (eds). *Dictatorship, Disorder and Decline in Myanmar*. Australian National University E Press, 2008.

Slim, Field Marshal the Viscount. *Defeat into Victory*. London: Cassell & Company, 1962.

Smith, Donald Eugene. *Religion and Politics in Burma*. Princeton: Princeton University Press, 1965.

Smith, Martin. *Burma: Insurgency and the Politics of Ethnicity*. Bangkok: White Lotus, 1991.

South, Ashley. *Ethnic Politics in Burma: States of Conflict*. New York: Routledge, Taylor & Francis Group, 2008.

Steve Martin, Mic Looby, Michael Clark and Joe Cummings. *Myanmar (Burma)*. Victoria: Lonely Planet Publications, 2002.

Steinberg, David I. *Turmoil in Burma: Contested Legitimacies in Myanmar*. Norwalk: EastBridge, 2006.

Steinberg, David I. and Hongwei Fan. *Modern China–Myanmar Relations – Dilemmas of Mutual Dependence*. Copenhagen: NIAS Press, 2012.

Steinberg, David I. *Burma/Myanmar: What Everyone Needs to Know*. New York: Oxford University Press, 2010.

———. *Burma: The State of Myanmar*. Washington DC: Georgetown University Press, 2001.

———. *Burma: Prospects for Political and Economic Reconstruction*. Cambridge: The World Peace Foundation, 1997.

246 Bibliography

———. *Burma's Road Toward Development: Growth and Ideology under Military Rule*. Colorado: Westview Press, 1981.

Suragamika. *The Roadmap: Documentary Fiction on Contemporary Burma*. Chiang Mai: Silkworm Books, 2011.

Swe, U Ba. *The Burmese Revolution*. Rangoon: Information Dept., Union of Burma, 1952.

Tagore, Rabindranath. *Letters from Java: Rabindranath Tagore's Tour of South-East Asia 1 927*. Kolkata: Visva Bharti Publishing Department, 2010.

Taylor, Robert H. *The State in Myanmar*. London: Hurst Publishers, 2009.

Tennyson, F. Jesse. *The Story of Burma*. London: Macmillan, 1945.

Than, Mya and Joseph L. H. Than (eds). *Myanmar Dilemmas and Options: The Challenge of Economic Transition in the 1990s*. Singapore: ISEAS, 1990.

Than, Tin Maung Maung. *State Dominance in Myanmar: The Political Economy of Industrialization*. Singapore: ISEAS Publishing, 2007.

Thant, U. *Toward World Peace: Addresses and Public Statements, 1957–1963*. New York: Thomas Yoseloff, 1964.

Tharoor, Shashi. *Pax Indica: India and the World of the 21st Century*. New Delhi: Allen Lane, 2012.

Thawnghmung, Ardeth Maung. *Behind the Teak Curtain: Authoritarianism, Agricultural Policies and Political Legitimacy in Rural Burma/Myanmar*. London: Kegan Paul, 2004.

Thwe, Pascal Khoo. *From the Land of Green Ghosts: A Burmese Odyssey*. New York: HarperCollins, 2002.

Tinker, Hugh. *The Union of Burma*. London: Oxford University Press, 1959.

Tint, Mya Than. *On the Road to Mandalay*. Bangkok: White Orchid Press, 1996.

Tiwari, Arun K., U Kyi Thein and P. Krishnam Raju. *Glitter N Gold*. New Delhi: Ocean Books Pvt. Ltd., 2005.

Trager, Frank N. *Burma: From Kingdom to Republic*. London: The Pall Mall Press Limited, 1966.

Trager, Helen G. *Burma through Alien Eyes*. Bombay: Popular Press, 1966.

Tucker, Shelby. *Burma – The Curse of Independence*. London: Pluto Press, 2001.

Tun, Sai Aung. *History of the Shan State: From Its Origins to 1962*. Chiang Mai: Silkworm Books, 2009.

Turnell, Sean. *Fiery Dragons: Banks, Moneylenders and Microfinance in Burma*. Copenhagen: NIAS Press, 2009.

Ullah, AKM Ahsan. *South and Southeast Asia: Dealing with History and Development*. VDM Verlag, 2008.

Victor, Barbara. *The Lady*. New York: Faber and Faber, 1998.

Webster, Donovan. *The Burma Road*. London: Macmillan, 2004.

Weller, Marc (ed.). *Democracy and Politics in Burma: A Collection of Documents*. The National Coalition Government of the Union of Burma, 1993.

Westad, Odd Arne. *Restless Empire: China and the World Since 1750*. London: The Bodley Head, 2012.

Wheeler, J. Talboys. *India and the Frontier States of Afghanistan, Nepal and Burma, Volume II*. New Delhi: Bhavana Books & Prints, 2000 (First Reprint).

Wilson, Trevor (ed.). *Myanmar's Long Road to National Reconciliation*. Singapore: ISEAS, 2006.

Win, Kanbawza. *Constructive Engagement in The Burmese Context*. Bangkok: CPDSK (Institute of), 1995.

Wintle, Justin. *Perfect Hostage: A Life of Aung San Suu Kyi*. London: Hutchinson, 2007.

Yhome, K. *Myanamr: Can the Generals Resist Change?* New Delhi: Rupa, 2008.

Yoe, Shway. *The Burman: His Life and Notions*. New York: The Norton Library, W.W. Morton, 1963.

Journals, Papers and Articles

"Burma's 2010 Elections: A Comprehensive Report." 31 Jan 2010.

Campbell, Kurt M. "The New U.S. Policy of Prgmatic Engagement." In *Myanmar/Burma: Inside Challenges, Outside Interests*, Lex Rieffel (ed.), 212.Washington, DC: Brookings Institution Press and the Konrad Adenauer Foundation, 2010.

Clapp, Priscilla. "Prospects for Rapprochement between the United States and Myanmar." *Contemporary Southeast Asia*, December 2010: 409–428.

Current Realities and Future Possibilites in Burma/Myanmar: Options for U.S. Policy. Asia Society Task Force Report, 2010.

Current Realities and Future Possibilites in Burma/Myanmar: Perspectives from Asia. Asia Society, March 2010.

Economist Intelleigence Unit Country Report. "Burma: Outlook for 2012–13." November 2011: 4–33.

Focus on India–Myanmar Relations. Embassy of India, Yangon. Yangon: Embassy of India, 2003.

Ganesan, N. "Myanmar's Foreign Relations: Reaching out to the World." In *Myanmar: Beyond Politics to Societal Imperatives*, Robert H. Taylor, Tin Maung Maung Than, Kyaw Yin Hlaing (eds), 212.Singapore: ISEAS, 2005.

Gandhi in Burma. India Information Service of Rangoon: Embassy of India, Burma.

Hlaing, Kyaw Yin. "Myanmar in 2004: Why Military Rule Continues." *Southeast Asian Affairs*, 2005: 231–256.

Hong, Zhao. *China and India Courting Myanmar For Good Relations*. EAI Background Brief no. 360, December 2007.

India–Burma Relations: Trends and Developments (1990–2011). New Delhi: Burma Centre Delhi, 2011.

Jagan, Larry. "Burma's Military: Purges and Coups Prevent Progress Towards Democracy." In *Myanmar's Long Road to National Reconciliation*, Trevor Wilson, (ed.), 29–37. Singapore: ISEAS, 2006.

248 Bibliography

Kaplan, Robert D. "Center Stage for the Twenty-first Century." *Foreign Affairs 88-2*, March/April 2009: 16–32.

Kanwal, Gurmeet. "A Strategic Perspective on India–Myanmar Relations." In *Myanmar/Burma: Inside Challenges, Outside Interests*, Alexis Rieffel, (ed.), 212. Washington, DC: Brookings Institution Press and the Konrad Adenauer Foundation, 2010.

Kumar Satish, (ed.), *India's National Security: Annual Review 2012*. New Delhi: Routledge, 2013.

Limaye, Satu P. "Introduction: America's Bilateral Relations with Southeast Asia – Constaints and Promise." *Contemporary Southeast Asia*, December 2010: 309–316.

Lin, Christina Y. "Militarisation of China's Energy Security Policy." *Institut für Strategie –Politik – Sicherheits – und Wirtschaftsberatung (ISPSW)*. June 18, 2008. se1.isn.ch/serviceengine/Files/ISN/56390/ . . . /StringPearls. pdf.

Matheo Falco (Chair). *Burma: Time for Change*. Report of an Independent Task Force, New York: Council on Foreign Relations, 2003.

Matthews, Bruce. "Myanmar: Beyond the Reach of International Relief?" *Southeast Asian Affairs*, 2001: 229–248.

Menon, Shivshankar. "Maritime Imperatives of Indian Foreign Policy." *Maritime Affairs*, Winter 2009: 5(2); 15–21.

Ministry of External Affairs, Government of India. *Visit of President Dr. A.P.J. Abdul Kalam to Myanmar and Mauritius: 8 to 13 March 2006*. New Delhi: Ministry of External Affairs, 2006.

Netaji and Burma. India Information Service of Rangoon: Embassy of India, 1979.

Niksch, Larry A. "Burma–U.S. Relations." In *Burma in Turmoil*, Alden T. Roycee, (ed.). 53–74. New York: Nova Science Publishers,, 2008.

Nyunt, Daw Thein Thein. *Rights of Myanmar Women Endowed by Myanmar Customs and Traditions*. Paper, Michigan: University Press, 2005.

Onn, Deepak Nair and Lee Poh (eds). "The Asean." *Regional Outlook: Southeast Asia*, 2005–2006: 36–115.

———. "The Asean." *Regional Outlook: Southeast Asia*, 2008–2009: 23–125.

Onn, Lee Poh and Ian J. Storey (eds). "The Asean." *Regional Outlook: Southeast Asia*, 2009–2010: 35–129.

Onn, Lee Poh and Michael J. Montesano (eds). "The Asean." *Regional Outlook: Southeast Asia*, 2010–2011: 42–145.

———. "The Asean." *Regional Outlook: Southeast Asia*, 2011–2012: 51–151.

Pandey, Ira (ed.). *India China: Neighbours Strangers*. New Delhi: India International Centre, 2009/2010.

Pedersen, Morten B. "Myanmar: The Future Takes Form – But Little Chnage in Sight." *Southeast Asian Affairs*, 2007: 217–254.

Pederson, Morten B. "A Comprehensive International Approach to Political and Economic Development in Burma/Myanmar." In *Myanmar's Long Road to National Reconciliation*, Wilson Trevor, (ed.), 276–290. Singapore: ISEAS, 2006.

Bibliography   249

Pederson, Morten B. "The Challenges of Transition in Myanmar." In *Myanmar: Beyond Politics to Societal Imperatives*, Robert H. Taylor, Tin Maung Maung Than, Kyaw Yin Hlaing (eds), 212. Singapore: ISEAS, 2005.

Prakash, Admiral Arun. "India's Maritime Growth: Rationale and Objectives." *Varuna Vak*, July 2011.

Rajah, Ananda. "Ethnicity and Civil War in Burma: What Is the Rationality?" In *Burma: Prospects for a Democratic Future*, Robert I. Rotberg (ed.), 308. Washington, DC: Brookings Institutions Press, 1998.

Ray, Prabir De and Jayanta Kumar. *India–Myanmar Connectivity: Current Status and Future Prospects*. IFPS/CPWAS Occasional Paper Series No. 4, New Delhi: KW Publishers, 2013.

Rohana Mahmood and Hans-Joachim Esderts (eds). "Myanmar and the Wider Southeast Asia." *Institute of Strategic and International Studies (ISIS) Malaysia*. Kuala Lumpur: ISIS, 1991. 63.

Russel Heng Hiang-Khng and Denis Hew (eds), "The Asean." *Regional Outlook: Southeast Asia*, 2003–2004: 26–69.

———. "The Asean." *Regional Outlook: Southeast Asia*, 2004–2005: 27–81.

Seekins, Donald M. "Myanmar: Secret Talks and Political Paralysis." *Southeast Asian Affairs*, 2002: 199–212.

Seshadri, V. S. 'Transforming Connectivity Corridors between India and Myanmar into Development Corridors', *Research and Information System for Developing Countries – RIS*, New Delhi: RIS, 2014.

Steinberg, David I. "Myanmar in 2010: The Elections Year and Beyond." *Southeast Asian Affairs*, 2011: 174–207.

———. "Myanmar: Reconciliation – Progress in the Process?" *Southeast Asian Affairs*, 2003: 171–188.

Taylor, Robert H. "Myanmar in 2009: On the Cusp of Normality?" *Southeast Asian Affairs*, 2010: 201–233.

———. "Myanmar in 2007: Growing Pressure for Change but the Regime remains Obdurate." *Southeast Asian Affairs*, 2008: 247–290.

———. "One Day, One Fathom, Bagan Won't Move": On the Myanmar Road to a Constitution." In *Myanmar's Long Road to National Reconciliation*, Trevor Wilson (ed.), 3–28. Singapore: ISEAS, 2006.

———. Myanmar: Roadmap to Where? *Southeast Asian Affairs*, 2004 171–184.

Than, Tin Maung Maung. "Myanmar." *Southeast Asian Affairs*, 2012–2013: 68–76.

———. "Myanmar in 2008: Weathering the Storm." *Southeast Asian Affairs*, 2009: 196–221.

———. "Myanmar: Challenges Galore but Opposition Failed to Score." *Southeast Asian Affairs*, 2006: 183–223.

———. "Myanmar's Energy Sector: Banking on Natural Gas." *Southeast Asian Affairs*, 2005: 257–289.

———. "Myanmar and China: A Special Relationship." *Southeast Asian Affairs*, 2003: 189–210.

250 Bibliography

Thuzar, Moe. "Myanmar: Facing the Future." *Southeast Asian Affairs*, 2012–2013: 115–118.

Venkateswaran, A. P. (Foreword). "India's Security Environment: Proceedings of Select Seminars held by Asia Centre Bangalore." Asia Centre Bangalore. New Delhi: Konark, 2007–12: 362.

Wilson, Trevor. "China, India and Myanmar's Elections: Strategic Contest or Friendly Neigbours?" Australian Institute of International Affairs Policy Commentary, November 2010: 33–42.

Yawnghwe, Harn. "United States–Myanmar Relations: On the Threshold of a Rapprochement." *Contemporary Southeast Asia*, December 2010: 427–433.

Zwa, U Kyaw. *The Role of Ramayana in Myanmar Society*. Paper, Illionois: Northern Illionois University, 2001.

Index

Act East Policy 149–50, 216
Air Services Agreement 131, 183
Anti-Fascist People's Freedom League (AFPFL) 28–9, 82
ASEAN–India Commemorative Summit 130, 146, 149
Association of South East Asian Nations (ASEAN) 3, 36–9; Australia's regional programme of assistance 48; Burma policy 38–9; 'China's satellite' 38; CLMV 36; Cyclone Nargis 37; degree of authoritarianism 36; and EU 44; 'flawed democratization process' 37; and Japan cooperation 48; Myanmar's membership 37; Nyapyitaw's plans 38; policymakers 4; policy of constructive engagement 34; pro-democracy movement 36–7; 'Saffron Revolution' 37; SPDC approach 39
Aung San 7, 18, 20, 24, 27, 28, 30, 76, 82, 91, 94
Aung San Suu Kyi 6, 19, 21, 40, 43, 108, 113, 120, 137, 144, 149, 153, 170, 200, 219
Australia 48–50; bilateral relations 49; middle-of-the-road policy 48; Myanmar history 48–9; 'The new policy' 49

Bangladesh 54–5; ITLOS 55; and Myanmar relations 54–5; Myanmar's internal problem 54–5; policy of oppression 54

Bangladesh, China, India and Myanmar (BCIM) Economic Corridor 5, 148, 168, 170, 206–7
Bangladesh, Sri Lanka, Maldives and Myanmar (BSM) division 3
Bhutan 51
Bilateral Investment Promotion Agreement (BIPA) 178
bilateral relationship: border region and ethnicity 165–6; China and India 161–2; China factor 168–9; connectivity 166–8; 2008 Constitution 218; constitutional reforms 218–19; economic cooperation 221–3; ethnic reconciliation 217; India and Burma/Myanmar 161; India–China equations 216; military rule 219; multifaceted relationship 169–86; national reconciliation process 217; NLD 217–18; North East angle 162–5; people-to-people contacts 223–4; politico-economic sphere, India 216; politico-strategic cooperation 220–1; 'the Sonia Gandhi model' 219; Thein Sein government 217; US–China equations 215–16
border region and ethnicity 165–6; artificial delineation 165; China–Myanmar border areas 166; impact of ethnicity 166; Indian security forces, attacks 166; Indo–Myanmar border region 166; insurgent groups

252 Index

165; pattern of ethnic linkages 165; self-help, approach of 165; Thai–Myanmar border 166

Bs (Brahmanism, Buddhism and British) 71

Burma and India: Some Aspects of Intellectual Life under Colonialism 139

Burma Independence Army (BIA) 82, 94

Burma National Army (BNA) 76

Burma Socialist Programme Party (BSPP) 29, 90, 97–8

Burmese Way to Socialism in April 1964 18, 32, 89, 94

China–Myanmar relations 168–9, 192–6; Burma's independence 192–3; Communist Party of Burma (CPB) 193; Cultural Revolution 193–4; Delhi and Beijing, interactions 193; 'Golden Land' 168; and India 161–2; India–Myanmar–China triangle 168; India's Myanmar policy 195; natural resources 196; Ne Win government 194; People's Republic of China 193; policies of China and India 195; SLORC and SPDC 194; Thein Sein's foreign policy 195–6

CLMV (Cambodia, Laos, Myanmar, Vietnam) 36, 64, 170, 216

connectivity 166–8; to China 167; economic cooperation 223; India's Eastern policy 168; Kaladan Multi-modal Transport project 166; NER policy 166–8; RIS 166–7; Trilateral Highway project 166

2008 Constitution 10, 19, 142, 218

Cultural Exchange Programme 133, 184

Cyclone Nargis 26, 37, 113, 184

defence/security cooperation 171–3; China and Myanmar 172; India's NER and Myanmar's north-western region 171–2; MoU on Border Cooperation with Myanmar 172; sports exchanges 173; terrorism and insurgency 172; Thein Sein government 172–3

development cooperation 181–2; hydroelectric power projects 181; Indian Space Research Organisation (ISRO) 181; Rhi-Tiddim road project 181–2; Telecommunications Consultants India Ltd. (TCIL) 181; Trilateral Highway project 181

Double Taxation Avoidance Agreement (DTAA) 178

economic cooperation 173–8; border trade 177; connectivity 223; India–Myanmar trade 173, 175; India's exports/imports from Myanmar 175–6; international competition 222; investment 177–8; Kaladan Multi-modal Transport project 222; Myanmar's trade with ASEAN 173–4; Strategic Economic Dialogue 222; 'suitable commercial strategies' 222; trade and investment cooperation 221–2; Trilateral Highway project 222–3

energy cooperation 178–80; after reforms 180; before reforms 178–80; MoU on cooperation in the petroleum sector 179; OVL and GAIL 178–80; 'Saffron Revolution' 179; shallow-water pipeline and direct shipping 179

EU policy 44–6; 'Building a Lasting EU–Myanmar Partnership' 45–6; Cameron, David 46; Council of European Union 44–5; EU–ASEAN relations 44; Generalised Scheme of Preferences (GSP) 44; government of Myanmar/Burma 45; Juppe, Alain 46; NLD 45–6; Suu Kyi 45

FESR *see* Framework for Economic and Social Reforms (FESR)

Fiery Dragons 74

Framework for Economic and Social Reforms (FESR) 32–3

Gas Authority of India Ltd. (GAIL) 178–80
Generalised Scheme of Preferences (GSP) 44

human resource development (HRD) cooperation 182–3; India–Myanmar Centres 182; training, ITEC programme 182–3
human settlement, Burma 64–5

India and Burma/Myanmar 65–6, 161
India–ASEAN Summit 149
India-assisted developmental projects 185–6
India–China relations 204–6; ICWA 205–6; Narendra Modi's foreign policy 205; Panchsheel phase 204; post–Ne Win military rule 205; Strategic Economic Dialogue 205
India–Myanmar–China triangle: BCIM Economic Corridor 206; Burmese diplomacy 191; Chinese community and immigration 199–200; cooperation in other areas 199; defence cooperation 197–8; economic relations 198; ICWA delegation 201, 203–4, 208; India–China relations 204–6; infrastructure 198–9; Japan's policy 202; Kachin Independence Army (KIA) 202; Maritime Silk Route (MSR) 206–7; Myanmar–China relations 192–6; Myanmar politics 201; Myanmar's foreign policy 192; Myitsone Dam project 202; NLD 204; Panchsheel or Five Principles of Peaceful Co-existence 206; political and diplomatic domain, proximity 197; 'pro-active engagement' 207–8; pro-democracy movement 200; rivalry, China and India in Myanmar 208; SLORC/SPDC era 200; strategic concerns and security 207; Thant Myint-U 209; Thein Sein's rule 200–1, 203
Indian Council of Cultural Relations (ICCR) 145
Indian Council of World Affairs (ICWA) delegation 151–3, 201, 203–6, 208
Indian leaders 74–7; Bose and Aung San 76; Japan's occupation of Burma 75–6; Jawaharlal Nehru 75–6; Mahatma Gandhi, advice to Indians 75; Rabindranath Tagore 74; Rajendra Prasad in Rangoon 91; Subhas Chandra Bose, 76
Indian National Army (INA) 76
Indian perspective, Myanmar: economy in transition: British Raj 31–2; Burma, Least Developed Country (LDC) 32; challenges 32; *Doing Business 2014* 33; economic growth 33; FESR 32–3; market economy, evolution of 32; regime of Ne Win 32; external relations: ASEAN 36–9; Australia 48–50; Bangladesh 54–5; Bhutan 51; EU policy 44–6; Five Principles of Peaceful Co-existence 35; foreign policy 35–6; Japan 46–8; MOFA 34–5; Nepal 51–2; Pakistan 52–4; perceptions, external/internal 33–4; Sri Lanka 50–1; US 39–44; internal politics 23–31; socio-cultural portrait 16–17
Indians, role of: Indian community, impact 73–4; Japanese troops in 1941 74; Rangoon, transformation 73
Indian Technical and Economic Cooperation (ITEC) programme 133
International Tribunal for the Law of the Sea (ITLOS) 55
ITLOS *see* International Tribunal for the Law of the Sea (ITLOS)

Japan: 'bifurcated policy' 47; and Burma 46; 'a carrot and stick policy' 47; Japan–ASEAN

254 Index

cooperation 48; Myanmar policy
47–8; Official Development Aid
(ODA) 47; 'Saffron Uprising' 47;
Thilawa Special Economic Zone
(SEZ) 48

Kachin Independence Army (KIA)
31, 202
Kaladan Multi-modal Transport
project 130, 166, 181, 222
Karen National Union (KNU) 8,
31
KIA *see* Kachin Independence Army
(KIA)
Kings, Burma 66–71; Ananda
Temple 67; attacks by
neighbouring 67; Buddhist
scriptures 67; dynasties 66;
East India Company 68; First
Anglo-Burmese War 68–9; river
communications with India 68;
Second Anglo–Burmese War 69;
Thibaw's reign 69–70; Third
Anglo–Burmese War 69; three
B's (Brahmanism, Buddhism and
British) 71; *Tripitaka* – 'the Three
Baskets of Laws' 67
KNU *see* Karen National Union
(KNU)
Krishna's visit 122

Look East Policy (LEP) 5, 52, 64,
101, 122, 127, 130, 144, 152,
168

Manmohan Singh's voyage
(Prime Minister): BIMSTEC
Summit 123–4; context 123–4;
evaluation: *The Hindu* 134;
The Indian Express 134; *The
Irrawaddy* 135; *New Light of
Myanmar,* 133; Renaud Egreteau
135; itinerary in Yangon 128;
joint statement 129–33; 'Border
Trade Committee' 132; culture
and human resource development
133; development cooperation
131–2; enhancing connectivity
131; human resource development
132; Initiative for ASEAN

Integration (IAI) 130; political
and security dimensions 129–30;
trade and investment 132;
reactions within India 124; speech
126–7
Maritime Silk Route (MSR) 168,
206–7
Ministry of Foreign Affairs (MOFA)
33–4
MOFA *see* Ministry of Foreign
Affairs (MOFA)
Mutual importance, India and
Myanmar: BCIM Economic
Corridor 5; The China factor
5; Japanese occupation of
Burma 4; Look East Policy
(LEP) 5; Myanmar, size and
economic attractiveness 5;
religion and ethnicity 3; respect
for India 3; tribes 4; 'truisms
of Indo-Myanmar relations of
contemporaneous history' 4
Myanma Economic Bank (MEB)
178
Myanma Foreign Trade Bank
(MFTB) 178
Myanma Investment Commercial
Bank (MICB) 178
Myanmar: ASEAN 3; BSM division
3; Burma, British colony 2;
economic liberalisation 8;
elections 6; Five Principles of
Peaceful Co-existence 6; foreign
policy 2; India's neighbours 2;
KNU 8; mutual importance 3–5;
NLD 6, 8–9; policy, re-appraisal
10–11; SPDC 6; Suu Kyi 8–9;
unity and diversity 2; USDP 7
Myanmar and the International
Community (seminar) 6
Myanmar Institute of Strategic
and International Studies
(MISIS) 7
Myitsone Dam project 199,
202
Myitsone hydroelectric dam project
8

Narendra Modi visit 149–50
National Convention process 26

Index 255

National League for Democracy
(NLD) 6, 8–9, 29–30, 45–6, 98,
204, 217–18
National Unity Party (NUP) 29, 98
nat worship 19
Nepal 51–2; British connection
51; 'the Burmese Nepali' 52;
Lord Buddha 51; political and
diplomatic relations 52
*Netaji Subhas Chandra Bose: The
Forgotten Hero* 106
New Delhi and Rangoon, relations
91
The New Light of Myanmar 122,
133, 224
NLD *see* National League for
Democracy (NLD)
North East 162–5; complex security
development paradigm 164–5;
Indian Insurgent Groups (IIGs)
163; India's Look East/Act East
Policy 162–3; India's NER 162–3;
job creation and development
164; Myanmar military 163

Official Development Aid (ODA) 47
Oil and Natural Gas Corporation
Videsh Ltd. (OVL) 178–80

Pakistan 52–4; Buddhist–Muslim
strife 53–4; and Burma 52;
India–Myanmar relations 52;
Mohammad Ali Jinnah 52;
Pakistan–Myanmar, bilateral
relationship 52–3; Shaheed
Benazir Bhutto Award for
Democracy 53
Panchsheel or Five Principles of
Peaceful Co-existence 6, 34–5,
169, 204, 206
Panglong arrangements 30
People's Union for Civil Liberties
(PUCL) of India 99
Persons of Indian Origin (PIO) 110,
183
political cooperation 169–71,
220–1; Agreements and MoUs
170; boundary management issues
170; Centre–state relations 221;
cooperation in institutions 171;

Five Principles of Peaceful
Co-existence 169; Foreign
Office Consultations (FOC)
170, 221; high-level bilateral
visits 169; Initiative for ASEAN
Integration (IAI) 221; '10-metre
no-construction zone' 170–1;
process of relationship building
170; regional and subregional
cooperation 170; 'a reluctant
power' 220–1; 'a strategic
partnership' 220; *Tatmadaw* 221;
training and capacity-building
assistance 221
politics (internal), Myanmar: carrot-
and-stick policy 28; ethnic groups
30–1; Constitution of 2008 30;
draft national ceasefire agreement
31; federalism 31; KIA and KNU
31; Panglong arrangements 30;
SLORC/SPDC 30; financial
resources 28; legitimacy 25–6;
democratic government 25;
National Convention process
26; Ne Win regime 25; political
legitimacy 26; Thein Sein
government 26; nation-building
23–5; authoritarian rule 24–5;
British administration 24; 'a
divided society' 23–4; freedom
movement 24; Konbaung dynasty
24; parties 28–30; AFPFL 28–9;
BSPP 29; 'The democracy era'
28–9; 'The king's party' 29;
multiparty system 29; NLD
29–30; NUP 29; pro-democracy
movement 29; SLORC/SPDC
period 29; political parties and
ethnic groups 27; SLORC and
SPDC era 26; *Tatmadaw* 27–8

reform period: ICWA delegation's
visit 151–3; Krishna's visit to
Myanmar 122; Manmohan
Singh's voyage (Prime Minister)
123–35; other visits 147–8;
people-to-people exchanges
150–1; President Thein Sein's visit
122; recent visits: Act East Policy
150; India–ASEAN Summit 149;

256 Index

Narendra Modi 149–50; Sushma Swaraj 149; 14th round of Foreign Office Consultations 148; Salman Khurshid visit 144–5; Suu Kyi's visit 136–44; Thein Sein's visit 146–7

Reliance Industries Ltd. (RIL) 180

Research and Information System for Developing Countries (RIS) 166–7

'Saffron Revolution' 37

'Saffron Uprising' 19, 47

Salman Khurshid visit 144–5; international conference on Buddhist cultural heritage in Yangon 144; speech 144–5

second Panglong Conference 20

separation, Burma from British India 72; 1937 and 1942 80–1; Anti-Fascist People's Freedom League (AFPFL) 82; assassination of Aung San 83; Burma Independence Army (BIA) 82; 'Burma Rebellion' 80; Burma Roundtable Conference, 1931 80; Burmese political movement 77; 1937 Constitution 81; dyarchy 78; Dyarchy from 1923 to 1936 80; General Council of Burma Association 78; independence in 1946–47, negitiations 82–3; Japanese rule 81; post-war reconstruction 82; Simon Commission to Burma, 1929 79; special Roundtable Conference in 1931 79; war period 81; Young Men's Buddhist Association (YMBA) 77

Shwedagon Pagoda 3, 74

Sitagu International Buddhist Academy 145

SLORC see State Law and Order Restoration Council (SLORC)

Socio-cultural portrait, Myanmar: Buddhism 17–18; Burmese ability 21; external influences and independent style 16–17; human migration 16; interrogation and imprisonment 22; long military rule 21–2; military's actions against Burmans 22; religion 17–19; 2008 Constitution 19; and history 17; *nat* worship 19; Ramayana, story of 17; 'the Saffron Uprising' 19; special characteristics 21; unity in diversity 19–21; 1947 Constitution 20–1; Frontier Areas 20; Ministerial Burma 20; national races 19–20; second Panglong Conference 20; women 22–3; Burmese woman 23; lower status 22; SPDC 23; Women's Day celebrations 23

'the Sonia Gandhi model' 219

South Asian Association for Regional Cooperation (SAARC) 2, 97, 148, 170–1

SPDC see State Peace and Development Council (SPDC)

Sri Lanka 50–1; bilateral cooperation 50; Buddhism 50; diplomatic relations 50; and Myanmar 50–1

State Law and Order Restoration Council (SLORC) 26, 29–30, 34, 40, 90, 97–8, 100–1, 194, 200

State Peace and Development Council (SPDC) 6, 23, 26, 29–30, 37, 39, 52–3, 89–90, 100, 104–6, 112, 114, 121–3, 169, 191, 194, 200–1

Sushma Swaraj visit 149

Suu Kyi's visit 136–44; discussions 139–41; India–Myanmar Friendship Society 100; interviews 141–4; critical analysis 141; ethnic cleansing 143; On President Thein Sein 142; situation in Burma 142; lecture 137–9; meeting with Prime Minister Singh 136; Nobel Prize in October 1991 100; programme 136–7

Suvarnabhumi or *Suvarnadvipa* 65

Than Shwe rule: 'the Burmese Way to Socialism' 94; Congress-led UPA government 106;

developments: Cyclone Nargis 113; Dr. A. P. J. Abdul Kalam's visit 111; Enlightened Society (Kalam) 111; Kalam's visit, public diplomacy 111; period of rapprochement 114; 'Saffron Uprising' 112; United Nations Human Rights Council (UNHRC) 113; VVIP visits 114; Indian community: L. M. Singhvi Committee on the Indian Diaspora 110; Persons of Indian Origin (PIOs) 110; status 110–11; India's high commissioner in Kenya 105; new phase: factors 103–4; growing dependency on China 104; India–Myanmar–Thailand Ministerial Meeting on Transport Linkages 105; leadership in MEA and PMO 104; National Democratic Alliance (NDA) 103; Shyam Saran and V. P. Malik 104–5; SPDC, contacts 104; Tamu–Kale-Kalewa highway, project 105; personages: Aung San Suu Kyi, meeting with 108; CII's 'Made in India Exhibition' 109; Daw Khin Kyi 108; information technology (IT) to Myanmar 109; Khin Nyunt 109; Than Shwe 107–8; policy review: change, reasons 102; convergence of views and coordination 101; Indian side, visits 102; role in Burma's governance 95; SPDC 100; UPA ministers, visits 106; visit of Chairman Than Shwe to India 106

The Energy and Resources Institute (TERI) 137

Thein Sein's (President) visit 122, 146–7; Multi-Sectoral Technical and Economic Cooperation (BIMSTEC) Summit 122; second visit 146–7; India–ASEAN Commemorative Summit 146; sojourn in Mumbai 146–7; tomb of King Thibaw 147

Theravada Buddhism 3, 66

Thilawa Special Economic Zone (SEZ) 48

transition 97–9; historic developments in 1988 97; house arrest of Suu Kyi 98; India–Burma/Myanmar relations 98; Indian Embassy, medical assistance 99; India's pro-active multilateral diplomacy 99; National League for Democracy (NLD) 98; Ne Win model of governance 98; 8888 Rising 97; United Nations High Commissioner for Refugees (UNHCR) 99

Treaty of Peace and Friendship, 1951 91

Tripitaka – 'the Three Baskets of Laws' 67

Union Solidarity and Development Association (USDA) 29

Union Solidarity and Development Party (USDP) 7, 29–30, 32, 38

U Nu era 90–4; Burma Immigration and Foreigners' Registration Act of 1957 92; cooperative relationship 91; economic cooperation 91; and Jawaharlal Nehru 90–1; Kuomintang troops in northern Burma 92; Land Nationalisation Act of 1948 92; New Delhi and Rangoon, cordial and friendly relations 91; observations 93–4; Sino–Burma boundary issues 93; Treaty of Peace and Friendship 91

US 39–44; Barack Obama administration 39–40, 42; 'dual-track' policy 41; international terrorism 40; Myanmar in Southeast Asia 41; Suu Kyi–Thein Sein meeting 42; US–Burma relations 40–3

USDA *see* Union Solidarity and Development Association (USDA)

USDP *see* Union Solidarity and Development Party (USDP)

Where China Meets India: Burma and the New Crossroads of Asia 192